THE
OLD SYRIAC ELEMENT
IN THE TEXT
OF
CODEX BEZAE.

THE
OLD SYRIAC ELEMENT

IN THE TEXT

OF

CODEX BEZAE

BY

FREDERIC HENRY CHASE, B.D.

LECTURER IN THEOLOGY AT CHRIST'S COLLEGE, AND
PRINCIPAL OF THE CLERGY TRAINING SCHOOL, CAMBRIDGE.

WIPF & STOCK · Eugene, Oregon

Wipf and Stock Publishers
199 W 8th Ave, Suite 3
Eugene, OR 97401

The Old Syriac Element in the Text of Codex Bezae
By Chase, F. H.
ISBN 13: 978-1-4982-8141-6
Publication date 2/23/2016
Previously published by Macmillan & Co., 1893

TO THE

RIGHT REVEREND BROOKE FOSS WESTCOTT D.D.

LORD BISHOP OF DURHAM

THIS ESSAY IS DEDICATED

AS A SLIGHT EXPRESSION

OF GRATITUDE FOR THE INSPIRATION OF HIS TEACHING

AND AS A TRIBUTE

OF REVERENCE FOR THE MEMORY OF

HIS TWO FRIENDS AND FELLOW-WORKERS

WITH WHOM HIS OWN NAME IS EVER CONNECTED

BISHOP LIGHTFOOT

AND

DR HORT

PREFACE.

THE following Essay contains a fresh investigation into the character of the text contained by the Cambridge Codex, Codex Bezae (Cod. D), and, since I have chosen the Book of the Acts for detailed examination, to a large extent into that contained by the Oxford Codex, Codex Laudianus (Cod. E).

It is, I trust, from no waywardness or ingratitude to others that I must claim to be an independent worker in this field. Few probably, who have reviewed the evidence with any care, would hold that the works on Codex Bezae hitherto published have foreclosed further discussion of the questions suggested by its eccentricities.

It is due to two of my immediate predecessors in the study of this MS. that I should briefly allude to their work.

Professor Ramsay has devoted some sections of his recent book, *The Church in the Roman Empire*, to a consideration of some of the readings of Codex Bezae in Acts xiii—xxi[1]. Though the volume did not come into my hands until my first chapter was already in type, I was able before the sheets were printed off to give to his conclusions on this subject that

[1] Professor Ramsay has described the scope and character of his work on the Codex in the notes on p. 88 f. of his book. I have ventured to criticise the Professor's work, p. 137 n.

careful consideration which any work of Professor Ramsay demands. My own views however remained absolutely unchanged.

On the other hand it was my friend Mr Rendel Harris' *Study of Codex Bezae* which first suggested to me the investigation, as to the results of which I now ask the criticism of those interested in these questions. I must say frankly, as I think that he would wish me to do, that I began to work at the Codex because I thought that his methods were unsatisfactory and his main conclusions untenable. As however an investigator is not necessarily a censor, my criticisms on the details of his work find expression (except on the rarest occasions) simply in my own presentation and examination of the facts.

It will, I believe, be convenient if I briefly record the stages of my work and explain my method.

When I read Mr Rendel Harris' book I was struck with the fact that several of the phenomena of the MS., to which he drew attention, could be explained by Syriac, just as easily as by Latin, influence; and I was led to believe that Syriac influence must have played some part in the genesis of the Bezan text.

The only satisfactory way of investigating the text of the MS. was, as it seemed to me, minutely to examine some section large enough to guarantee that no characteristic feature of the text would be left unnoted. Having a special interest in questions connected with the Acts, I chose for my purpose the earlier chapters of that Book. The first step was to mark in different ways (1) the variations from the common text in particular words and phrases; (2) changes of order; (3) interpolations; (4) omissions. This preliminary review over, I considered separately each variation thus marked, and tried to arrive at an explanation of it. Such problems as resisted solution were left for reconsideration in the light of further experience. In other cases provisional solutions were registered. I had not however gone very far when I became convinced that Syriac influence was a far more widely working factor in the genesis of the Bezan text than I had at first thought. I therefore commenced a third review of the characteristic readings of the Bezan text of the Acts, taking as a working hypothesis the theory of assimilation to a Syriac text. As one problem after another, which had previously seemed insoluble, yielded its secret to this method of interrogation, I became sure that Codex D and Codex E contained Syriacised texts. The study of the interpolations in the two MSS. and of those passages of Codex D in which the language becomes almost incoherent finally dissipated any lingering doubts as to this conclusion. I then decided that my work should take the form of a somewhat detailed examination of all, or almost all, the characteristic readings of the Codex till the commencement of the first lacuna (viii. 29), and of a briefer discussion of some selected passages in the remaining chapters in which the Greek text of the MS. is extant (x. 14—xxii. 29).

Two difficulties early presented themselves. On the one hand there appeared to be coincidences between the Bezan text and the Syriac Vulgate, which (like the Latin Vulgate) may in any particular place embody the reading of some older text of which it is the revision. But I was always conscious that it might be urged that these coincidences ought to be explained by the supposition that the Syriac Vulgate contains a text assimilated to a Greek text, this Greek text coinciding at times with that of Codex Bezae. Again, the Bezan text seemed to imply a Syriac text different from, and older than, that of the Syriac Vulgate. But here again my position was open to the obvious criticism, 'You are judging the Bezan text by a standard which you evolve out of the Bezan text itself. You are arguing in a vicious circle.'

The growing appreciation of these two difficulties made the earlier stages of the work peculiarly anxious and laborious. Many passages had to be investigated and reinvestigated yet again. My safe emergence, as I hope, from these labyrinths I owe to three clues. They are these: (1) The agreement of Codex E with Codex D in the insertion of a gloss, coupled with divergence in the wording of the gloss; (2) The occurrence of a Syriac idiom in any particular phrase in the Syriac text of the Acts of which the corresponding Bezan phrase seemed to be the equivalent; (3) The occurrence in such a phrase as that just indicated of a word or expression which the comparison of other passages in the Syriac N.T. proved to be characteristically Syriac. Each passage required a method of treatment in a sense peculiar to itself; but the conclusions arrived at in any particular case must not be isolated from the consideration of the whole series of passages.

My method of considering the characteristic readings of the Bezan text in the order in which they occur in the Book of the Acts itself, while I believe it to be the true scientific method, is peculiarly ill-adapted for the advocacy of a theory. The passages which supply the clearest evidence do not necessarily occur first. The most patient student will reasonably demand that I should make out a *prima facie* case before he consents to enter on a review of the evidence as a whole. I have therefore selected ten passages (where the phenomena are not specially complicated), the notes on which will, I hope, convince the student that the theories advanced are worthy of his consideration. The passages are ii. 17 ($αὐτῶν$), ii. 47 ($τὸν\ κόσμον$), iii. 13 f., iv. 32, vi. 1 vii., 24, viii. 27, xi. 27 f., xii. 10, xix. 28 f.

I am aware that my endeavours to unravel the tangles of the Bezan text will severely tax the patience of the most patient reader. But when everything depends on the careful examination of small points, I have discovered no way of avoiding what will seem to many a wearisome minuteness. Trustworthy results cannot be obtained unless all the phenomena of a passage are taken into account. It is an important truism that points which at first sight seem trivial are often of the highest value as guides to a true interpretation of the evidence.

The interest of an investigation into the Bezan text lies in its bearing on wider questions. I have therefore considered in a second chapter the three problems of the *date*, the *birthplace*, the *affinities* of the Bezan text. The conclusion as to the *first* of these questions supplies, I believe, a secure basis for further researches. A special instance will be found in the Appendix on [Mark] xvi. 9—20. In connexion with the *second* of these subjects I was led to examine the text of the newly-recovered fragment of 'the Gospel according to Peter[1].' In considering the *third* of these questions it was impossible not to take into view the Bezan text of the Gospels. In various parts of the Essay incidentally and in the Appendix I have treated of a sufficient number of passages from the Gospels to justify the assertion that the conclusions reached in the discussion of the Bezan text of the Acts hold good for the Bezan text of the Gospels also. I am bold enough to hope that scholars will recognise in this part of the Essay, as indeed in the Essay as a whole, the true solution of the problem of the 'Western' text.

Of my own work throughout I wish to speak with unfeigned diffidence. A pioneer cannot hope to escape many mistakes. Moreover I must state frankly that I make no pretensions to being a trained Syriac scholar. I have only that working

---

[1] I regret that I did not see Dr Th. Zahn's *Das Evangelium des Petrus* in time to make any use of it.

knowledge of Syriac which a student of the New Testament greatly needs and may very easily acquire. To several friends in Cambridge who have most kindly read through different parts of the proof-sheets I take this opportunity of tendering my warmest thanks. To Mr McLean, B.A., Fellow and Hebrew Lecturer of my own College, I owe an especial debt. His patient accuracy has enabled me to correct some more or less serious errors of my own in Syriac matters. He has not however seen all that I have written, so that the mistakes which will be found are not to be laid at his door. Nor is he responsible for any of my arguments or of my conclusions.

But if I speak with diffidence of my own work, I believe that I am justified in claiming for my results that they are of far-reaching importance. The light which they throw on many problems is, I believe, as clear as it is valuable. The chief of these questions, for the further examination of which I am not without hope that the results reached in this Essay may be found to supply a starting-point, I may be allowed to indicate:

(1) The Bezan text as a whole, especially that of the Gospels, will need fresh detailed examination.

(2) The early quotations (particularly in Justin, the Clementines, Irenaeus and Tertullian) from the N.T., especially the Gospels, will repay reinvestigation. Fresh knowledge as to the early history of the *text* of the Books of the N.T. forces us back to a date for the primitive text of these Books earlier than is always recognised.

(3) A more fruitful study of the 'Western' text, especially of the Old Latin authorities, is now, I believe, possible.

(4) Codex Bezae and the 'Western' text generally are made available as material for the critical study of the early Syriac text of the N.T.

(5) Information is gained as to the lines along which early Missionary efforts moved. Of these efforts Antioch was

still in the second century a chief centre. The connexion between Antioch and the Christianity of Carthage is especially worthy of note.

Anyone who has been led to work independently at, and has reached independent conclusions on, a subject which has engaged the attention of many generations of scholars must be deeply conscious of two feelings.

He knows his need of the cooperation of his fellow-students, their correction, their revision, their approval, if so it may be, of his work. The watchword συναθλοῦντες is the law of progress in Christian scholarship as it is in Christian evangelization.

He knows better than he knew before the greatness of the debt which he owes to those whom for many years he has regarded as his teachers.

By the kindness of the Bishop of Durham I am allowed to connect this Essay with his name and with those other two names to which his own is inseparably united in the reverent and thankful remembrance of Cambridge men. Thus an opportunity is afforded me of expressing, however inadequately, this ever-growing sense of gratitude.

CAMBRIDGE,
June, 1893.

TABLE OF CONTENTS.

PAGES

1. THE OLD SYRIAC ELEMENT IN THE BEZAN TEXT OF THE ACTS.   1—102

   Examination of the Bezan text.

2. THE BEZAN TEXT OF THE ACTS. DATE. BIRTHPLACE. AFFINITIES.   103—149

   (1) The date of Bezan text and of the underlying Syriac text.   103—115
      (i) Evidence of Tertullian [103—105]. (ii) Evidence of Irenaeus: Examination of quotations in the Latin translation of Iren. iii. xii. [105—108]: three reasons for the belief that the text of the Acts quoted in the Latin reproduces that quoted in the original Greek of Irenaeus, viz. (1) it is unlikely that the Latin translator would continuously substitute another text; (2) two passages from the Acts quoted where the Greek of Irenaeus is preserved contain peculiarities Bezan in character; (3) Irenaeus elsewhere uses a Syriacised text of N.T. [108—113]. Date of Iren. iii. [113]. (iii) Evidence of Theophilus of Antioch [113—115]. Conclusions [115].

   (2) The birthplace of the Bezan text.   115—131
      Antioch, its Greek and Syriac population [115 f.]. The supposition that Antioch was the birthplace of the Bezan text confirmed by examination of the fragment of 'the Gospel according to Peter,' which is marked by (i) assimilation to Scriptural passages [117—121]: (ii) signs of Syriac influence, especially that of the Diatessaron [121—131].

CONTENTS.

	PAGES

(3) Affinities of the Bezan text of the Acts.   131—149

(1) The Old Syriac text underlying the Bezan text of the Acts: its character, glosses [132 f.]: variations of reading; Cod E implies older Syriac text than does Cod. D; corruptions in Syriac text underlying the latter; implied early date [133].

(2) The Greek text of Cod. D and of Cod. E: they exhibit different modes of Syriacisation [134 f.]: two stages of Syriacisation [135 f.]: the two MSS. probably exhibit the Greek texts of two Graeco-Syriac bilingual MSS. [136]: such texts the result of gradual growth [136 f.].

(3) The origin of the 'Western' text of N.T.: wide influence of Syriacised texts [137—139]: this points to the rise of the 'Western' text at an influential centre [139]. Examination by the 'Reviewer' of theories as to birthplace [139—142]: his suggestion of Antioch; his arguments in support of this [142—148]: two further arguments [148 f.]. Antioch the birthplace of the Bezan text and of the 'Western' text [149].

APPENDIX.

Note on [Mark] xvi. 9—20.   150—157

Gloss from an Old Syriac version of [Mark] xvi. 15, 19 in the Bezan text of Acts i. 2 [150]. Conclusion as to date of Syriac and Greek texts of [Mark] xvi. [150 f.]. This confirmed by four pieces of evidence: (i) Codex Bezae gives a Syriacised text of [Mark] xvi. 9—15 [151—153]. Conclusion as to date [153]. (ii) Tatian in the Diatessaron used the section [153 f.]. (iii) Justin and probably Aristides knew the section [154 f.]. (iv) The section probably used in 'the Gospel according to Peter' [156]. Final result as to the *antiquity* of the section [156 f.]. Reasons for hesitating to infer *genuineness* [157]. The result confirmed by apparent coincidences with Col. Hebr. [157].

I.

THE OLD SYRIAC ELEMENT IN THE BEZAN TEXT OF THE ACTS.

IT seems advisable as a preliminary to the detailed examination of the Bezan text of the Acts that I should state with all brevity the main elements of the theory as to that text which I believe that this investigation will establish. They are three in number.

(1) The Bezan text of the Acts is the result of an assimilation of a Greek text to a Syriac text. The extent indeed to which this work of assimilation has been carried out varies in different parts of the Bezan text. It reveals itself sometimes in the addition of a gloss, sometimes in the reconstruction of a paragraph, sometimes in the alteration of a word or even of the form of a word. It never long remains inactive.

(2) A marked characteristic of this Syriac text is its constant tendency to harmonize the text of the Acts with other parts of Scripture; it weaves, that is, into its rendering of a particular passage phrases from other parts of the Acts, from the Gospels, the Pauline Epistles, and the Old Testament.

(3) This Syriac text of the Acts, on which large portions of the Bezan text are based, is not that of the Syriac Vulgate. It is that of an old Syriac Version, in which, when the evidence derived from Codex D is supplemented by that derived from other sources, we can, I believe, from time to time discern traces of variations of reading. The conclusion that it is an *Old* Syriac text which lies behind that of Codex D is founded on the consideration of two lines of evidence—*external* and *internal*. The *external* evidence I shall deal with in

a separate chapter. The *internal* evidence lies in the character of the Syriac text itself, when it is compared with that of the Syriac Vulgate. The evidence which falls under the latter head will come before us in our discussion of the several passages.

For the sake of convenience I shall from the first speak of 'the Old Syriac' text in dealing with Syriac readings which are not those of the Syriac Vulgate, fully realizing that I am thereby making an important assumption, an assumption however which will be gradually justified by the evidence which we shall consider. For a similar reason I shall use the term 'the Bezan scribe' to denote the scribe who in any particular passage assimilated the Greek text to the Syriac, and in that passage produced 'the Bezan text'. Taking however all the evidence into consideration, I am inclined to believe that the 'Syriacised' character of the Bezan text is the result not of one man's work but of a process carried out by successive workers. Again, I have employed the term 'the true text' to denote the common form of the Greek text, which, whatever doubt there may be as to smaller points of reading, stands in marked contrast to the eccentric Bezan text. I do not think that in any of the passages which I shall discuss the problem is complicated by serious textual difficulty. As 'the true text' in this sense I have printed that given in Dr Westcott and Dr Hort's edition of the New Testament.

I have not given the Bezan Latin except in a few cases. The evidence which I have brought together as to the character of the Greek text in Codex Bezae completely establishes, if I mistake not, Dr Hort's opinion (*Introduction*, p. 83) that 'for the criticism of the Greek text the Latin reading has here no independent authority'. To prove that the Bezan Greek text is moulded on a Syriac text is to disprove the theory of its Latinisation. In saying this I do not wish to deny that there may be a very few passages scattered up and down the MS. in which the scribe, allowing his eye to wander to the Latin copy before him while he wrote the Greek, may have been influenced by the Latin in his transcription of a word or phrase of the Greek[1]. But these instances of Latinisation (if such they can be called) are at most very rare; they are accidents of the particular transcription and do not affect the essential character of the text which the MS. presents.

For the Greek and Latin text of Codex Bezae I have relied on Dr Scrivener's characteristically excellent collation *Bezae Codex Cantabrigiensis*, Cambridge, 1864[2]. In quoting for the first time a passage from Codex D or Codex E (Codex Laudianus) I have always used small uncial type.

Acts i. 2. ΑΧΡΙ ΗC ΗΜΕΡΑC
ΑΝΕΛΗΜΦΘΗ ΕΝΤΕΙΛΑΜΕΝΟC ΤΟΙC ΑΠΟCΤΟΛΟΙC
ΔΙΑ ΠΝC ΑΓΙΟΥ ΟΥC ΕΞΕΛΕΞΑΤΟ ΚΑΙ ΕΚΕΛΕΥCΕ
ΚΗΡΥCCΕΙΝ ΤΟ ΕΥΑΓΓΕΛΙΟΝ.

The true text has ἄχρι ἧς ἡμέρας ἐντειλάμενος τοῖς ἀποστόλοις διὰ πνεύματος ἁγίου οὓς ἐξελέξατο ἀνελήμφθη.

Two points claim consideration—a change of order and an interpolation.

(1) It seems clear that the Bezan Latin ('usque in eum diem quem susceptus est quo praecepit apostolis') is an awkward translation, and not the original, of the Bezan Greek. On the other hand the Syriac seems to offer an explanation of the variation in order from the common Greek text. The Syriac is always obliged to remodel a sentence in which an aorist participle plays an important part (see e.g. v. 40); in some way the participle must be paraphrased. Here the Syriac Vulgate translates quite naturally thus: 'Until that day in-which He-was-taken-up after He-had-commanded (ܡܢ ܒܬܪ ܕܦܩܕ ܗܘܐ) them (even) those Apostles whom-He-chose in the Holy Ghost.' The order in the Bezan

---

[1] An instance is found in Acts xiii. 10 ΥΙΟΙ ΔΙΑΒΟΛΟΥ | fili diabole.

[2] For my own satisfaction I have compared Dr Scrivener's printed text with that of the MS. itself in all the important passages, with which I have to deal. The only result of my inspection is to confirm my confidence in the patient and minute accuracy of that great scholar.

Greek is the same as that in the Syriac except that the former retains the true Greek order διὰ πν. ἁγ. οὓς ἐξελ. (2) What of the interpolated words καὶ ἐκέλευσεν κηρύσσειν τὸ εὐαγγέλιον? Among the Curetonian fragments of the Old Syriac version of the Gospels the last four verses (17—20) of [Mc.] xvi. have a place. In *v.* 19 we read 'But our-Lord Jesus after that He had-*commanded* (ܡܢ ܕܟܪܙ ܦܩܕ)[1] His-disciples, was-exalted to-heaven.' Further, in *v.* 15 (where the Curetonian fragments fail us, but where there is but little room for variation in translation) we read in the Greek text: κηρύξατε τὸ εὐαγγέλιον πάσῃ τῇ κτίσει. We cannot doubt that the Bezan interpolation is originally Syriac. The word ܦܩܕ in Acts i. 2 at once called to mind the ܦܩܕ in the Old Syriac of [Mc.] xvi. 19. The passage of the Gospel seemed to supply what was lacking in the text of the Acts: it suggested the substance of the Lord's parting commands. Hence in the text of Acts i. 2 the interpolation of the important words of [Mc.] xvi. 15, 19.

Two remarks must be added before we leave the passage.

In the interpolated words we should perhaps have expected κηρύξαι (Mc. *l.c.* κηρύξατε). But the imperative, infinitive, and participle of Syriac verbs are tenseless. When the Bezan scribe therefore is following the Syriac, his constant tendency is to replace an aorist by a present in his Greek. Thus, to take one example, in Matt. x. 27 κηρυςςεται takes the place of the true Greek κηρύξατε.

The Bezan Greek, it will be noticed, preserves the true Greek text ἐντειλάμενος, but represents the second Syriac 'commanded' by ἐκέλευσεν. The Latin on the other hand has *praecepit* in both places. At first sight it might seem possible that in this passage the Latin preserves a Syrism which does not appear in the Greek. If indeed the original scribe wrote out his Latin version, modelling it on the Greek,

---

[1] No doubt the 'commanded' of [Mc.] xvi. 19 is due to harmonizing with Matt. xxviii. 20 (comp. Jn. xv. 14, 17). Cureton's printed text has ܕܟܪܙ. Is this the error of his transcription or of the MS. itself?

just after he had written out his Greek text, modelling that on the Syriac, it would not be unnatural that from time to time such cases should occur. But a study of such passages as iv. 32, xi. 26, 27, xv. 29 shews that the Latin scribe had no clue to the meaning of an enigmatical Greek rendering of a Syriac gloss, and that therefore the formation of the Bezan Latin must be independent of, and later in time than, the formation of the Bezan Greek, and further, that we have no ground for thinking that the birthplace of the one is the birthplace of the other.

i. 3. ΤΕϹϹΕΡΑΚΟΝΤΑ ΗΜΕΡⲰΝ.

The true text has δι' ἡμερῶν τεσσεράκοντα, which is roughly represented by the Bezan Latin 'post dies quadraginta'. The Bezan Greek on the other hand omits the preposition and changes the order of the words. (1) As to the latter point, the true text in Mc. i. 13 has τεσσερ. ἡμ., while the order in Matt. iv. 2, Lc. iv. 2 is ἡμ. τεσσερ. But the Old and the Vulgate Syriac alike reverse the usual order in Matt. iv. 2[1]. (2) Though the Syriac Vulgate has here the preposition ܒ (in), the Old Syriac may well have used no preposition partly that it might avoid translating the difficult διά of the Greek. This suggestion is confirmed by the interpolation ΗΜΕΡΑϹ Μ̄ in x. 41 (a verse which we can refer back to the Old Syriac; see note on xi. 27). Both changes, the variation of order and the omission of the preposition, are probably due to the same cause, viz. assimilation to Matt. iv. 2 (ܐܪܒܥܝܢ ܝܘܡܝܢ), which, as having a place in the Diatessaron (Ciasca, p. 8), would be specially familiar to a Syriac scribe. The Bezan scribe, it must be added, has but half done his work; for he leaves the genitive ἡμερῶν unaltered.

i. 3. ΤΑϹ ΠΕΡΙ ΤΗϹ ΒΑϹΙΛΕΙΑϹ ΤΟΥ Θ͞Υ.

The true text has τὰ περὶ κ.τ.λ. The Bezan Latin is 'ea quae sunt de regno'. It is of course possible that the

---

[1] 'Die Voranstellung des Zahlworts ist häufiger' (Nöldeke, *Syr. Gram.*, p. 164).

quae of the Latin was taken as a feminine plural and gave rise to the Greek τάς. But there is another explanation, which further knowledge of the Bezan text will confirm. In Syriac, as in Hebrew, there is no neuter; for the neuter the feminine is commonly used. Thus, though here the Syriac Vulgate has simply 'speaking about the kingdom of God', the Philoxenian Version has the plural of the feminine pronoun (ܐ ܡܝܢ). The Syriac Vulgate translates Lc. xix. 42 τὰ πρὸς εἰρήνην σου thus: ܐܝܠܝܢ ܕܐܝܬܝܗܝܢ ܕܫܠܡܟܝ. We may feel that it is probable that the Old Syriac had some similar phrase here, and that the Bezan text was influenced by it.

i. 4. ΚΑΙ CΥΝΑΛΙϹΚΟΜΕΝΟϹ ΜΕΤ ΑΥΤѠΝ.

The true text is καὶ συναλιζόμενος.

The συναλισκόμενος is an emendation reproducing the sound of the word in the true text. But what of the added μετ' αὐτῶν? There are no compound verbs in Syriac, and consequently in the Syriac Versions some paraphrase is employed in rendering Greek compounds. Thus, the phrase συνευδοκῶν τῇ ἀναιρέσει αὐτοῦ (viii. 1) becomes in Syriac 'was willing and was participating in-his-murder'; συνφυεῖσαι (Lc. viii. 7) becomes 'they-sprang-up with-it (ܥܡܗ)'; συνεσταυρώθη (Rom. vi. 6) 'was-crucified with-him (ܥܡܗ)'. In our present passage therefore the Syriac according to its wont represents the συν- of the compound verb by the preposition with a pronominal suffix—'and-when He-had-eaten with-them (ܥܡܗܘܢ) bread'. This 'with-them', necessary in the Syriac rendering of the Greek, reappears in the μετ' αὐτῶν of Codex Bezae.

The same explanation is to be given of ϹΥΝΕΦΑΓΕϹ ϹΥΝ ΑΥΤΟΙϹ (xi. 3), where the σύν is added to correspond with the 'with-them' of the Syriac.

Comp. the Syriac of e.g. Phil. i. 27, 2 Cor. vii. 3 and, in the light of the Syriac of Jn. iii. 3, Heb. vi. 6, the Bezan text of Acts x. 16 (ΠΑΛΙΝ). Note also Acts x. 44, xi. 15 in Cod. D.

i. 4. ΗΝ ΗΚΟΥϹΑ ΦΗϹΙΝ ΔΙΑ ΤΟΥ ϹΤΟΜΑΤΟϹ ΜΟΥ.

The true text is ἣν ἠκούσατέ μου. The Bezan Latin has 'quam audistis de ore meo'. I believe that φησίν is a Greek addition. The words διὰ τοῦ στόματός μου are due to assimilation to xv. 7, where the Syriac Vulgate has 'from-my-mouth'. But what of ἤκουσα? If the Old Syriac were ܡܢ ܦܘܡܝ ܕܫܡܥܬܘܢ (which-ye-heard from my-mouth), it would be very easy in a badly written MS. for the ܘ- to fall out before ܡ and leave ܕܫܡܥܬ (I-heard) remaining.

i. 5. ΚΑΙ Ο ΜΕΛΛΕΤΑΙ ΛΑΜΒΑΝΕΙΝ.

This is an interpolation from Jn. vii. 39. The καὶ ὅ may be an instance of superficial Latinisation, the Bezan Latin being 'et eum'. I believe however that it is due to the Bezan scribe wavering in his reading of ܕ (which), easily in a MS. confused with ܘ (and) (see notes on ii. 6 f., xix. 29), his indecision ending in a double rendering (see note on iii. 2).

i. 5. ΕΩϹ ΤΗϹ ΠΕΝΤΗΚΟϹΤΗϹ.

This is another interpolation. Compare 1 Cor. xvi. 8 ἐπιμένω δὲ ἐν Ἐφέσῳ ἕως τῆς πεντηκοστῆς. Was this phrase 'until Pentecost' interpolated in Lc. xxiv. 49 in some form of the Old Syriac? The Syriac Vulgate uses the same verb to render καθίσατε (Lc.) and ἐπιμένω (1 Cor.), and the two passages read in the Syriac are not dissimilar. Such an interpolation is in the manner of that version (see note on vi. 10). If so, the interpolation would naturally pass from Lc. into our present passage. I venture to make the suggestion because the words here do not fit into the context and have the appearance of being taken from the Gospels (see i. 2, viii. 1). But I have no evidence to produce in support of the suggestion. We have not the Old Syriac of Lc. xxiv. beyond *v*. 44, and the words do not occur in the Arabic Tatian (Ciasca, p. 98).

In connexion with this suggestion as to Lc. xxiv. 49 I will briefly discuss another passage of the Gospels which seems to be assimilated to a phrase of an Epistle. The passage to which we turn has a special interest, inasmuch as it would appear that the eccentric reading in this place was the reason why Codex Bezae was taken to the Council of Trent (Scrivener, p. viii, Rendel Harris, p. 36). In the Bezan text of Jn. xxi. 22 we read ⲉⲁⲛ ⲁⲩⲧⲟⲛ ⲑⲉⲗⲱ ⲙⲉⲛⲉⲓⲛ ⲟⲩⲧⲱⲥ ⲉⲱⲥ ⲉⲣⲭⲟⲙⲁⲓ ⲧⲓ ⲡⲣⲟⲥ ⲥⲉ. The οὕτως has no place in the true text. Is the word an interpolation introduced from 1 Cor. vii. 40 μακαριωτέρα δέ ἐστιν ἐὰν οὕτως μείνῃ? Before further considering this question let us turn to the Syriac. The Vulgate in Jn. xxi. 21 f. is as follows: 'Him (ܠܗܢܐ) when Cephas saw, he-said to-Jesus, My-Lord and-this-man (ܘܗܢܐ) what? Jesus said to-him, If I will that this-man tarry (ܕܢܩܘܐ ܗܢܐ), until I-come, to-thee what to-thee?' The ܗܢܐ in the last sentence, it will be remarked, is quite natural: the word has occurred twice before in the passage; it here has a special point as connecting the answer of Christ with the question of St Peter. It cannot be doubted that it is the original Syriac reading. But in the Old Syriac MS. used by the Bezan scribe I believe that ܗܢܐ (this-man) had been changed into ܗܟܢܐ (thus). The change may be an unthinking emendation[1]. But it is also possible that it was deliberately made in the interests of asceticism in order to conform the passage to 1 Cor. vii. 40 ' But happy-is-she if thus she-shall-tarry (ܗܟܢܐ ܬܩܘܐ).' In the latter case, as the passage has a place in the Diatessaron (Ciasca, p. 98)[2], is the emendation due to the Encratite Tatian? Between these two alternatives of accident or asceticism it is perhaps impossible to decide without

[1] Comp. Acts xv. 15 Syr. Vulg. ܘܠܗܕܐ (and-to-this-thing), Cod. D ⲕⲁⲓ ⲟⲩⲧⲱⲥ.

[2] Ciasca's Latin is: 'Si eum uolo manere, donec ueniam: quid ad te?' The Syriac text, of which the Arabic is a translation, has been, it appears, generally assimilated to the text of the Peshitto. Hence the fact that 'thus' has no place in the Arabic Tatian is no argument that it did not occur there in the original Diatessaron.

further evidence. One point however still remains. Jerome *adv. Jovin.* i. (Migne *P. L.* 23 col. 246) quotes the passage in this form 'Quid ad te si eum uolo sic esse?' Is Jerome simply paraphrasing? Or is he in the *esse* quoting an Old Latin reading? In the latter case it may be plausibly suggested that the reading *esse* is ultimately due to a confusion between ܢܩܘܐ (that-he-should-tarry) and ܢܗܘܐ (that-he-should-be).

i. 9. ΚΑΥΤΑ ΕΙΠΟΝΤΟC ΑΥΤΟΥ
ΝΕΦΕΛΗ ΥΠΕΒΑΛΕΝ ΑΥΤΟΝ
ΚΑΙ ΑΠΗΡΘΗ ΑΠΟ ΟΦΘΑΛΜΩΝ ΑΥΤΩΝ.

The true text has καὶ ταῦτα εἰπὼν βλεπόντων αὐτῶν ἐπήρθη, καὶ νεφέλη ὑπέλαβεν αὐτὸν ἀπὸ τῶν ὀφθαλμῶν αὐτῶν. The Syriac Vulgate is as follows: 'And-when (ܘܟܕ) these-things He-(had-)spoken, when (ܟܕ) looking (were they) at-Him, He-was-taken-up, and-a-cloud received-Him, and-He-was-hidden from-their-eyes.' Comparing the Bezan reading with the Syriac we notice the following points. (1) If we suppose that the Bezan scribe is translating from the Syriac, we can account for his variation from the true Greek text in the first line. See below on ii. 1, 2. (2) In the Syriac we can see why the clause 'when they were looking' would fall out; it begins with ܟܕ (when) and the former clause began with ܘܟܕ (and-when). (3) If the Bezan scribe is attending to the Syriac rather than transcribing the Greek, we can explain ὑπέβαλεν instead of the ὑπέλαβεν of the true text: the former is an inaccurate reminiscence of the latter (see on ἀπήρθη). (4) In the last words 'And-a-cloud received-Him, and-He-was-hidden from-their-eyes' we have a characteristic Syriac amplification and also a characteristic assimilation to a passage from the Gospel (Lc. xix. 42). The Bezan text seems derived from the Syriac, the word 'He-was-taken-up' being omitted, and ἀπήρθη (an inaccurate reminiscence of ἐπήρθη in the true text) being made to do duty as a representation of 'He-was-hidden'.

i. 13. καὶ οτε εἰcηλθεν ἀνεβηcaν εἰ το ὑπερωον.

The true text has καὶ ὅτε εἰσῆλθον, εἰς τὸ ὑπερῷον ἀνέβησαν.
Two points claim attention. (1) It is quite possible that εἰσῆλθεν is to be explained as an *itacism* for εἰσῆλθον. But another explanation may be suggested. The 3rd person plural of the perfect of the Syriac verb ends in a *vav* (ܘ), which however, except in the case of the ܐ verbs, is not sounded. There is nothing in the pronunciation to distinguish between the singular and the plural of the 3rd person in the perfect. A scribe therefore writing the Greek text but at the same time recalling the sound of the Syriac would be liable constantly to substitute the 3rd singular for the 3rd plural of the perfect. I think we probably have such an error here. The same account may be given of i. 23 (ἔστησεν), ii. 4 (ἤρξατο). In a somewhat similar way, as indeed Harvey (Irenaeus i. p. 83 n. 5) points out, we may explain the early and important variation in Jn. i. 13 (ὃς...ἐγεννήθη). (2) The order of the words ἀνέβησαν εἰς τὸ ὑπερῷον agrees with the Syriac. 'They went up into that upper-room in which &c.' In the Syriac this order is necessary so that the relative may stand side by side with the noun to which it refers.

i. 13. ιακωβος ο του αλφαιου.

The true text has not ὁ τοῦ.
The Bezan Latin is able to translate the true Greek literally—'iacobus alphei'. The Syriac however cannot reproduce the brevity of the Greek—Ἰάκωβος Ἀλφαίου. It is obliged to add 'the-son', 'the-son of', explicitly. Thus below it has 'Judas the-son of-James' (where the Bezan text is not affected), and all through the long list of names Lc. iii. 23—38 the word 'the-son' is inserted. The ὁ τοῦ of the Bezan text represents the Syriac phrase 'the-son of'. The same explanation applies to Acts xiii. 22, Jn. xxi. 2.

i. 14. CYN ΤΑΙC ΓΥΝΑΙΖΙΝ ΚΑΙ ΤΕΚΝΟΙC.

Here Cod. D adds ταῖς and καὶ τέκνοις to the true Greek text. Compare xxi. 5 σὺν γυναιξὶ καὶ τέκνοις. But what is the rationale of the interpolation? Its explanation comes to us in a reading which Cod. E preserves in the following verse. In place of the true text ἦν τε ὄχλος ὀνομάτων Cod. E reads ΗΝ ΤΕ ΟΧΛΟC ΑΝΔΡѠΝ. The same expression appears in the Syriac Vulgate—ܟܢܫܐ ܕܓܒܪܐ. But when we find that the same reading—'turba hominum'—has a place in the Latin Vulgate of this passage and in Cyprian *Ep.* 68, our first impression is that the cause of Latinisation, at least in regard to this passage, is triumphant. But a prudent man will hesitate when he remembers in how many Syriac paraphrastic expressions the word 'men' plays a part. On further investigation he will discover that the Old Syriac renders διὰ τὸν ὄχλον (Lc. viii. 19) by 'on-account-of the-multitude *of-men*'; ὄχλου ὄντος ἐν τῷ τόπῳ (Jn. v. 13) by the same phrase; that the Syriac Vulgate has the phrase 'send-away the-multitudes *of-men*' (where the only difference is in the vocalization of ܓܒܪܐ) to translate ἀπόλυσον τοὺς ὄχλους (Matt. xiv. 15), and 'the-multitude *of-men*, who believed' to represent τοῦ δὲ πλήθους τῶν πιστευόντων (Acts iv. 32). He will discover, that is, that in four passages the phrase 'the-multitude *of-men*' intrudes itself into the Syriac N.T. where there is nothing either in the Greek to require it or (so far as I know) in any Latin rendering to suggest it. He will not doubt that it is a characteristic Syriac phrase, and that in Acts i. 15 it comes into 'Western' texts from the Syriac, not from any 'Western' text into the Syriac.

It is impossible not to connect with this specific mention of 'men' in *v.* 15 the interpolation in the previous verse which refers to 'women and children' (Matt. xiv. 21, xv. 38, in the latter verse however the word for 'men' is different), or to doubt that in *v.* 14 we have a Syriac gloss which, though it has not survived in the Syriac Vulgate, had a place in an Old Syriac text. We shall find other instances where the evidence of

Cod. E supplements that of Cod. D in regard to a gloss certainly Syriac (see e.g. iv. 32, v. 12).

i. 16. ΔΕΙ ΠΛΗΡΩΘΗΝΑΙ
ΤΗΝ ΓΡΑΦΗΝ ΤΑΥΤΗΝ ΗΝ ΠΡΟΕΙΠΕΝ ΤΟ ΠΝΑ ΤΟ ΑΓΙΟ.

The true text has ἔδει, and reads τὴν γραφὴν ἥν. The ταύτην answers to the Syriac ܗܕܐ. The Syriac relative ܕ is in a very large number of cases preceded by a demonstrative pronoun. Thus in this verse we have 'that Judas who'. Comp. e.g. i. 2 (that day), 13 (that upper-room), ii. 2 (that house), iii. 15 (that prince), iv. 22 (that man).

ii. 1 f. ΟΝΤΩΝ ΑΥΤΩΝ ΠΑΝΤΩΝ ΕΠΙ ΤΟ ΑΥΤΟ
ΚΑΙ ΕΙΔΟΥ ΕΓΕΝΕΤΟ Κ.Τ.Λ.

The true text has ἦσαν πάντες ὁμοῦ ἐπὶ τὸ αὐτό, καὶ ἐγένετο κ.τ.λ.

Here we have a complete reshaping of a sentence—not a wholly unusual phenomenon in the Bezan text. The Latin ('erant simul omnes in unum et factum est') clearly lends us no aid in our endeavour to account for the peculiarities of the Bezan Greek. We turn to the Syriac Vulgate. There we read 'When assembled (ܟܢܝܫܝܢ) were-they all-of-them (ܟܠܗܘܢ) together.' This appears to be a natural Syriac representation of the true Greek text. (1) It is true that the clauses are differently arranged in the Syriac and in the true Greek text. But the Syriac is fond of coordinate sentences beginning with 'when', and the slight rearrangement at this point is, I think, quite in accordance with the style of the Syriac Version. (2) In the true Greek text two words are used to express the *unity* of the Disciples—ὁμοῦ (*v. l.* ὁμοθυμαδόν) and ἐπὶ τὸ αὐτό. In the Syriac text the latter of these two words has its exact equivalent; the former is represented by 'assembled'. This last word is used in translating ὁμοθυμαδόν in v. 12 and xii. 20. (3) The Syriac could only express πάντες by 'all-of-them' (see v. 12, Mc. i. 27, vi. 42, xii. 44 &c. &c.). We conclude then that the

Syriac is the natural and idiomatic rendering of the true Greek text. But it is no less clear that the Bezan Greek is, except for the omission of any word answering to the Syriac 'assembled', a close translation of the Syriac. The genitive absolute is, as so often, the equivalent of the Syriac 'when...'; the idiomatic Syriac 'all-of-them' reappears with absolute literalness in the Bezan αὐτῶν πάντων.

In the next line the Bezan text has καὶ ειδογ (= ἰδού) εγενετο. The Bezan Latin has no *ecce*, so that the intruder cannot come into the Greek from that source. But the Syriac is very fond of interpolating ܗܐ ('behold'); compare ii. 15 'for *behold*, it is now the third hour', ii. 33 'which *behold* ye see and hear', iii. 2, iv. 16, x. 33, xiii. 32 f. and (a characteristic passage from the Old Syriac) Lc. xxiii. 40 f. 'Art not thou even afraid of God, because *behold*, we also are in the same judgment? And *behold*, we as those who are worthy.' In this last passage, the twice repeated 'behold' of the Old Syriac has no place in the Syriac Vulgate. What happened in Lc. xxiii. 40 f.[1] happened, I believe, in our present passage. In its ἰδού Cod. Bezae preserves a trait of the Old Syriac of the Acts, a trait which has disappeared in the Vulgate.

In the same verse notice ὅλον τὸν οἶκον (true Greek text) = ܟܠܗ ܒܝܬܐ = ΠΑΝΤΑ ΤΟΝ ΟΙΚΟΝ (Cod. D). The Bezan Latin has 'totam domum'. Note the converse change in xiii. 44.

ii. 6 f. ΚΑΙ ΗΚΟΥΟΝ ΕΙC ΕΚΑCΤΟC
ΛΑΛΟΥΝΤΑC ΤΑΙC ΓΛΩCCΑΙC ΑΥΤΩΝ
ΕΞΕΙCΤΑΝΤΟ ΔΕ ΚΑΙ ΕΘΑΥΜΑΖΟΝ
ΛΕΓΟΝΤΕC ΠΡΟC ΑΛΛΗΛΟΥC

The true Greek text is ὅτι ἤκουσεν εἷς ἕκαστος τῇ ἰδίᾳ

---

[1] Comp. (in the Curetonian fragments) Lc. xxii. 12 '*Behold*, he sheweth to you one large upper room'; 27 '*Behold*, am not I as a minister among you?' In the former verse the Vulgate has, in the latter it omits, the 'behold'. Note also xxiv. 21 'And *behold* three days *behold* since all these things were'. The Vulgate retains the former 'behold' only.

διαλέκτῳ λαλούντων αὐτῶν· ἐξίσταντο δὲ καὶ ἐθαύμαζον λέγοντες.

The Bezan Latin has: 'qui audiebant...lingua sua...dicentes ad alterutrum'.

The Syriac is as follows: 'Because (ܕ ܡܛܠ) hearing was each man (ܐܢܫ ܐܢܫ) of-them that-speaking were-they in-their-tongues (ܒܠܫܢܝܗܘܢ). Amazed were-they all-of-them and-wondering while saying one to-another (ܚܕ ܠܚܕ).'

Comparing the Syriac and the Bezan texts I notice the following points. (1) The Syriac phrase 'that-speaking were-they' Cod. D naturally renders by the participle, but equally naturally uses the accusative, not the genitive of the true text. It conforms to the Syriac order, placing λαλοῦντας first in the clause. (2) The Peshitto uses the word 'tongue' in representing διάλεκτος. This word it has in i. 19 (in-the-tongue of-the-place), ii. 8, in both which places the Bezan text retains διάλεκτος. Here however it conforms to the Syriac. (3) Syriac has no precise equivalent to ἴδιος[1]. Accordingly the Bezan text omits the word ἴδιος in ii. 8 (contrast the Bezan Latin 'propria lingua nostra') and here. The word ἴδιος in such a passage as this has the notion of *possession* and of *distribution*. The former idea the Syriac represents by the pronominal suffix 'their'; the latter it loosely expresses by the change of the singular διαλέκτῳ into the plural 'tongues'. In both these necessary turns of expression the Bezan text here follows the Syriac. (4) The Syriac phrase used here ܐܡܪ ܚܕ ܠܚܕ is common: see v. 12, Mc. iv. 41, Lc. viii. 25, and (with the addition of ܗܘܐ) Lc. xxiv. 32, Jn. xi. 56, xii. 19, xvi. 17, Acts iv. 15. On the other hand the Bezan phrase in this passage λέγοντες πρὸς ἀλλήλους is found, I believe, only in Lc. viii. 25. Hence we have grounds for saying that the 'one to-another' of the present passage is a natural Syriac interpolation.

[1] Compare in the Curetonian fragments, e.g. Matt. xxii. 5 'And one went to-the-farm, and one went to-the-merchandise'; Jn. v. 18 'Because He had called God my-Father'.

As we look back then over the passage we see that the Bezan text is an exact rendering of all the idiomatic Syriac phrases.

Does the Bezan text diverge from the Syriac text when at the beginning of the passage it alters the true Greek ὅτι ἤκουσεν into καὶ ἤκουον? In discussing xix. 29 (see also note on i. 5) we shall find what I think is a certain instance of a confusion between ܐ and ܘ. Further in Acts xvii. 18 the expression ܓܒܪ ܓܒܪ (each man) is used with the 3rd person plural. I conclude therefore that the Bezan text is here following an Old Syriac text which read ܐܫܬܡܥܐ.

ii. 9. ΚΑΙ ΕΛΑΜΕΙΤΑΙ
ΟΙ ΚΑΤΟΙΚΟΥΝΤΕϹ ΤΗΝ ΜΕϹΟΠΟΤΑΜΙΑΝ.

The true Greek text has καὶ Ἐλαμεῖται καὶ οἱ κατοικοῦντες κ.τ.λ., with which the Bezan Latin agrees 'et qui inhabitant'. The Syriac has 'And-Elamites (ܘܥܝܠܡܝܐ) and-those (ܘܐܝܠܝܢ) who-dwell between the-Rivers.' The word ܘܐܝܠܝܢ (and-those) would very easily fall out after the word ܘܥܝܠܡܝܐ (and-Elamites), and thus the Bezan reading would be generated.

ii. 10. ΦΡΥΓΙΑΝ
ΚΑΙ ΠΑΜΦΥΛΙΑΝ ΑΙΓΥΠΤΟΝ ΤΕ

The true Greek text has Φρυγίαν τε καὶ Παμφυλίαν, Αἴγυπτον. The Syriac is: 'And-who-(are)-from the-region of-Phrygia, and-of-Pamphylia, and-of-Egypt.' In this paraphrastic rendering the *and* is necessary before *of-Egypt*. This *and* reappears in the Bezan text (contrast the Bezan Latin 'et pamphyliam aegyptum'), which also omits the τε after φρυγίαν.

ii. 13. ΕΤΕΡΟΙ ΔΕ ΔΙΕΧΛΕΥΑΖΟΝ ΛΕΓΟΝΤΕϹ
ΟΤΙ ΓΛΕΥΚΟΥϹ ΟΥΤΟΙ ΜΕΜΕϹΤΩΜΕΝΟΙ ΕΙϹΙΝ.

The true text is ἕτεροι δὲ διαχλευάζοντες ἔλεγον ὅτι Γλεύκους μεμεστωμένοι εἰσίν.

To deal with the first clause, the Syriac has: 'But others mocking were (ܘܗܘܘ ܡܒܙܚܝܢ) at-them while saying (ܟܕ ܐܡܪܝܢ).' This is the normal Syriac rendering of such a Greek sentence. Compare Lc. xxii. 65 βλασφημοῦντες ἔλεγον, where the Syriac is: 'blaspheming were-they and-saying (ܘܐܡܪܝܢ)'; Matt. xxvii. 41 ἐμπαίζοντες...ἔλεγον, where the Syriac is: 'mocking were-they...and-saying'. This idiomatic Syriac rendering of the true Greek text the Bezan scribe *more suo* translates back literally into Greek. My position, I would add, is completely confirmed when it is noticed that in his version of Matt. xxvii. 41 he carries his literalness a stage further, making shipwreck thereby of his Greek; for there he has οι αρχιερεις ενπαιζοντες μετα των γραμματειων και φαρισαιων λεγοντες αλλογς εςωςεν.

In regard to the second line, the Syriac, with its love for pronouns (Duval, *Traité de Gram. Syriaque*, p. 287 f.), idiomatically begins the clause with ܗܠܝܢ. This reappears in the οὗτοι of the Bezan text.

ii. 14.   τοτε ϲταθειϲ δε ο πετροϲ
          ϲγν τοιϲ δεκα αποϲτολοιϲ
          επηρεν πρωτοϲ την φωνην αγτογ και ειπε͞.

The true text has: σταθεὶς δὲ ὁ Πέτρος σὺν τοῖς ἕνδεκα ἐπῆρεν τὴν φωνὴν αὐτοῦ καὶ ἀπεφθέγξατο αὐτοῖς.

I take the points which require consideration in order. (1) The τότε of the Bezan Greek, to which nothing in the Bezan Latin corresponds, remains still, as it were, outside the sentence, the δέ barring its entrance. Plainly it is an adventurer from some other text, caught in the act of breaking into the Bezan Greek. Its native place is the Syriac, which here reads: 'And-afterwards (ܘܒܬܪܟܢ) Simon Cephas with the-eleven Apostles.' An interpolated τότε is found in v. 19, x. 21, 48 (cf. xi. 26), the Syriac in each place having ܗܝܕܝܢ (then)[1]; in vii. 30 we may reasonably conclude that the Bezan

[1] Probably the Syriac 'then' in these passages is meant to represent δέ. Cod. D has a curious reading in xix. 26 ο παγλοϲ ογτοϲ τιϲ τοτε πιϲαϲ. Whence

μετὰ ταῦτα, though it answers to nothing in the Syriac Vulgate, yet represents some word or words of the Old Syriac. (2) The curious reading τοῖς δέκα ἀποστόλοις may be due to a scribe whose nervous anxiety for accuracy made him for the moment forget the election of St Matthias; compare i. 26 ܬܘܢ ܝܒ ܐܦܘܣܬܘܠܘܢ. But a reference to the Syriac suggests another explanation. The words for 'with the-eleven' are ܝܡܢ.ܬܘ ܥܡ. Would not the similarity of ܥܡ and ܥܣܪ cause a hasty reader to pass over the intermediate ܬܘ? If he did so, the reading 'with the-ten' would result. It will be noticed that the Bezan text agrees with the Syriac in inserting the word 'Apostles'. (3) After ἐπῆρεν Cod. D has an interpolated πρῶτος, Cod. E after τὴν φωνὴν αὐτοῦ an interpolated προτερον. Is there any Syriac word likely to be inserted here which could be represented equally well by either of these two Greek words? I believe that ܩܕܡ answers all the requirements. It is a favourite word in the Syriac N.T., being commonly used to express the προ- of compound verbs (see on viii. 19) and being employed in Mc. i. 35 (πρωὶ ἔννυχα λίαν), Lc. xxi. 38 (ὤρθριζεν), xxiv. 22 (ὀρθριναί), to express the idea of *earliness*. The Greek word of Cod. D or that of Cod. E well represents it. We conclude that an Old Syriac copy of the Acts read here ܩܕܡ ܐܪܝܡ ܩܠܗ (lit. he-was-early he-lifted-up his-voice, i.e. he spoke at once). Compare Matt. xvii. 25 (Greek and Syriac). (4) Why is the forcible ἀπεφθέγξατο driven out and its place taken by the feeble εἶπεν? The word ἀποφθέγγεσθαι occurs twice elsewhere in the N.T., viz. Acts ii. 4, xxvi. 25. In both these passages the Syriac renders it by the extremely common word ܠܡܠܠܘ (to-speak). Here it has the appropriate but equally common comes this τις τότε? Just below are the words 'that-not Gods (are) they those (ܗܢܘܢ ܐܠܗܐ: note ΟΥΤΟΙ in Cod. D) who-by-hands &c.' I would suggest that the two Syriac words given above in some badly written MS. slipped up a line and took their place after the Syriac word 'Paul'; that then an emendation, favoured, if not caused, by transcriptional corruption, was made and the two words became ܩܕܡ ܐܡܪ.

word ܐܡܪ, introducing St Peter's speech. Hence the Bezan εἶπεν.

In the clause which follows the Syriac has: 'All-of-them who-dwelling (are) in-Jerusalem.' The 'all-of-them' must have the first place in the sentence. Hence the Bezan reading πΑΝΤΕϹ ΟΙ ΚΑΤΟΙΚΟΥΝΤΕϹ ΙΕΡΟΥϹΑΛΗΜ, as against the true text οἱ κατοικ. Ἰερ. πάντες.

ii. 17. εϹΤΑΙ.

The true text prefixes καί. A reference to the following passages in the Syriac, in which in the Greek a καί or a δέ begins a quotation, viz. Rom. i. 17, Gal. iii. 16, Hebr. i. 6, (comp. Matt. ii. 6), seems to shew that the Syriac regularly omits the particle of connexion in a quotation from the O.T. It omits it here.

ii. 17.   ΕΠΙ ΠΑϹΑϹ ϹΑΡΚΑϹ
ΚΑΙ ΠΡΟΦΗΤΕΥϹΟΥϹΙΝ ΟΙ ΥΙΟΙ ΑΥΤΩΝ
ΚΑΙ ΘΥΓΑΤΕΡΕϹ ΑΥΤΩΝ.

The true text has ἐπὶ πᾶσαν σάρκα, καὶ προφ. οἱ υἱοὶ ὑμῶν καὶ αἱ θυγατέρες ὑμῶν. (1) The reading σάρκας may conceivably be due to the influence of the LXX. where the plural σάρκες is fairly common. But another explanation seems more in harmony with the phenomena of the Bezan text. The Syriac Vulgate has ܒܣܪ, but probably an Old Syriac text had ܒܣܪܐ, which could be taken as singular (as generally) or as plural (Jude 7, Apoc. xix. 18, 21). Here the plural might seem natural in view of the enumeration which follows. (2) The genesis of the reading οἱ υἱοὶ αὐτῶν κ. θυγ. αὐτῶν, so inexplicable in the 'Western' text, Greek and Latin, becomes obvious when we write side by side ܒܢܝܟܘܢ (your-sons) and ܒܢܝܗܘܢ (their-sons). Compare xiv. 17 ὑμῖν...τὰς καρδίας ὑμῶν, where the Syriac is... ܠܗܘܢ ܠܒܗܘܬܗܘܢ (to-them...their-hearts).

There are several variations from the true text in the Bezan text of the quotation from Joel. They are chiefly omissions. The easiest explanation of them, I believe, is that we have here a Greek representation of an early Syriac text. I will give one argument in support of this suggestion. We read in the true text (v. 18) καί γε ἐπὶ τοὺς δούλους μου καὶ ἐπὶ τὰς δούλας μου [ἐν ταῖς ἡμέραις ἐκείναις] ἐκχεῶ ἀπὸ τοῦ πνεύματός μου[, καὶ προφητεύσουσιν]. The Bezan text omits the two clauses which I have bracketed. The Syriac Vulgate has the passage in this form (the words omitted in the Bezan text are again in brackets): 'And-on my-servants and-on my-handmaids will-I-pour-out my-Spirit [in those days, and-they-shall-prophesy].' The omitted words, it will be seen come together in the Syriac, and the double omission in Greek becomes a single omission in Syriac.

ii. 23. εκδοτον λαβοντες.

The last word, which is found also in Cod. E, has no place in the true text. The worthlessness of the Bezan Latin for the criticism of the Bezan Greek is well illustrated by its relation to this particular textual problem. It reads: 'prouidentia dī auditum accepistis'. It is not the source of λαβόντες. Having got *traditum accepistis* from the Greek, the Latin scribe apparently interpreted it to mean 'Ye have received as handed down by tradition.' Hence for the word *traditum* he substituted a mental gloss upon it, and so wrote 'auditum accepistis'.

But have we here a case, such as will meet us several times in the Bezan text of the Acts, of assimilation to the Passion story of the Gospels? We turn to St John xix. 6, 'Pilate saith unto them, *Take* (λάβετε) him yourselves and *crucify* (σταυρώσατε) him... 16. Then therefore he *delivered* (παρέδωκεν) him unto them to be *crucified* (ἵνα σταυρωθῇ). 17. They *took* (παρέλαβον) Jesus therefore.'

There can, I think, be little doubt that the interpolated λαβόντες comes from Jn. xix. But the question remains whether it is originally Greek or whether it comes through an Old Syriac Version? There are several reasons which induce me to decide for the latter alternative. (1) If this gloss stood alone, it might be conceded that it is Greek. But it can hardly be separated from other clauses from the Passion story in the Gospels interpolated in the Bezan text of the Acts, which, I believe, can be shewn to come through an Old Syriac Version (see iii. 13, v. 21).   (2) It is when we think of the coincidences of Acts ii. with Jn. xix. from the point of view of an English rendering, that their force appears greatest. For then we seem to have a twofold resemblance between Acts ii. 23 and Jn. xix. 6, 16 f.—'having taken' (Acts), 'take' (Jn. xix. 6), 'took' (v. 17); 'crucified' (Acts), 'crucify' (Jn. xix. 6), 'to be crucified' (v. 16). But the moment we look at the Greek, much of the likeness between the three verses melts away. For on the one hand Jn. xix. 17 has the compound $\pi\alpha\rho\acute{\epsilon}\lambda\alpha\beta\text{ον}$; and on the other hand St John uses $\sigma\tau\alpha\upsilon\rho\acute{\omega}\sigma\alpha\tau\epsilon$, $\H{ι}\nu\alpha$ $\sigma\tau\alpha\upsilon\rho\omega\theta\hat{\eta}$, the Acts has $\pi\rho\sigma$-$\pi\eta\xi\alpha\nu\tau\epsilon\varsigma$. When however we turn to the Syriac, all those points of contact which struck us in the English, but of which a reference to the Greek robbed us, are restored to us again. The same word for 'crucify' is used in the three verses; the Syriac, having no compounds, uses the simple word 'take' in Jn. xix. 17[1]. Thus the resemblance between the passage in the Acts and that in the history of the Passion would strike a Syriac reader far more than a student of the original Greek.   (3) These verses in Jn. xix. had a place in the Diatessaron (Ciasca, p. 90 f.). They would therefore be specially familiar to Syrian Christians in early times. Indeed, though the Syriac Vulgate has not retained the word 'when they had taken' (= $\lambda\alpha\beta\acute{ο}\nu\tau\epsilon\varsigma$ Codd. DE), yet it has another word derived apparently from the same source. Its words are these: 'Him who-separated was for this same thing [comp. 1 Pet. i. 20] in the foreknowledge and-will of-God ye-*delivered* in(to)-the-hands of-wicked-men and-*crucified* and-

---

[1] The full phrase here is: 'They-took Jesus *and-made-Him-go-out*.' The italicised word may be intended roughly to represent the $\pi\alpha\rho\alpha$- of the compound verb (see note on viii. 19), but it is more probably due to assimilation to Mc. xv. 20.

slew.' The italicised words indicate the coincidences between the Syriac Vulgate in Acts ii. 23 and in Jn. xix. 6, 16, 17. We may reasonably conclude that an Old Syriac text of Acts ii. 23 contained the interpolation 'when they-had-taken', and we may further surmise that this interpolation from Jn. xix. brought into the Syriac Vulgate from the same source another interpolation viz., 'ye-delivered', though it lost its own position in the passage.

ii. 24. ΛΥϹΑϹ ΤΑϹ ωΔΙΝΑϹ ΤΟΥ ΑΙΔΟΥ.

The true text has τοῦ θανάτου (comp. Ps. xviii. 4, cxvi. 3). I do not myself doubt that in this particular case the reading τοῦ ᾅδου comes from the Syriac. For the Syriac Vulgate here reads: 'God...loosed the-pangs of-Sheol, because it was impossible that-He-should-be-held in-Sheol'; and this word *Sheol* is very natural in the Syriac N.T., comp. (in the Syriac Vulgate) Rom. x. 7 'Who descended into-the-abyss of-Sheol?' 1 Pet. iii. 19 'He preached to-the-souls which-were-held in-Sheol.' But a reading so obvious in itself in view of *v*. 31 (οὔτε ἐνκατελείφθη εἰς ᾅδην), which might too be suggested by the LXX. of Ps. xviii. 6, may well have arisen independently in different authorities. When therefore we read in the Epistle of Polycarp *c*. i. ὃν ἤγειρεν ὁ θεὸς λύσας τὰς ὠδῖνας τοῦ ᾅδου, we have no right to draw the conclusion that Polycarp was using a 'Syriacised' text.

ii. 25. προορωμην τον κυριον μου.

The true text does not add the μου. Its addition may have been suggested by *v*. 34 τῷ κυρίῳ μου. It is worth noticing however that 'my Lord' is here the Syriac reading, and the expansion of 'Lord' into 'my-Lord' is very frequent in the Syriac version: see e.g. (where the case is the vocative) Matt. vii. 21, xviii. 21, Lc. xiv. 22, Jn. xi. 32; xii. 38, Acts ix. 10, and (where the case is not the vocative) 2 Tim. iii. 11, Hebr. xiii. 6. The expansion of 'Lord' into 'our-Lord' is extremely common: see e.g. Acts i. 6, 21, ii. 47, iii. 6, xi. 24.

ii. 30. ΕΚ ΚΑΡΠΟΥ ΤΗC ΚΑΡΔΙΑC ΑΥΤΟΥ
ΚΑΤΑ CΑΡΚΑ ΑΝΑCΤΗCΑΙ ΤΟΝ X̄P̄N̄
ΚΑΙ ΚΑΘΙCΑΙ Κ.Τ.Λ.

The true text has ἐκ καρποῦ τῆς ὀσφύος αὐτοῦ καθίσαι. The Bezan text presents us with a variant and a gloss. (1) What is to be said of the very singular reading τῆς καρδίας? I believe that it is due to assimilation to v. 26 ηὐφράνθη ἡ καρδία μου. Note ἡ σάρξ μου of v. 26 and the κατὰ σάρκα of the Bezan gloss. If the passage be taken by itself, there is little or nothing to indicate whether the reading first arose in Greek or in Syriac. It is perhaps worth noticing that the Syriac Vulgate incorporates the very words of the Ps. cxxxi. 13 'Of the-fruit of-*thy-belly* will-I-make-to-sit upon thy-throne,' as though it were obliterating an error in an earlier Syriac text. But such an argument as this cannot be pressed. (2) The gloss possibly arose to limit and define the meaning of 'the fruit of thy heart'. The κατὰ σάρκα appears Pauline (Rom. i. 3, ix. 5, 1 Cor. x. 17, 2 Cor. v. 16). Nothing certain can be said of the latter part of the gloss, nor does it yield any suggestion as to its original language.

In v. 31 the words προϊδὼν ἐλάλησεν περὶ are omitted in Cod. D. The omission is obviously an accidental one. It may be due simply to the scribe dropping a line of his Greek. But it is worth noting that if the Syriac words 'on his-throne' stood over the Syriac words 'about (*lit.* on) the-resurrection', thus—

ܥܠ ܟܘܪܣܝܗ

ܥܠ ܩܝܡܬܐ

a scribe writing Greek, but following in Syriac, would very easily omit the words in question.

ii. 37. ΤΟΤΕ ΠΑΝΤΕC ΟΙ CΥΝΕΛΘΟΝΤΕC
ΚΑΙ ΑΚΟΥCΑΝΤΕC ΚΑΤΕΝΥΓΗCΑΝ ΤΗ ΚΑΡΔΙΑ
ΚΑΙ ΤΙΝΕC ΕΞ ΑΥΤΩΝ ΕΙΠΑΝ
ΠΡΟC ΤΟΝ ΠΕΤΡΟΝ ΚΑΙ ΤΟΥC ΑΠΟCΤΟΛΟΥC

ΤΙ ΟΥΝ ΠΟΙΗΣΩΜΕΝ ΑΝΔΡΕΣ ΑΔΕΛΦΟΙ
ΥΠΟΔΕΙΞΑΤΕ ΗΜΕΙΝ.

The true text has ἀκούσαντες δὲ κατενύγησαν τὴν καρδίαν, εἶπάν τε πρὸς τὸν Πέτρον καὶ τοὺς λοιποὺς ἀποστόλους Τί ποιήσωμεν, ἄνδρες ἀδελφοί; I will deal with the several points of the passage in order. (1) I have already pointed out that 'then' seems to be a favourite particle of connexion in Syriac (see above on v. 14). The interpolated words which follow are to be explained as an instance of assimilation, and, as will, I think, clearly appear, must be referred back to an Old Syriac text of the Acts. The conscience-stricken multitude of Jews on the day of Pentecost recalled the conscience-stricken multitude of Jews on the day of the Crucifixion. Let us place the Bezan text of Acts ii. 37 side by side with the Old Syriac rendering of Lc. xxiii. 48:

LUKE.	ACTS.
And all those that were assembled there,	Then all those that came together,
and saw what was done,	and heard,
were smiting upon their breast,	were pricked in the heart,
and saying.	and some of them said.

Though the Greek of Lc. *l. c.* (καὶ πάντες οἱ συνπαραγενόμενοι ὄχλοι) bears no resemblance to the language of our Bezan gloss, the phrase used in the Old Syriac

ܘܟܠܗܘܢ ܗܢܘܢ ܕܐܬܟܢܫܘ ܬܡܢ

(lit. and-all-of-them those who-assembled there) on the one hand is an exact representation in Syriac of the Bezan gloss, and on the other admirably fits in with the Syriac word which follows, as suggested by the Bezan text; ܘܫܡܥܘ (and-heard) in Acts answering to ܘܚܙܘ (and-saw) in Luke: the Vulgate in Acts has ܫܡܥܘ ܕܝܢ. It should be added that Lc. xxiii. 48 had a place in the Diatessaron (Ciasca, p. 93). (2) καί τινες ἐξ αὐτῶν εἶπαν. The gloss contained in this clause might in itself be Greek. The whole phrase (except the particle of connexion) occurs in Jn. xi. 37 τινὲς δὲ ἐξ αὐτῶν εἶπαν (Syr. 'Men however of-them said'). But the same phrase is found, as we shall see, four verses lower down (v. 41), where nothing in the Greek answers to it, in the Syriac Vulgate; and this, added to the fact that the first words of v. 37 are proved (as I believe) to come from the Old Syriac of the Acts, justifies us in holding that in the words τινὲς ἐξ αὐτῶν we have another phrase of the same venerable document. (3) Of the omission of λοιπούς before ἀποστόλους I will only remark that I believe that the palaeographical explanation of the omission is easier in Syriac than in Greek—ܠܫܡܥܘܢ (to-Simon), ܘܠܫܪܟܐ (and-to-the-residue)[1]. (4) The interpolated words in the last two lines viz....οὖν...ὑποδείξατε ἡμῖν (Cod. E ΥΠΟΔΙΞΑΤΕ ΗΜΙΝ), as those in the first line, are to be referred to assimilation. The anxious enquiry of the crowds and the answer of the Apostles 'repent' are analogous to the questioning of the multitudes by the Jordan at an earlier day of decision and the Baptist's answer to them—see Matt. iii. 7 (comp. Lc. iii. 7) τίς ὑπέδειξεν ὑμῖν; Lc. iii. 10 τί οὖν ποιήσωμεν; Possibly the οὖν is a Greek addition. As to ὑποδείξατε ἡμῖν, if we were to consider this Bezan interpolation by itself, we should say that it is certainly Greek. But taking account of its surroundings and of the fact that Cod. E several times (e.g. iii. 13, iv. 32, 39, vi. 10) joins with Cod. D in preserving a gloss which undoubtedly comes from the Old Syriac of the Acts, it will be allowed that this gloss may be referable to the same source. This verdict appears to be confirmed when it is added that the Old Syriac of Matt. iii. 7 and Lc. iii. 7 (ܡܢܘ ܚܘܝܟܘܢ) is a literal rendering of the Greek; that the same version has nothing to answer to οὖν in Lc. iii. 10; and that Matt. iii. 7, Lc. iii. 10 have a place in the Diatessaron, but not Lc. iii. 7 (Ciasca, p. 7).

ii. 41. ΟΙ ΜΕΝ ΟΥΝ ΠΙΣΤΕΥΣΑΝΤΕΣ ΤΟΝ ΛΟΓΟΝ ΑΥΤΟΥ.

The true text has ἀποδεξάμενοι. The Syriac Vulgate

---

[1] Probably the Old Syriac read ܘܠܫܪܟܗܘܢ (and-to-their-residue: see Acts xv. 17).

has: 'And-some of-them readily received his-word and-believed.' Here the 'some of-them' enables us to see why the word 'and-believed' is added. The gloss is the product, I believe, of assimilation. The result of St Peter's words at Jerusalem must needs be coordinated with the result of St Paul's words at Athens. We compare this verse and xvii. 34 as they stand in the Syriac Vulgate:

ii. 41.	xvii. 34.
And-some of-them readily received his-word and-believed.	And-some of-them clave-to-him and-believed.

For another case of assimilation to xvii. see iv. 2; and for passages where the account of St Peter's work is harmonised with that of St Paul's see v. 15, xi. 2.

Codex Bezae may, I believe, be taken as a witness that the Old Syriac had the word 'believed'. But the evidence does not enable us to decide whether the Old Syriac copy used by the Bezan scribe had an epitomised form of the full Syriac text, or whether the Bezan scribe epitomised the Old Syriac text before him. It is of course possible that the Syriac Vulgate here is an amplification of a simpler reading in the Old Syriac, represented by the Bezan Greek.

ii. 45 f. 45. καὶ ὁcοι κτηματα ειχον
η ϒπαρζεις επιπραcκον
καὶ διεμεριζον αϒτα καθημεραν πaci
τοις αν τις χρειαν ειχεν
46. παντες τε προcεκαρτεροϒν εν τω ιερω
καὶ κατοικοϒcαν επι το αϒτο κλωντες τε αρτο κ.τ.λ.

The true text is καὶ τὰ κτήματα καὶ τὰς ὑπάρξεις ἐπίπρασκον καὶ διεμέριζον αὐτὰ πᾶσιν καθότι ἄν τις χρείαν εἶχεν· καθ᾽ ἡμέραν τε προσκαρτεροῦντες ὁμοθυμαδὸν ἐν τῷ ἱερῷ, κλῶντές τε κατ᾽ οἶκον ἄρτον.

Of this passage and of the preceding clause the Vulgate Syriac has the following rendering: 44. 'And-all-of-them those who-had-believed together were, and-every-thing which-was to-them of-community was-it. 45. And-those to-whom there was a-possession selling were-they it, and dividing were-they to-each man according to what he-needing was (ܡܕܡ ܐܝܟ ܡܐ ܕܣܢܝܩ ܗܘܐ). 46. And-every-day (ܠܟܠܝܘܡ) continuing were-they in-the-temple in-one soul and-in-the-house breaking were-they bread.'

This passage in the Bezan text is a tangled one. Its difficulties arise from the fact that, often diverging from the true Greek text and coinciding with the Syriac Vulgate, it sometimes diverges from both and, as I believe, implies an Old Syriac text. I will take the points *seriatim*.

(1) The Syriac makes a change in the form of *v*. 44 ('and-every-thing...of-community was-it') which breaks in upon the construction. When it comes to the words of *v*. 45 the subject of the verbs, which has been obscured by the construction adopted in *v*. 44, must be made clear. Hence using up the words τὰ κτήματα it fashions a new clause and harmonises its opening words (ܐܝܠܝܢ ܕ) with the parallel passage in iv. 34. In all this it is exactly followed by the Bezan text, the only point of divergence being that the Bezan text has ἢ ὑπάρξεις, the Syriac equivalent of which may well have had a place in the Old Syriac. (2) In the words καθ᾽ ἡμέραν πᾶσι τοῖς ἄν τις χρείαν εἶχεν, the Bezan text differs alike from the true Greek and from the Syriac Vulgate. The Bezan chaos appears to point back to an Old Syriac text, and in some way, about which it seems impossible to dogmatise, to depend on a confusion between two pairs of Syriac words (*a*) ܟܠܗܘܢ (all-of-them) and ܟܠܝܘܡ (every-day), see below; (*b*) ܐܝܠܝܢ ܕ (those who) and ܕ ܐܝܟܡܐ (according as). (3) πάντες τε in the Bezan text corresponds with καθ᾽ ἡμέραν of the true text (with which the Syriac Vulgate (ܟܠܝܘܡ) agrees). Evidently the confusion between ܟܠܗܘܢ and ܟܠܝܘܡ noted above has been at work, but whether in the genesis of the Old Syriac text or in the mind of the Bezan scribe it is impossible to say for certain. The truth I suspect is that the two words

simply changed places in the two successive clauses of the Old Syriac. (4) The Syriac, unable to represent the long participial clauses of the Greek (προσκαρτεροῦντες... κλῶντές τε), is obliged to turn them into substantive clauses ('continuing were-they...breaking were-they bread'). This arrangement the Bezan scribe exactly follows, until in the κλῶντές τε ἄρτον he relapses again into conformity with the true Greek text. (5) The Bezan text omits ὁμοθυμαδόν, which should come after προσεκαρτέρουν. Its Syriac equivalent 'in-one soul' occurs in the Syriac Vulgate *after* 'in-the-temple'. *Either* then the Old Syriac did not render the word (probably because, as we shall see, it had a somewhat similar phrase 'they-were together' in the next sentence), and the revised (i.e. the Vulgate) version inserted it at the end of the clause, *or* the Bezan scribe, not finding the word in its usual place, did not insert it in its novel position (i.e. *after* 'in-the-temple'). Of these two alternatives a consideration of all the phenomena of the passage leads us to choose the former. (6) κατοικουσαν is for κατ᾽ οἴκους ἦσαν, just as εθορυΒογcan in xvii. 5 must be resolved into ἐθορύβουν ἦσαν (see note *in loc.*). Hence we have the reading κατ᾽ οἴκους ἦσαν ἐπὶ τὸ αὐτό. What of the ἦσαν ἐπὶ τὸ αὐτό? Two verses above (*v.* 44) the Vulgate Syriac introduces this very phrase 'those who-had believed *together* were (ܗܢܘܢ ܕܗܝܡܢܘ ܗܘܘ ܐܟܚܕܐ) and-every-thing &c.' (= πάντες δὲ οἱ πιστεύσαντες ἐπὶ τὸ αὐτὸ εἶχον κ.τ.λ.). Does it not seem likely *either* that the Old Syriac repeated this phrase, and inserted it where the Bezan Greek has it, perhaps intending it there to be a representative of ὁμοθυμαδόν (to which it otherwise has nothing to answer), and that in the revised Syriac it was omitted as having already occurred in the context; *or* that the Old Syriac brought down the phrase from *v.* 44 and utilised it in *v.* 46?

So we come to an end of the long process of unravelling this Bezan tangle. Until we obtain a direct authority for the Old Syriac text of the Acts, some points must still remain in obscurity. But the whole structure of the Bezan passage becomes, I believe, intelligible if, and only if, we regard it as a rendering of a Syriac Version.

ii. 47. καὶ ἐχοντες χαριν προς ολον τον κοcμον.

Instead of κόσμον the true text has λαόν. In Syriac 'the people' is ܥܡܐ, 'the world' is ܥܠܡܐ. The change from the former to the latter in Syriac would be very easy and, when the sense in any degree favoured it, natural. In two passages in the Syriac N.T. it has taken place. The Old Syriac of Matt. i. 21 reads 'He-shall-save *the-world* (ܠܥܠܡܐ) from its-sins', where the Syriac Vulgate has ܠܥܡܗ (his-people), thus conforming with the true Greek text. Again, the Syriac Vulgate (as yet the Old Syriac has not been recovered in this passage) has this version of the Angel's message (Lc. ii. 10): 'For behold I announce to you great joy which shall be to all *the world* (ܥܠܡܐ).' For the hyperbolism thus imported into the text compare the Syriac rendering of Acts xvi. 37 (δείραντες ἡμᾶς δημοσίᾳ) 'They-beat-us before all *the-world* (ܩܕܡ ܥܠܡܐ ܟܠܗ).' Note too the Syriac in xvii. 26 'From one blood He-made all *the-world* of-men.' I venture to think that there can be no doubt that the Bezan reading here preserves for us that of the Old Syriac. The Syriac Vulgate here, as in Matt. i. 21, restored conformity with the Greek text by reading ܥܡܐ (people).

ii. 47. ο Δε κ̄c̄ προcετιθει τουc cωζομενουc
καθημεραν επι το αυτο εν τη εκκληcια.

The true text has no ἐν τῇ ἐκκλησίᾳ. This expression is, I believe, the result of assimilation. The blessing which rested on St Peter's work at Jerusalem must needs be compared with the blessing which rested on the work of Barnabas and Saul at Antioch. See Acts xi. 24 'And much people was added unto the Lord...26. And it came to pass, that even for a whole year they were gathered together in the church.'

The last words indeed of this extract, as we read them in the Greek (ἐγένετο δὲ αὐτοῖς...συναχθῆναι ἐν τῇ ἐκκλησίᾳ), present no points of contact with Acts ii. 47. But it is otherwise with the Syriac, which is as follows: '*Together* assembled were-they *in-the-church* (ܐܟܚܕܐ ܐܬܟܢܫܘ ܒܥܕܬܐ)'. It is from this passage, I believe, that the expression 'in-the-church' was imported into the Old Syriac of Acts ii. 47.

It is worth while to note, as far as we can trace it, the sequel of this intrusion. The stages, I think, are three. (1) Either in the Greek or in the Syriac the words 'together' and 'in-the-church' were transposed. It doubtless seemed right to bring the latter expression into closer connexion with 'were being saved (*Syriac*, were living)' and 'the Lord was adding'. (2) Then, apparently in the Greek, the expression ἐπὶ τὸ αὐτό stepped over the boundary line and took its place in the history of the miracle at the Beautiful Gate. Thus we get the familiar 'Textus Receptus' ἐπὶ τὸ αὐτὸ δὲ Πέτρος καὶ Ἰωάννης. (3) We come now to the revision of the Syriac text. In the Old Syriac there was, it seems, at the beginning of Acts iii. an interpolated introductory clause. It probably took different forms. The form preserved in Cod. D is 'And in these days'; that retained in the Syriac Vulgate is simply 'And-it-came-to-pass'. These two authorities very probably present us each with a portion of a fuller gloss, and it is likely that in some Old Syriac texts Acts iii., like Acts ii. (see Cod. D), began with the formula 'And it came to pass in these (those) days'. When then the Old Syriac came to be revised and, as it would appear, conformed, at least partially, to the Greek 'Syrian' text (see Dr Hort, *Introduction*, pp. 84, 156), the word 'together' had to be taken into the history of the miracle, while yet an introductory formula, varying possibly in different Old Syriac texts, had established itself at the beginning of that history. The word 'together' is inserted late in the opening sentence, which runs as follows: 'And-it-came-to-pass that-when going-up (were) Simon Cephas and-John *together* into-the-temple

&c.' Thus in the Syriac Versions the word 'together' introduced the expression 'in-the-church' into ii. 47, and then was itself caught by the tide of textual revision and carried far away from its chosen companion. The history, which we have tried to follow out, repays us for the labour, if it shews us, as I believe it does, the character of the Syriac Vulgate as a revised text when compared with the Old Syriac, which we are learning to look upon as the basis of no small part of the Bezan text.

iii. 1. πετρος και ϊωανης ανεβαινον εις το ιερον
το δειλεινον επι την ωραν ενατη τη προσευχης.

There is nothing to answer to τὸ δειλινόν in the true Greek text.

Here once more an interpolation is due to assimilation, in this case to assimilation of the beginning to a later stage of the history. In iv. 3, after the healing of the man and St Peter's speech to the people, we read that it was now evening, ἦν γὰρ ἑσπέρα ἤδη. The connexion of this clause with the interpolated τὸ δειλινόν does not appear. But let us appeal to the Syriac. In iv. 3 the Syriac Vulgate has ܪܡܫܐ ܠܗ ܗܘܐ ܩܪܒ (there-had-drawn-nigh the-evening). Did the Old Syriac interpolate in iii. 1 the word ܒܪܡܫܐ (in-the-evening)? The phrase τὸ δειλινόν occurs in the sense of *evening* in the LXX. version of Gen. iii. 8 (= 'in the cool of the day'), Exod. xxix. 39, 41, Lev. vi. 20, 2 Kings xviii. 29 ('the offering of the *evening* oblation'), comp. 2 Chron. xxxi. 3 (τὰς ὁλοκαυτώσεις...τὴν δειλινήν). In the Syriac Version of all these passages except Gen. *l. c.*, 2 Kings *l. c.*, the word ܪܡܫܐ is found; it is in fact the common, if not the only, Syriac word for *evening*. It is impossible to doubt that ܒܪܡܫܐ was intruded into the Old Syriac of Acts iii. 1, and that the Bezan scribe employs an unusual word to represent it, as he does in the case of other Syriac glosses (see v. 39, vi. 10).

iii. 2. τογ αιτειν ελεημοcγνην παρ αγτων
εicπορεγομενων αγτων εic το ϊερον.

Here the strange phrase παρ' αὐτῶν εἴσπορ. αὐτῶν takes the place of the true text παρὰ τῶν εἰσπορευομένων. In the Syriac Vulgate the clause stands thus: 'that-he-might-be asking alms from those (ܡܢ ܐܝܠܝܢ) who-entering (were) into-the-temple'. This is the natural Syriac rendering of the true Greek text; and the Bezan Greek is an almost literal translation of the Syriac. The second αὐτῶν will be noticed. This may be intended to represent ܡܢܗܘܢ, which the Old Syriac may have idiomatically appended to the verb expressing motion. But it is more likely that the Bezan scribe carelessly rendered ܡܢ ܐܝܠܝܢ twice. Such an explanation must be given of the repeated τοῦτο in v. 12, and is the most probable account of και εκαθιcαν τε (ii. 3) and και αριθμοc τε (iv. 4).

iii. 3 ff. 3. ογτοc ατενιcαc τοιc οφθαλμοιc αγτογ
και ιδων πετρον και ϊωανην
μελλονταc ειναι εic το ιερον
ηρωτα αγτογc ελεημοcγνην
4. εμβλεψαc δε ο πετροc εic αγτον
cγν ϊωανην και ειπεν ατενειcον εic ημαc
5. ο δε ατενειcαc αγτοιc
προcδοκων τι λαβειν παρ αγτων.

The important words in the true text are: 3. ὃς ἰδὼν... εἰσιέναι... ἠρώτα ἐλεημοσύνην λαβεῖν. 4. ἀτενίσας δὲ Π.... σὺν τῷ Ἰωάνῃ εἶπεν Βλέψον εἰς ἡμᾶς. 5. ὁ δὲ ἐπεῖχεν αὐτοῖς προσδοκῶν τι παρ' αὐτῶν λαβεῖν.

The different points in this passage must be taken in order. (1) The Syriac relative ܕ is weak. The Syriac naturally renders ὅς by ܗܢܐ (this-man). Hence the Bezan οὗτος. (2) The variation of the words expressing *sight* in the different authorities is instructive:

True Greek.	Bezan Latin.	Bezan Greek.	Syriac.
v. 3 ἰδών	uidit	ἰδών	ܚܳܪ
v. 4 ἀτενίσας	intuitus	ἐμβλέψας	ܚܳܪ ܒܗ
βλέψον εἰς...	aspice	ἀτένισον	ܚܽܘܪ
v. 5 ἐπεῖχεν	adtendebat	ἀτενίσας	ܚܳܪ

The Syriac ܚܪ, denoting an earnest gaze, is the common rendering of ἀτενίσαι. It translates βλέψαι εἰς in the three passages in which it occurs (Mc. xii. 14, Lc. ix. 62, Jn. xiii. 22). It is perhaps the most natural word in such a context as this to render ἐπεῖχεν, which does not occur again in the N.T. exactly in this sense[1]. The Syriac is characteristically courageous in its repetition of a word, and here it has the courage of its character. It is impossible, I think, to resist the conclusion that the Bezan text simply renders the Syriac words expressing sight. (3) But what of the interpolated phrase in v. 3 ἀτενίσας τοῖς ὀφθαλμοῖς αὐτοῦ? 'To see with the eyes' is an O.T. phrase. It occurs e.g. in 2 Kings vii. 2, Ps. xci. 8, Ezek. xl. 4, where the Syriac verb is ܚܪ. The Old Syriac, as we shall see, is fond of interpolating O.T. phrases (see on iv. 24, v. 38, vii. 43). It would naturally enough here interpolate the words ܟܕ ܚܪ ܒܥܝܢܘܗܝ (when he-had-looked with-his-eyes). (4) In v. 3 the Syriac perforce renders the compound εἰσιέναι by the simple verb ܥܠ (enter). Hence the Bezan text has the simple verb ειναι (= ἰέναι). (5) The interpolated αὐτούς in the next line answers to the Syriac ܡܫܐܠ ܗܘܐ (' asking was-he from-them '). Further, λαβεῖν is omitted, there being nothing in the Syriac to answer to it. Cod. E reads ΛΑΒΕΙΝ ΠΑΡ ΑΥΤΩΝ. (6) In v. 4 σὺν Ἰωάνην, probably because of the unvarying Syriac form ܥܡ ܝܘܚܢܢ. Cod. E has CYN TW IωANHN. We have probably other examples of the influence on the Bezan Greek of the *sound* of Syriac terminations in iv. 14 CYN AYTωN (ܥܡܗܘܢ), vii. 2 ΑΝΔΡΕC ΑΔΕΛΦΗ (plur. in ܐ̄—).

[1] In the Philoxenian Version this verb is used to translate προσέχειν in Matt. xvi. 6, 11, 12, Lc. xii. 1, Acts viii. 10, 1 Tim. iv. 3.

Similarly we may explain xviii. 2 διΑ τὸ τεταχέναι κλαύδιος, for, though here ܣܘܢܛܠܘ (Claudius) is the subject of the sentence, the name is of course unalterable in Syriac. (7) Note ὁ δὲ ἀτενίσας...προσδοκῶν. The Bezan scribe is rendering a construction of the Old Syriac: his Greek has no construction. (8) In v. 5 the Syriac has: 'Since hoping was-he to-receive from-them something.' This order in Syriac is the natural one, that the infinitive with ܠ may stand immediately after the verb on which it depends. The Bezan text adopts the Syriac order, except that τι retains its place next after προσδοκῶν. Cod. E still more closely follows the Syriac, ΠΡΟϹΔΟΚΩΝ ΛΑΒΕΙΝ ΤΙ ΠΑΡ ΑΥΤΩΝ.

The number and variety of the ways in which the Bezan text is in this passage brought into conformity with the Syriac precludes, I venture to think, any possibility of disagreement as to our verdict.

iii. 7 f. 7. ΚΑΙ ΠΙΑϹΑϹ ΑΥΤΟΝ ΤΗϹ ΔΕΞΙΑϹ ΧΕΙΡΟϹ ΗΓΕΙΡΕΝ
ΚΑΙ ΠΑΡΑΧΡΗΜΑ ΕϹΤΑΘΗ
ΚΑΙ ΕϹΤΑΙΡΕΩΘΗϹΑΝ ΑΥΤΟΥ
8. ΑΙ ΒΑϹΕΙϹ ΚΑΙ ΤΑ ϹΦΥΡΑ ΚΑΙ ΕΞΑΛΛΟΜΕΝΟϹ ΕϹΤΗ
ΚΑΙ ΠΕΡΙΕΠΑΤΕΙ ΧΑΙΡΟΜΕΝΟϹ
ΚΑΙ ΕΙϹΗΛΘΕΝ ϹΥΝ ΑΥΤΟΙϹ ΕΙϹ ΤΟ ΙΕΡΟΝ
ΑΙΝΩΝ ΤΟΝ ΘΝ.

The true text has: καὶ πιάσας...ἤγειρεν αὐτόν· παραχρῆμα δὲ ἐστερεώθησαν αἱ βάσεις αὐτοῦ καὶ...καὶ περιεπάτει καὶ εἰσῆλθεν σὺν αὐτοῖς εἰς τὸ ἱερὸν περιπατῶν καὶ ἁλλόμενος καὶ αἰνῶν τὸν θεόν.

Again I take seriatim the several points of the passage.

(1) The αὐτόν is omitted (as it is by Cod. E) after ἤγειρεν, probably because in the Syriac it is represented by the suffix, and as part of the verb it was easily (especially after the previous αὐτόν) passed over by the Bezan scribe. (2) What of the interpolated word ἐστάθη? If we turn to Lc. vi. 8 we read (in a similar context) ἀναστὰς ἔστη; for the latter word Cod. D has ἐστάθη; the Syriac is ܩܡ. The Old

Syriac then probably read in Acts iii. 7 'and-immediately he-stood-up'. This interpolated word is due to assimilation. The miracle of the disciple must be conformed to the miracle of the Master. In Mc. ix. 27 we read κρατήσας τῆς χειρὸς αὐτοῦ ἤγειρεν αὐτόν, καὶ ἀνέστη. There is no verbal resemblance between the Greek of Mc. ix. 27 and the Bezan Greek of Acts iii. 7. Let us compare the two passages in Syriac:

[ܩܡ]	ܘܐܩܝܡܗ	ܒܐܝܕܗ	ܐܚܕܗ Mc.
[and-he-stood-up]	and-lifted-him-up	by-his-hand	He-took-him

ܘܐܩܝܡܗ	ܕܝܡܝܢܐ	ܒܐܝܕܗ	ܐܚܕܗ Acts
and-lifted-him-up	of-the-right-side	by-his-hand	he-took-him

The correspondence is here complete, and there can be no doubt that Mc. ix. 27 (which has a place in the Diatessaron, Ciasca, p. 44) is the source of the gloss in the Old Syriac. It is probable that this version, inserting ܩܡ ('he-arose') in Acts iii. 7, omitted it in the following verse, where it answers to ἔστη, but that the Bezan scribe retained it in conformity with the true Greek text. The Syriac Vulgate indeed in Mc. ix. 27 omits the word ܩܡܘ (and-he-arose), possibly assimilating that passage to the true text of Acts iii. 7, and the text of Ciasca's Diatessaron is conformed to that of the Vulgate. But it cannot be doubted that an Old Syriac text rendered the ἀνέστη of the Greek, and that it adopted what is, I believe, the invariable Syriac equivalent of that Greek verb, viz. ܩܡ (see Matt. ix. 9, Mc. i. 35, ii. 14, v. 42, vii. 24, x. 1[1], &c.). (3) The word χαιρόμενος (Cod. E has ΧΑΙΡωΝ) is an insertion. The form does not encourage us to maintain a Greek origin for the gloss. We have, I believe, again a case of assimilation in the Old Syriac. See Acts viii. 39, 'He went on his way rejoicing (ܒܕ ܚܕܐ).' This phrase is parallel in structure to the Syriac rendering of αἰνῶν τὸν

---

[1] In Mc. x. 50 ܩܡ=ἀναπηδήσας. In Acts x. 25 the Bezan reading ο δε κορνηλιος εκπηδησας και συναντησας αυτω represents, I believe, an Old Syriac text ܐܪܥܗ ܩܡ (he-arose and-met-him). This Syriac text is perhaps due to assimilation to Jn. xi. 29 (ܩܡܬ), 30 (ܐܪܥܗ).

θεόν (ܐܬܚܝܠ ... ܗܘ). (4) We have seen reason to think it probable that the Old Syriac, having already used the word, omitted the Syriac equivalent of ἔστη in *v*. 8. But, this word being eliminated, the natural Syriac rendering of ἐξαλλόμενος περιεπάτει would be: 'leaping was-he and-walking'. If this be allowed, we have an explanation of the fact that, whereas the Syriac Vulgate has 'And-he-entered with-them into-the-temple, while *walking and-leaping* and-praising God', the Old Syriac, as represented by Cod. D, omits these participles 'walking and-leaping'; since, in the reverse order, they had occurred just above.

We conclude therefore that the Old Syriac of *v*. 8 was as follows:

'Leaping was-he and-walking,
While rejoicing:
And-he-entered with-them into-the-temple,
While praising God.'

The result of this attempt to restore the Old Syriac in this verse seems to justify itself by the parallelism which it introduces into the text.

iii. 10. ΕΠΙ ΤΩ ΓΕΓΕΝΗΜΕΝΩ ΑΥΤΩ.

The τῷ συμβεβηκότι of the true text is naturally rendered (comp. Mc. x. 32, 1 Pet. iv. 12) in the Syriac by ܕܗܘܐ (which-was). The Bezan scribe no less naturally translates the Syriac by τῷ γεγενημένῳ.

iii. 11. ΕΚΠΟΡΕΥΟΜΕΝΟΥ ΔΕ ΤΟΥ ΠΕΤΡΟΥ ΚΑΙ ΙΩΑΝΟΥ
ΣΥΝΕΞΕΠΟΡΕΥΕΤΟ ΚΡΑΤΩΝ ΑΥΤΟΥΣ
ΟΙ ΔΕ ΘΑΜΒΗΘΕΝΤΕΣ ΕΣΤΗΣΑΝ
ΕΝ ΤΗ ΣΤΟΑ Η ΚΑΛΟΥΜΕΝΗ ΣΟΛΟΜΩΝΟΣ ΕΚΘΑΜΒΟΙ.

The true text has κρατοῦντος δὲ αὐτοῦ τὸν Πέτρον καὶ τὸν Ἰωάνην συνέδραμεν πᾶς ὁ λαὸς πρὸς αὐτοὺς ἐπὶ τῇ στοᾷ τῇ καλουμένῃ Σολομῶνος ἔκθαμβοι.

In the Bezan text the whole passage is reshaped. (1) The man's *entrance into* the temple *with the Apostles* (*v*. 8) seemed to imply his *going out with them* (comp. xii. 21, 23 Cod. D). This desire for fulness of detail was reinforced by the constant wish for assimilation to passages of the Gospels. There is no passage in the Greek Gospels which would supply the phraseology of this passage; but in the Syriac Version (where ἀκολουθεῖν αὐτῷ becomes 'to-go with- (behind-)him') there are several which might do so. Thus Lc. xxii. 39 καὶ ἐξελθὼν ἐπορεύθη...ἠκολούθησαν δὲ αὐτῷ καὶ οἱ μαθηταί is thus rendered in the Old Syriac: 'And-going-out was-He and-He-went (ܘܐܙܠ ܗܘܐ ܢܦܩ)...and-there-went (ܘܐܙܠܘ) with-Him also His-disciples.' For the Syriac phrase compare the Old Syriac of Matt. xx. 29 and the Vulgate of Acts x. 23. (2) The second interpolation οἱ δὲ θαμβηθέντες ἔστησαν is due to assimilation in the Old Syriac to Acts ix. 7 'standing were-they while wondering (ܡܬܕܡܪܝܢ),' where the Greek is ἱστήκεισαν ἐνεοί. Compare the Syriac Vulgate of Lc. i. 21 'But the-people *standing* (ܩܐܡ) was and-waiting for-Zacharias and-wondering (ܡܬܕܡܪܝܢ)'. The word ܬܡܗ (wonder) has occurred in iii. 10, and ܬܡܗ is a twin word with ܕܡܪ, which the Syriac Vulgate uses to render ἔκθαμβοι (see the Syriac of x. 45). (3) In τῇ στοᾷ τῇ καλουμένῃ we have a literal rendering of the Syriac ܕܡܬܩܪܐ. Compare the Hebraistic language of the Apocalypse, e.g. ii. 20 τὴν γυναῖκα Ἰεζάβελ, ἡ λέγουσα.

iii. 12.   ΑΠΟΚΡΙΘΕΙϹ ΔΕ Ο ΠΕΤΡΟϹ ΕΙΠΕΝ ΠΡΟϹ ΑΥΤΟΥϹ.

The true text has ἰδὼν δὲ ὁ Πέτρος ἀπεκρίνατο πρὸς τὸν λαόν.
The Bezan text seems to point back to an Old Syriac text; for (*a*) the intrusion of εἶπεν (see ix. 13, x. 47, xi. 9, xxii. 28, xxiv. 10) and that of the pronoun ('to-them') are, I believe, both characteristically Syriac changes; (*b*) the Syriac Vulgate has: 'And-when Simon saw, he-answered and-said to-them'—a reading which has the appearance of being a conflation of the reading of the true Greek text and that of the Old Syriac.

iii. 12. ωc HMων TH ιΔιΑ ΔγΝΑΜι H εγcεβιΑ
τογτο πεποιηκοτων τογτο περιπατειν αγτο.

The true text has ὡς ἰδίᾳ δυνάμει ἢ εὐσεβείᾳ πεποιηκόσιν τοῦ περιπατεῖν αὐτόν. The Syriac Vulgate has: 'As-if by-the-power which-is-ours (ܕ) or by-our-authority we-have-done this-thing (ܗܢܐ) that this-man should-walk.' The Bezan text (*a*) represents the Syriac 'this-thing' both before and after πεποιηκότων (see on iii. 2); (*b*) translating more or less independently from the Syriac diverges from the construction of the true Greek. It is possible that the Old Syriac read here ܐܝܟ ܗܘ ܕܚܢܢ (as-if we-ourselves).

iii. 13 f. 13. ον ημεις παρεΔωκατε εις κρισιν
και απηρνηςαςθαι αγτον
κατα προςωπον πειλατογ
τογ κριναντος εκεινογ
απολγειν αγτον θελοντος
14. γμεις Δε τον Αγιον και Δικαιον
εβαργνατε και ητηςατε ανΔρα φονεια.

The true text has ὃν ὑμεῖς μὲν παρεδώκατε καὶ ἠρνήσασθε κατὰ πρόσωπον Πειλάτου, κρίναντος ἐκείνου ἀπολύειν· ὑμεῖς δὲ τὸν ἅγιον καὶ δίκαιον ἠρνήσασθε, καὶ ᾐτήσασθε ἄνδρα φονέα χαρισθῆναι ὑμῖν.

There are several points here of peculiar interest. (1) What of the interpolated words εἰς κρίσιν? Cod. E has παρεΔωκατε εις κριτηριον. There are three passages in the Syriac Versions where this verb 'to-give-up' is followed by 'to-judgment (ܠܕܝܢܐ)'. Both the Old and the Vulgate Syriac so translate Lc. xxiv. 20 παρέδωκαν αὐτόν...εἰς κρίμα θανάτου —'They-gave-Him-up to-the-judgment of-death.' In Mc. xiii. 9 (where the Old Syriac has not been yet recovered) the Syriac Vulgate has 'They-shall-give-you-up to-judgments (ܠܕܝܢܐ)' as its rendering of παραδώσουσιν ὑμᾶς εἰς συνέδρια. Again, the Syriac Vulgate in Lc. xx. 20 (παραδοῦναι αὐτὸν τῇ ἀρχῇ...τοῦ ἡγεμόνος) has the same phrase 'that-they-might-

give-Him-up to-judgment and-to-the-power of-the-Governor'
(where it should be noticed that the Old Syriac and Cod. D
have simply 'give Him up to the Governor'). The evidence
then is overwhelming that 'to-give-up to-judgment' is a
characteristic Syriac phrase used in the Gospels. The word
ܕܝܢܐ (judgment), it should be added, renders κρίσις in
Matt. v. 21 f., x. 15, xi. 22 &c., and κριτήριον in 1 Cor. vi. 2, 4.
Thus Cod. D and Cod. E each gives a different but quite
natural translation of the same Syriac word. (2) The
gloss αὐτὸν θέλοντος may be accounted for by Lc. xxiii.
20 θέλων ἀπολῦσαι τὸν Ἰησοῦν. But it will be noticed that
in the Syriac Vulgate the phrase occurs also in Jn. xix. 12
'Pilate wishing was (ܗܘܐ ܨܒܐ) that-he-might-release-Him
(ἐζήτει ἀπολῦσαι αὐτόν).' Both passages had a place in the
Diatessaron (Ciasca, p. 89 f.).   (3) The ἠρνήσασθε of the
true text was literally translated by ܟܦܪܬܘܢ. This either
had been in the Old Syriac corrupted into ܟܒܪܬܘܢ or
was so read by the Bezan scribe[1]. For instances of this
word used *in malam partem* see Payne Smith, *Thes. Syr.*, sub
voce.

I may be allowed to refer to a passage in the Gospels in
which, as I believe, a corruption in the Syriac text has
generated an almost meaningless reading in Cod. D and in
several Old Latin MSS. In Cod. D we read in Mc. ix. 15,

ΠΑϹ ΟΧΛΟϹ ΕΙΔΟΝΤΕϹ ΤΟΝ ΙΗΝ ΕΘΑΜΒΗϹΑΝ
ΚΑΙ ΠΡΟϹΧΕΡΟΝΤΕϹ ΗϹΠΑΖΟΝΤΟ ΑΥΤΟΝ.

In the Syriac Vulgate the words are : 'They-saw-Him and-
wondered and-ran (ܪܗܛܘ) and-saluted Him.' In the Old
Syriac copy, on which the text of Cod. D is ultimately based, I
believe that the place of ܪܗܛܘ (and-they-ran) was taken
by ܪܘܙܘ (and-they-exulted). In the Arabic Tatian we
read (Ciasca, p. 43) 'et prae gaudio properantes'. If this
reading is indeed that of the Diatessaron (and the divergence

---

[1] This suggestion was made by Harvey, *Irenaeus*, ii. p. 55.

iii. 16, 17] IN THE BEZAN TEXT OF THE ACTS. 39

from the Syriac Vulgate, to which the text of the Arabic Tatian is usually conformed, makes this probable), then the blunder ܐܝܐܝܐ must go back to the days before Tatian; for Tatian's text involves a conflation of the two words 'and-they-ran' and 'and-they-exulted'. In other words the Syriac text of the Gospels had already a history in Tatian's time. And this fact, if fact it be, implies the existence of a Syriac St Mark far back in the Second Century.

iii. 16. ΤΟΥΤΟΝ ΘΕωΡΕΙΤΕ ΚΑΙ ΟΙΔΑΤΕ
ΟΤΙ ΕCΤΕΡΕωCΕΝ ΤΟ ΟΝΟΜΑ ΑΥΤΟΥ.

The true text has τοῦτον ὃν θεωρεῖτε καὶ οἴδατε ἐστερέωσεν τὸ ὄνομα αὐτοῦ. The true text is followed by the Bezan Latin, and (as far as the construction goes) by the Syriac Vulgate. There can, I think, be little doubt that the ὅτι of the Bezan Greek answers to an ambiguous ܕ in Syriac, and that the Old Syriac was as follows: 'This-man (ܗܢܐ) seeing (are-)ye and-knowing (are-)ye whom-it-strengthened (ܕܐܫܪܗ) (even-)His-name.' The Syriac Vulgate has 'Him...He (ܗܘ) strengthened and-healed', the last word coming from the Gospel history (e.g. Matt. iv. 24, xii. 15, xiv. 14, xv. 30, xix. 2, xxi. 14).

iii. 17. ΚΑΙ ΝΥΝ ΑΝΔΡΕC ΑΔΕΛΦΟΙ ΕΠΙCΤΑΜΕΘΑ
ΟΤΙ ΥΜΕΙC ΜΕΝ ΚΑΤΑ ΑΓΝΟΙΑΝ ΕΠΡΑΞΑΤΕ ΠΟΝΗΡΟ͞Ν.

The true text has καὶ νῦν, ἀδελφοί, οἶδα ὅτι κατὰ ἄγνοιαν ἐπράξατε.

The reading of the Syriac Vulgate is: 'But now, my-brethren, knowing (am) I (ܐܢܐ ܝܕܥ) that-in-error ye-did this-thing (ܗܕܐ ܣܥܪܬܘܢ).'

Here note the following points. (1) ἐπιστάμεθα seems to imply either that the Old Syriac had, or that the Bezan scribe read it as having, the common participial form ܝܕܥܝܢܢ (knowing(-are)-we): see e.g. Matt. xxi. 27, xxii. 16, Mc. xi. 33. It might arise from ܝܕܥܢܐ (knowing(-am)-I: 2 Cor.

xii. 2). (2) The ὑμεῖς μέν of the Bezan text suggests that the Old Syriac read ܐܢܬܘܢ ... ܐܢܬܘܢ܁ (that-ye...did) just as the Vulgate Syriac has in v. 13 ܐܢܬܘܢ ܐܢܬܘܢ܁ (that-ye...gave-up), and in v. 14 ܐܢܬܘܢ ... ܐܢܬܘܢ (ye...denied), i.e. that the Old Syriac emphasises the *you* in the words of extenuation as it had done in the words of accusation. Compare on v. 39. (3) About the interpolated πονηρόν we remark (*a*) that the 'this' of the Syriac Vulgate shews that the Syriac 'ye-did' could not well stand without some defining word; (*b*) that the words ܥܒܕ (do) and ܒܝܫ (evil) are very commonly used together; see the Syriac rendering of κακοποιῆσαι (Mc. iii. 4, Lc. vi. 9), of κακοποιός (1 Pet. iv. 15, cf. Jn. xviii. 30), of οἱ τὰ φαῦλα πράξαντες (Jn. v. 29), and compare Matt. xxvii. 23 || Mc., Lc.; Lc. xxiii. 32 f., 39, Rom. vii. 19, xiii. 4. See also the Bezan text in v. 4, viii. 24, Lc. xxiii. 41 ΟΥΤΟϹ ΔΕ ΟΥΔΕΝ ΠΟΝΗΡΟΝ ΕΠΡΑΞΕΝ.

iii. 19. ΟΠΩϹ ΑΝ ΕΠΕΛΘΩϹΙΝ ΚΑΙΡΟΙ.

The true text has the simple verb ἔλθωσιν, with which the Bezan Latin ('ut ueniant tempora') agrees.

The Syriac Vulgate has: 'that-there-may-come to-you (ܠܟܘܢ ܐܬܝܢ)'. Compare the Vulgate of Lc. xix. 43 'The-days shall-come to-thee (ܠܟܝ ܐܬܝܢ)'. The 'to-you', so natural an addition in the pronoun-loving Syriac, is literally represented in Cod. E ΟΠΩϹ ΑΝ ΕΛΘΩϹΙΝ ΚΑΙΡΟΙ ΑΝΑΨΥΞΕΩϹ ΥΜΙΝ. Cod. D represents it by the compound verb, so that here we have the converse of the case noted in i. 4.

iii. 21. ΔΙΑ ϹΤΟΜΑΤΟϹ ΤΩΝ ΑΓΙΩΝ ΑΥΤΟΥ ΤΩΝ ΠΡΟΦΗΤΩΝ.

The true text has ἀπ' αἰῶνος after τῶν ἁγίων. In the Syriac Vulgate the words ܕܡܢ ܥܠܡ (who-(were)-from eternity) stand at the end of the clause. The words therefore may have easily fallen out in the Old Syriac, or the Bezan scribe, as the words come out of order when compared with the Greek, may have omitted them. The latter is perhaps the preferable alternative, since Cod. E reads παντων των αγιων των απ αιωνος αυτου προφητων. But Cod. D and Cod. E may represent here, as we shall see that they seem to do in some other passages, slightly differing forms of the Old Syriac text. It is instructive to compare Lc. i. 70. There the true Greek text and the Syriac Vulgate are the same as here, and there the Bezan text exactly represents the Syriac phrase—δια στοματος αγιων προφητων αυτου των απ αιωνος.

iii. 22.   ως εμου αυτου ακουςεςθαι.

The true text has προφήτην ὑμῖν ἀναστήσει...ὡς ἐμέ· αὐτοῦ ἀκούσεσθε.

If the Bezan scribe is here following the Syriac, his mistake might easily arise if the division of lines, or the erasure of the dividing point, brought together the words ܐܘܢ ܠܝ ܫܡܥܘܢ (like-me him hear-ye).

iii. 24.   ο ελαλησεν.

The true text has ὅσοι ἐλάλησαν.

It is impossible to disprove the suggestion that the quod-quod (= quotquot) of the Bezan Latin generated the ὅ in the Bezan Greek. But this suggestion, it will be noticed, does not account for ἐλάλησεν. I believe that the Old Syriac represented ὅσοι ἐλάλησαν by ܡܠܠܘ; that the Bezan scribe translated the verb as singular according to the sound (see on i. 13) and carelessly translated ܕ by ὅ. Notice that ܡܠܠ occurs just before in v. 21.

iv. 1 f.   1.   λαλουντων δε αυτων
προς τον λαον τα ρηματα ταυτα
επεστησαν οι ιερεις και οι σαδδουκαιοι
2.   καιαπονουμενοι
δια το διδασκειν αυτους τον λαον

ΚΑΙ ΑΝΑΓΓΕΛΛΕΙΝ ΤΟΝ ΙΗΝ
ΕΝ ΤΗ ΑΝΑΣΤΑΣΕΙ ΤΩΝ ΝΕΚΡΩΝ.

The true text has λαλούντων δὲ αὐτῶν πρὸς τὸν λαὸν ἐπέστησαν αὐτοῖς οἱ ἀρχιερεῖς καὶ ὁ στρατηγὸς τοῦ ἱεροῦ καὶ οἱ Σαδδουκαῖοι, διαπονούμενοι διὰ τὸ διδάσκειν αὐτοὺς τὸν λαὸν καὶ καταγγέλλειν ἐν τῷ Ἰησοῦ τὴν ἀνάστασιν τὴν ἐκ νεκρῶν. The points in the passage are these. (1) The Syriac Vulgate has: 'And-while these words speaking (ܡܠܐ ܟܕ ܗܠܝܢ) were-they'. The addition of 'these words' is natural in Syriac because of the Semitic love for 'cognate accusatives'. The Bezan text and that of Cod. E (ΤΑΥΤΑ ΤΑ ΡΗΜΑΤΑ) follow the Syriac. (2) For ἐπέστησαν αὐτοῖς the Syriac Vulgate has 'there-rose against-them'. The Bezan text is contented with the compound verb without the pronoun, probably for the reason given above (see on iii. 19). (3) The Bezan text omits καὶ ὁ στρατ. τοῦ ἱεροῦ. The omission, I think, can be easily explained when we turn to the Syriac. The Syriac word ܪܒܝ ܟܗܢܐ (captain or captains) is pointed as a plural in the Syriac Vulgate here and v. 24, 26 (in the latter verse it goes with a verb which is in the plural)[1]. But it will be noticed that there is a similarity in form between the words, ܘܪܒܝ ܟܗܢܐ (καὶ οἱ στρατηγοί) and ܘܙܕܘܩܝܐ (καὶ οἱ Σαδδουκαῖοι), so that the eye of a scribe might easily pass from the former to the latter, and the phrase 'and-the-captains of-the-temple' fall out. That this omission was actually made in the Old Syriac text we have independent evidence in the fact that the Syriac Vulgate has here: 'the-Priests and-the-Sadducees and-the-captains of-the-temple'. When the Old Syriac was revised, the omitted words were added, but added at the end of the clause. (4) What of the remarkable reading in v. 2 καὶ ἀναγγέλλειν κ.τ.λ.? In an earlier passage (ii. 41) we

---

[1] In Lc. xxii. 52 (στρατηγοὺς τοῦ ἱεροῦ) the Old and the Vulgate Syriac in different ways avoid the word.

found reason to think that the Syriac text followed by Cod. D assimilated the account of St Peter's preaching to that of St Paul's preaching in xvii. (*v.* 33). In the present passage the Syriac Vulgate has: 'And-preaching (ܘܡܟܪܙܝܢ)(-were) in-Christ about (ܥܠ) the-resurrection'. In xvii. 18 it has: 'Because that Jesus and-His-resurrection preaching was-he (ܡܣܒܪ ܠܗܘܢ ܘܠܩܝܡܬܗ ܠܝܫܘܥ) to-them'. The use of the same verb in the two passages, while the Greek verbs differ, is probably a survival of fuller assimilation in the Old Syriac. If the Old Syriac of xvii. 18 had 'Because that-about Jesus and-the-resurrection (ܡܛܠ ܕܥܠ ܝܫܘܥ ܘܩܝܡܬܗ) preaching was-he to-them', the reading ܒܩܝܡܬܐ (in-the-resurrection) would very easily arise and pass into our present passage. I venture to offer this suggestion as to the genesis of this reading, fully acknowledging that it is very largely conjectural.

iv. 5. επι την αγριον ημεραν.

The ἡμέραν is an addition to the true text. The Syriac Vulgate has ܐܚܪܢܐ ܠܝܘܡܐ, where the word 'day' is necessary.

iv. 6. ιωναθας.

The true text has Ἰωάννης.

The difference between the two names in Greek is much more considerable than that between ܝܘܚܢܢ (John) and ܝܘܢܬܢ (Jonathan). In xiii. 8 there is a remarkable variation in a name due to Syriac influence. Cod. D has ετ ιμας (= ετοιμας, as is clear from the Bezan Latin 'etoemas'). A confusion between *l* and *t* would be easy in Latin; but the fresh transliteration remains to be accounted for. The variation therefore is probably to be traced to a confusion of ܠ and ܛ in Syriac, which produced the reading ܐܛܝܡܘܣ.

iv. 9. ανακρεινομεθα αφ γμω.

The ἀφ' ὑμῶν, absent from the true Greek text, but found in Cod. E, is a literal rendering of the Syriac ܡܢܟܘܢ.

iv. 12. ΚΑΙ ΟΥΚ ΕCΤΙΝ ΕΝ ΑΛΛω ΟΥΔΕΝΙ
ΟΥ ΓΑΡ ΕCΤΙΝ ΕΤΕΡΟΝ ΟΝΟΜΑ ΥΠΟ ΤΟΝ ΟΥΡΑΝΟ͂
Ο ΔΕΔΟΜΕΝΟΝ ΑΝΘΡωΠΟΙC.

The true text has καὶ οὐκ ἔστιν ἐν ἄλλῳ οὐδενὶ ἡ σωτηρία, οὐδὲ γὰρ ὄνομά ἐστιν ἕτερον ὑπὸ τὸν οὐρανὸν τὸ δεδομένον ἐν ἀνθρώποις. The points to be considered are these. (1) What of the omission of ἡ σωτηρία? In v. 10 Cod. E reads ΕΝ ΤΟΥΤω ΟΥΤΟC ΠΑΡΕCΤΗΚΕΝ ΕΝωΠΙΟΝ ΥΜωΝ CΗΜΕΡΟΝ ΥΓΙΗC ΚΑΙ ΕΝ ΑΛΛω ΟΥΔΕΝΙ. Here there are two interpolations (a) σήμερον from v. 9 and (b) ἐν ἄλλῳ οὐδενί from v. 12. Preserved in Cod. E we may well suspect that these two interpolations are of Syriac origin. Further, they are both consonant with what we have learned to be a characteristic of the Old Syriac text of the Acts, viz. its love of fulness and of assimilation. But again, the Syriac Vulgate of v. 10 in its emphatic rendering of ἐν τούτῳ—'in Him Himself (ܒܗ ܒܗ)'—seems to preserve an indication that this gloss once followed in the Syriac—'in Him Himself...and in no other'. We may then conclude that in all probability the Old Syriac ended v. 10 with the words ܘܠܐ ܒܐܢܫ ܐܚܪܝܢ (and-not in-a-man another). Now if these words of v. 10 were in a scribe's mind, when he came to v. 12 ܘܠܝܬ ܒܐܢܫ ܐܚܪܝܢ (and-there-is-not in-a-man another) he would be very likely to omit the word 'salvation' which did not occur in v. 10. (2) The Syriac Vulgate has for the two last lines: 'For there-is not a-name another-one under heaven which-has-been-given (ܕܐܬܝܗܒ) to-men.' With this the Bezan Greek exactly corresponds, except that it has the order ἕτερον ὄνομα and that it retains the δεδομένον of the true Greek, and by its retention of it makes shipwreck of the grammar. As to the last point however it is not unlikely that the Old Syriac has ܕܐܬܝܗܒ. Compare v. 25 ος...ΛΑΛΗCΑC.

iv. 14. ΟΥΔΕΝ ΕΙΧΟΝ ΠΟΙΗCΑΙ Η ΑΝΤΙΠΕΙΝ.

The true text has nothing to answer to ποιῆσαι ἤ.

With it the Bezan Latin ('nihil habebant contradicere') agrees. The Syriac Vulgate has: 'And-not able (ܡܫܟܚܝܢ) were-they anything to-say against-them'. The Syriac participle here used means either 'finding' (e.g. Matt. xi. 29, xxii. 9) or 'able' (e.g. Matt. ix. 15, x. 28). This phrase then of the Bezan text has affinities with several passages in the N.T., when Syriac is the medium of comparison, affinities which at once vanish if the Greek is referred to. Thus the interpolated words may be due to assimilation to Lc. xix. 48 'And-not finding (ܡܫܟܚܝܢ) were-they what they-*might-do*.' Compare Jn. xv. 5 'Because without me *not able* (ܡܫܟܚܝܢ) (are-)ye *to-do anything*'; Acts xix. 36 'Since therefore against this one is *not able* (ܡܫܟܚ) *to speak*, it-is-right for-you that-ye-be quiet and-*do* not *anything* in-haste.' It should be specially noticed that the same word is interpolated in the Syriac of 2 Cor. xiii. 8 (οὐ γὰρ δυνάμεθά τι κατὰ τῆς ἀληθείας), which runs thus: 'For *not able-are*-we (ܡܫܟܚܝܢ) that-we-*should-do anything* (ܢܥܒܕ ܡܕܡ) against the-truth.' The word interpolated in our passage has a Syriac ring, when we compare the context with other passages, and we may with confidence conclude that it was inserted in the Old Syriac Version.

iv. 15. εξω τογ cγνεδριογ απαχθηναι.

For the last word the true text has ἀπελθεῖν; so the Bezan Latin 'extra concilium habire'. The Syriac Vulgate, employing the idiom of the 'indeterminate third person' plural (comp. Gesen. *Hebr. Gram.* § 137), has: 'Then they-commanded that-they-should-cause-to-go-out them from their-council.' For the word ܐܦܩ in this connexion compare Jn. xix. 13, 16, Acts vii. 58. Thus the Bezan text gives a very fair Greek equivalent of the Syriac idiom[1].

[1] The reading of Cod. E in *v*. 17 (εινα μη επι πλιον διανεμηθη εις τον λαον τα ρηματα ταγτα) is interesting in connexion with the Syriac Vulgate: 'But that-no further there-go-forth this report (ܛܒܐ).'

iv. 18.   CYNKATATIΘEMENωN ΔE AYTωN TH ΓNωMH
          ΦωNHCANTEC AYTOYC ΠAPHΓΓEIΛANTO.

The true text has καὶ καλέσαντες αὐτοὺς παρήγγειλαν. To take the points separately: (1) The first line is a gloss. There are obvious points of contact and of contrast between Joseph of Arimathea and Gamaliel. The position of the latter towards the Apostles recalls that of the former in regard to Christ. This then is a harmonising gloss adapted from Lc. xxiii. 51 (οὗτος οὐκ ἦν συνκατατεθειμένος τῇ βουλῇ καὶ τῇ πράξει αὐτῶν). The words τῇ γνώμῃ shew (especially when this gloss is considered as one of a series, see e.g. v. 32) that it is not a Greek gloss but goes back to the Old Syriac text of the Acts (τῇ βουλῇ = ܒܨܒܝܢܐ = τῇ γνώμῃ)¹. In regard to Lc. xxiii. 51 it should be noticed that (a) the Syriac Vulgate has: 'This-man was not consenting to-their-will and-to-their-deed'; this very probably represents one form of the Old Syriac; (b) the form of the Old Syriac as preserved in the Curetonian fragments varies considerably from this last text—'This man who did not equal his-mind with the-accusers'; (c) the passage has a place in the Diatessaron—'Non consenserat autem consilio et actibus perditorum' (Ciasca, p. 93). (2) On φωνήσαντες, see below p. 64.

iv. 24.   OI MEN OYN AKOYCANTEC KAI EΠIΓNONTEC
          THN TOY ΘῩ ENEPΓEIAN.

The true text has simply οἱ δὲ ἀκούσαντες.

Can we by reference to the Syriac throw any light upon the remarkable gloss, with which the line concludes? The Syriac word which in Eph. i. 19, iii. 7, Col. i. 29, 2 Thess. ii. 9, 11 represents ἐνέργεια is ܡܥܒܕܢܘܬܐ. In Col. i. 29 however, owing to a confusion between like words, in place of ܡܥܒܕܢܘܬܐ (operation) all MSS. but one read ܡܥܕܪܢܘܬܐ (help). This latter word, according to Payne Smith, Syr.

---

¹ γνώμῃ is rendered by ܨܒܝܢܐ in the Hexapla, Ps. lxxxii. 3, Prov. ii. 16.

Thes., is found elsewhere in Scripture only in 3 Esdras viii. 27 and 2 Cor. i. 11 ('By-the-help of-your-prayer'). I believe then that, while for some reason in Col. i. 29 the rarer was substituted for the commoner word, in the case of this gloss the converse process has been at work, and that behind the Bezan gloss there lies an Old Syriac gloss—'And they when they heard and recognised the *help* of God.' The arguments for this suggestion, which, I admit, appear to me strong, are these: (1) The gloss thus restored makes excellent sense. It forms a most appropriate preface to the prayer which immediately follows. (2) In this prayer Ps. ii. is quoted and made the basis of petition. Now this thought of God's help is characteristic of the Psalms. In numberless passages of the Syriac Psalter words of this root are used in reference to divine assistance. Take, for example, Ps. xlvi., a companion Psalm to Ps. ii.: there we read *v.* 1 'O-our-God...our-helper.' *v.* 5 'God shall-help-her.' *v.* 7 'Our-helper the-God of-Jacob.' Compare e.g. cxvii. 6 quoted in Hebr. xiii. 6. Note too Ps. xx. 6 '*Known* it-is that God rescueth His-anointed' (Ps. ii. 2, cf. Acts iv. 26). (3) The gloss thus read links the history of St Peter and the Eleven with the history of St Paul: see Acts xxvi. 21 f. 'The-Jews were wishing to-kill-me, but God helped-me (ܥܕܪܢܝ).'

This restoration of the Old Syriac will be confirmed when in later passages we have clear instances of that version inserting O.T. phrases, see v. 38, vii. 43, xii. 10, xix. 29.

iv. 31. ΚΑΙ ΕΛΑΛΟΥΝ ΤΟΝ ΛΟΓΟΝ ΤΟΥ ΘΥ ΜΕΤΑ ΠΑΡΡΗϹΙΑϹ ΠΑΝΤΙ ΤΩ ΘΕΛΟΝΤΙ ΠΙϹΤΕΥΕΙΝ.

The last line is a gloss, which occurs in Cod. E in the same form. I suspect that it, like most of the other glosses in the Bezan text of the Acts, is due to assimilation. But I have not been able to trace it to its source. If it stood alone, we might suppose it to be originally Greek and compare the words which in 'The Preaching of Peter' (preserved by Clement, *Strom.* vi. 43, see Hilgenfeld, *Nov. Test. extra Canonem*, p. 56) are put into our Lord's mouth: ἐὰν μὲν οὖν τις θελήσῃ τοῦ Ἰσραὴλ μετανοῆσαι διὰ τοῦ ὀνόματός μου πιστεύων (v. l. [τοῦ] πιστεύειν, see Bp. Westcott, *Introduction to the Study of the Gospels*, p. 459) ἐπὶ τὸν θεόν κ.τ.λ. But this gloss cannot be isolated from other glosses; and when we consider (*a*) how frequently the word ܨܒܐ (to-will) is used in the Syriac N.T.; it occurs as the equivalent of no less than nine Greek words; (*b*) that it is inserted, when there is nothing in the Greek to answer to it, in the Vulgate Syriac of Acts x. 33 (so Cod. D), xxv. 26, cf. xxviii. 16; (*c*) that Cod. E has the gloss, a MS. which preserves Old Syriac glosses found also in Cod. D, often in a different form (see on *v.* 32), we must allow that it is at least probable that this gloss goes back to the Old Syriac text of the Acts. The phrase 'he who willeth to believe' may well have occurred in some passage in the Old Syriac of the Gospels, which as yet has not been recovered.

iv. 32. ΚΑΙ ΟΥΚ ΗΝ ΔΙΑΚΡΙϹΙϹ ΕΝ ΑΥΤΟΙϹ ΟΥΔΕΜΙΑ.

These words are an addition to the true text.

Cod. E has ΚΑΙ ΟΥΚ ΗΝ ΧΩΡΙϹΜΟϹ ΕΝ ΑΥΤΟΙϹ ΤΙϹ.

It appears certain that the two Codices present two translations of the same phrase. Can we refer this gloss to the influence of assimilation? Can we point to any clause in the Syriac Gospels which could naturally bear these two renderings? We turn to Jn. ix. 16, a verse which has a place in the Diatessaron (Ciasca, p. 64). There we read: 'And-a-division was there among-them (ܐܝܬ ܦܠܓܘܬܐ ܗܘܬ ܒܗܘܢ)', comp. Jn. vii. 43, x. 19. This phrase completely fulfils the conditions, if ܐܝܬ is changed into the corresponding negative ܠܝܬ, and if, as the οὐδεμία of Cod. D and the τις of Cod. E seem to suggest, there are added such words as ܐܦ ܠܐ ܚܕ (see Jn. xix. 11 Gr. and Syr.). The word ܦܠܓܘܬܐ is used as the equivalent of σχίσμα in Jn. *ll. cc.*, 1 Cor. xii. 25; of διαμερισμός in Lc. xii. 51; in Jas. iii. 17 it is used in translating ἀδιάκριτος ('without division is-it').

It is instructive to notice that the Bezan Latin ('et non erat *accusatio* in eis ulla') is based on a misunderstanding of διάκρισις[1].

iv. 34. ΟΥΔΕ ΓΑΡ ΕΝΔΕΗC ΤΙC ΥΠΗΡΧΕΝ ΕΝ ΑΥΤΟΙC
ΟCΟΙ ΓΑΡ ΚΤΗΤΟΡΕC ΗCΑΝ ΧΩΡΙΩΝ
Η ΟΙΚΕΙΩΝ ΥΠΗΡΧΟΝ ΠΩΛΟΥΝΤΕC
[Κ]ΑΙ ΦΕΡΟΝΤΕC ΤΕΙΜΑC ΤΩΝ ΠΙΠΡΑCΚΟ[ΜΕΝ]ΩΝ
ΚΑΙ ΕΤΙΘΟΥΝ.

The true text has οὐδὲ γὰρ ἐνδεής τις ἦν ἐν αὐτοῖς· ὅσοι γὰρ κτήτορες χωρίων ἢ οἰκιῶν ὑπῆρχον, πωλοῦντες ἔφερον τὰς τιμὰς τῶν πιπρασκομένων καὶ ἐτίθουν. The passage in the Syriac Vulgate runs thus: 'And-one *there was not* (ܗܘܐ ܕܠܐ ܐܢܫ) among-them who-lacked; for those who-possessing *were* fields and-houses *selling were-they and-bringing* the prices of any-thing which(-was-being)-sold, and-placing (it) were-they &c.' The Bezan text is, it will be seen, a conflation of the true Greek and a Greek rendering of the Syriac. (1) In the first line the Bezan scribe renders ܗܘܐ ܕܠܐ by the emphatic οὐδὲ...ὑπῆρχεν. (2) In the second line his κτήτορες ἦσαν precisely corresponds with the Syriac 'possessing were'. (3) In the third and fourth lines he literally translates the Syriac 'selling were-they and-bringing'. The only difference is one of order. The Syriac has 'selling were-they', the Bezan text ὑπῆρχον πωλοῦντες. But this is easily explained. The ὑπῆρχον comes from the true Greek text, where it is attached to the previous clause ὅσοι γάρ κ.τ.λ. In the Bezan text its place in that clause has been already taken by ἦσαν; hence the ὑπῆρχον is left free to go with πωλοῦντες, and with it to represent the Syriac 'selling were-they'. The whole passage is an instructive example of the union of revolutionary and conservative elements in the Bezan text. The Bezan scribe pulls down the fabric of the true Greek text, but he uses the fragments of it as he rears a new structure, Greek in vocabulary but largely Syriac in idiom.

[1] Origen *in loco* (Cramer, *Cat.*, p. 82) knew the gloss: ὅπου σχίσμα, ὅπου διαίρεσις καὶ ἀσυμφωνία...κακίας εἰσὶ γνωρίσματα· ὅπου δὲ ἑνότης καὶ ὁμόνοια... ἀρετῆς γνωρίσματα.

V. 9.   Ο ΔΕ ΠΕΤΡΟC ΑΥΤΗΝ ΤΙ ΟΤΙ
           CΥΝΕΦΩΝΗCΕΝ ΥΜΕΙΝ[1].

The true text has ὁ δὲ Π. πρὸς αὐτήν Τί ὅτι συνεφωνήθη ὑμῖν...;
The Bezan Latin has: 'quid utique conuenit uobis'. It is of course open to any one to hold that the Bezan Greek is here assimilated to the Bezan Latin.

But, when we keep in view the proved characteristics of the Bezan text, we cannot but think it probable that the Bezan συνεφώνησεν represents some phrase of the Old Syriac. The Syriac Vulgate has: 'Since ye-made-yourselves-equal to-tempt the-Spirit of-the-Lord, behold &c.' Compare the Old Syriac rendering of Lc. xxiii. 51: 'This man who did not equal his-mind with the-accusers'. The Philoxenian Version of Acts v. 9 however renders συνεφωνήθη ὑμῖν by means of the idiomatic use of the impersonal 3rd fem. sing. of the verb— ܐܫܬܘܝܬ. Compare e.g. the use of ܟܪܝܐ (it-was-sad) in 2 Cor. vii. 9 ܟܪܝܐ ܠܟܘܢ (it-was-sad to-you), Matt. xiv. 9, xvii. 23, xviii. 31. Other examples of this Syriac idiom may be found in Nöldeke, *Syr. Gram.*, p. 176. But no more mechanically literal translation of this ܐܫܬܘܝܬ ܠܟܘܢ could be given than the Bezan συνεφώνησεν ὑμῖν. If then we may suppose that the words of the Philoxenian Version reproduce, or coincide with, the Old Syriac rendering of συνεφωνήθη ὑμῖν, the problem suggested by the Bezan συνεφώνησεν ὑμῖν finds a natural solution.

V. 12.   ΚΑΙ ΗCΑΝ ΟΜΟΘΥΜΑΔΟΝ ΑΠΑΝΤΕC
           ΕΝ ΤΩ ΙΕΡΩ ΕΝ ΤΗ CΤΟΑ ΤΗ CΟΛΟΜΩΝΟC.

The true text has καὶ ἦσαν ὁμοθυμαδὸν πάντες ἐν τῇ Στοᾷ Σολομῶντος.
What of the interpolation ἐν τῷ ἱερῷ? Cod. E reads here ΚΑΙ ΗCΑΝ ΟΜΟΘΥΜΑΔΟΝ ΠΑΝΤΕC ΕΝ ΤΩ ΝΑΩ CΥΝΗΓΜΕΝΟΙ ΕΝ ΤΗ CΤΟΑ

---

[1] Cod. E begins ch. v., ΕΝ ΑΥΤΩ ΔΕ ΤΩ ΚΑΙΡΩ. The phrase is an exact translation of the Syriac clause with which c. xii. begins. The same Greek however occurs in I.c. xiii. 1.

v. 15] IN THE BEZAN TEXT OF THE ACTS. 51

Coλομωνoc. The Syriac Vulgate reads: 'And-all-of-them assembled (ܐܬܟܢܫ) were together'. The addition of 'assembled' is quite in the manner of the Syriac, which, as we have seen (on ii. 1 f.), more than once uses the word in rendering ὁμοθυμαδόν. But this Syriac word appears in the συνηγμένοι of Cod. E. When then we have to deal with the gloss 'in the temple', we can say with something like certainty that it comes from the Old Syriac, partly because it occurs in Cod. E by the side of a literal representation of a Syriac word, partly because the difference between Cod. D (ἐν τῷ ἱερῷ) and Cod. E (ἐν τῷ ναῷ) points back to a common original, which previous experience shews us to be an Old Syriac Version. Probably various influences combined to suggest the interpolated ܒܗܝܟܠܐ (in-the-temple)—(1) It assimilates this passage to Lc. xxiv. 53, Acts ii. 46. (2) It is an obvious gloss on 'in Solomon's porch'. (3) It is very natural in connexion with the word 'assembled'; compare the Syriac of Jn. xviii. 20 'I taught in-the-synagogue (ܒܟܢܘܫܬܐ) and-in-the-temple whither all the Jews assemble (ܡܬܟܢܫܝܢ = συνέρχονται)'.

v. 15. ΙΝΑ ΕΡΧΟΜΕΝΟΥ ΠΕΤΡΟΥ ΚΑΝ Η CΚΙΑ ΕΠΙCΚΙΑCΗ
ΤΙΝΙ ΑΥΤΩΝ ΑΠΗΛΛΑCCΟΝΤΟ ΓΑΡ
ΑΠΟ ΠΑCΗC ΑCΘΕΝΙΑC
ΩC ΕΙΧΕΝ ΕΚΑCΤΟC ΑΥΤΩΝ.

The words ἀπηλλάσσοντο γὰρ κ.τ.λ. are an interpolation. Cod. E has και ργcθωcιν απο παcηc αcθενιαc ηc ειχον.

Previous experience will have encouraged us to look for passages in the Gospels and the Acts which would suggest a gloss answering to the Greek both of Cod. D and of Cod. E. It is well to state clearly the conditions of the problem. The Syriac gloss must be such as will account for (*a*) the difference of construction at the beginning; (*b*) the variation in the ending; (*c*) the readings ἀπηλλάσσοντο and ῥυσθῶσιν; (*d*) the variations ὡς and ἧς.

In xix. 12 (ὥστε...καὶ ἀπαλλάσσεσθαι ἀπ' αὐτῶν τὰς

4—2

νόσους) we have in the Vulgate Syriac: 'and-departing (ܘܦܪܝܢ) were-they from-them (even) the-infirmities'. But the word ܦܪܩ is used in two senses (1) to deliver, (2) to depart. In the first sense it occurs in Vulgate of Lc. xi. 4 (= ῥῦσαι ἡμᾶς); in 1 Pet. ii. 9 the passive participle is found in the phrase ܥܡܐ ܦܪܝܩܐ ('a redeemed people'). We may look then to xix. 12 to supply us with part of the Old Syriac gloss, viz. ܟܘܪܗܢܐ (infirmity) and ܦܪܩܝܢ (delivered). In this part of the gloss the Syriac scribe was actuated by the desire (which some modern critics have freely ascribed to the author of the Acts himself) to equalize the miracles and ministry of St Peter and of St Paul (comp. e.g. the gloss in xi. 2).

But we must turn to another passage, viz., the interpolated clause of Jn. v. 4, a clause which has no place in the Old Syriac, but which may well have been current in some extra-Canonical Syriac authority (see below on *v.* 18). We are only concerned with the last words of that clause. In the printed text of the Syriac Vulgate it stands thus: ܟܠ ܟܐܒܐ ܐܝܟܐ ܕܐܝܬ ܗܘܐ ܠܗ (every disease which (lit. that which-)was to-him).

From a remembrance of these two passages I believe that the following gloss sprang up in the Old Syriac of Acts v. 15—

ܘܦܪܩܝܢ	ܗܘܘ	ܡܢ	ܟܠ	ܟܘܪܗܢܐ	ܐܝܟܐ	ܕܐܝܬ	ܗܘܐ
and-delivered	from	every		infirmity	that		which-was

ܠܐܢܫ	ܐܢܫ	ܡܢܗܘܢ
to-each		of-them

This gloss, as we have endeavoured to reconstruct it, satisfies each of the conditions laid down above. (*a*) The preceding context of the gloss in the Syriac is as follows: 'So that in-the-streets bringing-out were-they the-sick laid on-beds, that-when there-was going (by) Simon even his-shadow might-rest (ܬܛܠ) upon-them'. If at this point the gloss followed, it might be taken *either* (as in Cod. E) as part of the subordinate clause, *or* (as in Cod. D) as part of the main narrative. In the latter MS., since the Greek sentence, of which the gloss is to form a part, has the form ὥστε... ἐκφέρειν, the scribe dovetails the gloss into its place by the γάρ. (*b*) The closing words of the Syriac gloss could only be translated into Greek paraphrastically. Cod. D follows the Syriac more closely. Cod. E is content to render the compound phrase by the 3rd person plural. (*c*) The Syriac word 'delivered' is equally well translated by ῥύεσθαι and ἀπαλλάσσεσθαι, the latter word being suggested by its use (though in a different sense) in xix. 12. (*d*) Cod. E rightly translated ܕ ܐܝܬ by ἧς. Owing to an easy confusion of like words (see on ii. 45) the Bezan scribe seems either to have had before him in the Old Syriac, or else to have thought that he had before him, ܕ ܐܝܟ, and this he naturally (see 1 Cor. v. 7) renders by ὡς.

If this restoration of the Old Syriac text at this point is correct, it has a special interest as indicating that the extra-Canonical words, which later became embodied in Jn. v. 4, were known when this early Version was made.

v. 18. καὶ ἐπορεύθη εἰς ἕκαστος εἰς τὰ ἴδια.

This gloss appears, like a portion of the last, to be derived from an extra-Canonical source, viz. the *pericope adulterae*. The words in the common Greek text of [Jn.] vii. 53 are ἐπορεύθησαν (Cod. D ἐπορεύθη) ἕκαστος εἰς τὸν οἶκον αὐτοῦ. The gloss in Acts v. 18 taken by itself might be considered as originally Greek. But when we reflect (*a*) that it can hardly be separated from the gloss which occurred three verses earlier and from other glosses, which appear to be Syriac in origin ; (*b*) that the words which follow in the Bezan text τοτε διa νυκτοc αγγελοc κυ agree, with regard both to the inserted τότε (see on ii. 14) and to the order of the words, with the Syriac Vulgate as against the true Greek text ; (*c*) that in two points (viz. εἷς ἕκαστος and εἰς τὰ ἴδια) the Bezan gloss diverges from the Greek text of [Jn.] vii. 53, we must allow that this gloss probably goes back to the Old Syriac of the Acts. The few fragments of the Old Syriac of the Gospels privately printed

54 THE OLD SYRIAC ELEMENT [v. 21

by the late Prof. Wright include Jn. vii. 37—viii. 19. But, as he observes, 'the whole *pericope* ch. vii. 53—viii. 11 is omitted in this version as well as in the Pĕshīttā'. Though however as yet the *pericope* had not won its way into the Gospels, it may well have been current. Indeed the fact that two extra-Canonical narratives connected with St John's Gospel appear to be drawn upon in two (apparently) Syriac glosses (*vv.* 15, 18) lying close together, makes it, I venture to think, a plausible conjecture that some well known Syriac book (perhaps a Syriac translation of Papias) contained both the account of the Pool of Siloam and the history of the Woman taken in adultery[1].

It should be added that the printed editions of the Syriac Vulgate have the following words (which may be derived from an ancient authority) in [Jn.] vii. 53: 'There-went (ܐܙܠ) therefore each-one (ܠܒܝܬܗ) to-his-house'. About this we may notice that (*a*) the singular verb here agrees with the ἐπορεύθη of Cod. D in [Jn.] vii. 53 and Acts v. 18; (*b*) the εἷς ἕκαστος of Cod. D in the latter passage may be intended to represent the Syriac ܠܒܝܬܗ, the phrase ἕκαστος εἰς τὰ ἴδια being probably used because it occurs in Jn. xvi. 32.

v. 21. ΕΓΕΡΘΕΝΤΕΣ ΤΟ ΠΡωΪ
ΚΑΙ ΣΥΓΚΑΛΕΣΑΜΕΝΟΙ ΤΟ ΣΥΝΕΔΡΙΟΝ.

The true Greek text has συνεκάλεσαν τὸ συνέδριον.

The intention of the gloss is obviously to harmonize the account of the Apostles' trial with the history of the Lord's trial. In Matt. xxvii. 1 (πρωίας δὲ γενομένης), Mc. xv. 1 (εὐθὺς πρωί), Jn. xviii. 28 (ἦν δὲ πρωί) we have mention of the *early* meeting of the Jewish authorities. In Lc. xxiii. 1 we read καὶ ἀναστὰν (= the Old Syriac ܩܡܘ) ἅπαν τὸ πλῆθος αὐτῶν κ.τ.λ. Here then we have the material for the gloss. Was it not then originally Greek? I think not, and for these reasons. (*a*) The word for *arose* in Lc. *l. c.* is ἀναστάν, not ἐγερθέν. It is singular, not plural. The Old Syriac has ܩܡܘ ('and-

[1] Compare the Section on the man working on the Sabbath inserted by Cod. D in Lc. vi. 5.

they-arose'), which would give the ἐγερθέντες of our gloss. (*b*) The phrase τὸ πρωί is not found in the N.T. (*c*) We shall be able to connect the gloss with a passage in the Diatessaron. (*d*) The context in the Bezan text of Acts v. 21 shews signs of Syriac influence. If then we join together the Syriac of ἀναστάν (Lc.) and of πρωί (Mc.), we get the words ܒܨܦܪܐ ܩܡܘ which, retranslated into Greek, give ἐγερθέντες τὸ πρωί. It remains to justify two arguments urged above, (*c*), (*d*). As to (*c*), in Ciasca's Latin of the Diatessaron (p. 88) we read: 'Et surgens uniuersum concilium eorum apprehenderunt[1] Iesum et adduxerunt eum uinctum in praetorium'. This is a conflation of Mc. xv. 1, Lc. xxiii. 1 and Jn. xviii. 28. The word 'early' is not found in the form of the Diatessaron given by Ciasca. As it occurs in three out of the four Gospels, it is probable that it had a place in the Diatessaron, and if so, then it must have been inserted just at this point. It is not unlikely that our Bezan gloss comes straight from the Diatessaron. As to (*d*), when we remark the broken construction of the Bezan text of Acts v. 21 (ἐγερθέντες...καὶ συνκαλεσάμενοι...καὶ ἀπέστειλαν), it seems clear that the scribe *more suo* translated from the Syriac, and then relapsed into transcription of the common Greek text.

v. 26. ΤΟΤΕ ΑΠΕΛΘωΝ Ο CΤΡΑΤΗΓΟC CΥΝ ΤΟΙC ΥΠΗΡΕΤΑΙC
ΗΓΑΓΟΝ ΑΥΤΟΥC ΜΕΤΑ ΒΙΑC
ΦΟΒΟΥΜΕΝΟΙ ΓΑΡ ΤΟΝ ΛΑΟΝ ΜΗ ΛΙΘΑCΘωCΙΝ.

The true text is τότε...ὑπηρέταις ἦγεν αὐτούς, οὐ μετὰ βίας, ἐφοβοῦντο γὰρ κ.τ.λ.

The Syriac Vulgate has: 'Then there-went *the-Captains* with the-officers that-they-might-bring them, not with-violence, for fearing were-they &c.' The Bezan text follows the Syriac in two points[2]—(1) The word ܐܪܟܘܢܐ is pointed

---

[1] The 'apprehenderunt' seems due to assimilation to Jn. xix. 17 (Syriac: see above on ii. 23).

[2] The omission of οὐ in the second line is, I think, a mistake in the transcription of the Greek. Perhaps it is due to the preceding -ΟΥC.

plural (see on iv. 1), and here takes plural verbs. The Bezan scribe retains the singular ὁ στρατηγός, but in ἤγαγον lapses into the plural of the Syriac. (2) φοβούμενοι is simply a translation of the Syriac participle.

v. 28 f. 28. καὶ βογλεσθαι εφαγαγειν εφ ημας
το αιμα τογ ανθρωπογ εκεινογ
29. πειθαρχειν δε θω μαλλον η ανθρωποις
ο δε πετρος ειπεν προς αγτογς
30. ο θc̄ των πατερων κ.τ.λ.

The true text is καὶ βούλεσθε...τοῦ ἀνθρώπου τούτου. ἀποκριθεὶς δὲ Πέτρος καὶ οἱ ἀπόστολοι εἶπαν Πειθαρχεῖν δεῖ θεῷ μᾶλλον ἢ ἀνθρώποις. ὁ θεὸς τῶν πατέρων κ.τ.λ. At first sight the change of δεῖ into δέ seems to suggest that the Bezan arrangement of the clauses is originally Greek. It certainly is not Latin, for the *oportet* remains a resolute obstacle in the way of transformation. But the cluster of changes in this passage must not be isolated from those in many other passages, which, as we have seen conclusive reason to believe, are Syriac. And further, if we try to work through the problem here in terms of the Syriac, we shall, I think, find that the stages of change are natural and easy. These stages are, I believe, the following. (1) The Old Syriac text, which lies behind that of Cod. D, rejoices on the one hand in a fulness of connecting clauses (see e.g. ii. 1, 37, iii. 1), and on the other aims at giving definiteness and accuracy, whether by addition or correction, to statements about the *personae dramatis* (e.g. i. 26, ii. 14, xiii. 44). Now the speech *vv*. 30—32 is evidently that of one apostle speaking for his fellows. And who could be the spokesman but St Peter (comp. ii. 14, iii. 12, iv. 8)? Hence before *v.* 30 the words are interpolated 'And Peter said to them'. (2) Noting the order in the true Greek and in the Syriac Vulgate, we may assume that the Old Syriac rendering of the clause πειθαρχεῖν δεῖ θεῷ began thus: ܘܐܠܗܐ ܠܡܫܡܥ ܘܠܐ (it-is-necessary to-God to-hearken). Now the word ܘܠܐ

v. 32]   IN THE BEZAN TEXT OF THE ACTS.   57

consists of the first two letters of ܐܠܗܐ with ܘ prefixed. Out of these two words then standing side by side the reading ܘܐܠܗܐ (and-to-God) would almost inevitably arise[1]. In the Syriac Vulgate (a revision of the Old Syriac text) the prefixed ܘ is eliminated, though the position of ܐܠܗܐ as the first word in the sentence is maintained, and ܠܐ ܘ stands second.   (3)   Thus we have seen how, through easy and obvious changes, the following collocation of clauses may be conceived of as arising: 'Ye intend to bring this man's blood upon us. But Peter answered and the Apostles and said. To God to hearken more than to men. And Peter said to them. The God of our Fathers &c.' In these circumstances the clause 'But Peter answered and the Apostles and said' would necessarily fall out, for it would appear (*a*) to break the sequence of the infinitives 'to bring this man's blood upon us...and to hearken', and (*b*) to be an erroneous anticipation of the clause ('And Peter said to them') two lines lower down, which introduces the speech. Hence, as I believe, there naturally arose the Old Syriac text at this point, which the Bezan text, through the happy emendation of δέ for δεῖ, faithfully represented in Greek. The words 'Ye intend...to hearken to God more than to men' are to be taken as an ironical statement of the supposed pretensions of the Apostles.

v. 32.   ΤΟ ΠΝΑ ΤΟ ΑΓΙΟΝ ΟΝ ΕΔΩΚΕΝ Ο ΘC.

The Latin has: sp̄m sanctum quem dedit d̄s.   The altera-

[1] Cod. D is a witness that in xiii. 46 the same Syriac word ܠܐ ܘ fell out in an old Syriac text, though for quite a different reason. Cod. D has ΥΜΕΙΝ ΠΡΩ- ΤΟΝ ΗΝ ΛΑΛΗΘΗΝΑΙ ΤΟΝ ΛΟΝ ΤΟΥ Θ͞Υ. The Syriac Vulgate, exactly representing the true Greek, has

ܠܟܘܢ ܘܠܐ ܗܘܐ ܙܕܩ ܗܘܐ ܕܢܬܡܠܠ ܡܠܬܗ ܕܐܠܗܐ.

In some Old Syriac MS. ܙܕܩ (3rd pers. fem. of the verb) was written in place of the adverb ܙܕܩ. This change necessitated the excision of the now meaningless ܗܘܐ ܠܐ, and so produced an Old Syriac reading, which Cod. D (using the words of the true Greek text) accurately renders.

tion of the ὅ of the true text into the Bezan ὅν may therefore come from the Latin. But if the scribe were following the Syriac, he would write ὅν, for the Syriac Vulgate uses here the emphatic mode of expressing the masculine relative— ܐ ܗܘ ܕܙܩܦ܂ ܚܕ. Codex E also has ὅν.

v. 34. ΑΝΑϹΤΑϹ ΔΕ ΤΙϹ ΕΚ ΤΟΥ ϹΥΝΕΔΡΙΟΥ ΦΑΡΙϹΑΙΟϹ.

The true text has ἀναστὰς δέ τις ἐν τῷ συνεδρίῳ Φαρισαῖος. Cod. E has the same reading as Cod. D except that it adds αὐτῶν after συνεδρίου. This reading of Cod. E clearly points to a Syriac text, for the Syriac has '*their*-council' in Mc. xiv. 55, Acts iv. 15, xxiii. 1, 20, xxiv. 20, where there is nothing in the Greek to require the suffix. The Old Syriac then probably read: 'And there arose one from their-council (a) Pharisee (ܦܪܝܫܐ ܡܢ ܟܢܘܫܬܗܘܢ ܚܕ)'. From this the reading in the Syriac Vulgate would easily arise— 'And there arose one from the-Pharisees (ܦܪܝܫܐ ܡܢ ܚܕ)'. For in a badly written MS. ܟܢܘܫܬܗܘܢ (their-council) would easily fall out before ܦܪܝܫܐ (a-Pharisee), and the word ܦܪܝܫܐ would then be read as a plural.

v. 35. ΠΡΟϹ ΤΟΥϹ ΑΡΧΟΝΤΑϹ ΚΑΙ ΤΟΥϹ ϹΥΝΕΔΡΙΟΥϹ.

The true text has πρὸς αὐτούς.

The gloss is evidently one of precision. Its character seems to stamp it as Syriac. But what of the Bezan καὶ τοὺς συνεδρίους (sic)? I conjecture that the Old Syriac read ܘܐܝܠܝܢ ܕܒܟܢܘܫܬܐ ('and-those who(-were)-in-the-council': comp. vi. 15, xxiii. 6). The ܒ (in) would very easily fall out, and the reading ܕܟܢܘܫܬܐ be generated. This rendered into Greek with the literalness of the Bezan scribe would be τοὺς συνεδρίου, whence by a mechanical error of transcription the actual Bezan reading.

v. 36. ΟϹ ΔΙΕΛΥΘΗ ΑΥΤΟϹ ΔΙ ΑΥΤΟΥ ΚΑΙ ΠΑΝΤΕϹ Κ.Τ.Λ.

The true Greek text has ὃς ἀνῃρέθη καὶ πάντες......διελύθησαν.

v. 38]   IN THE BEZAN TEXT OF THE ACTS.   59

I conjecture that the Bezan text is a characteristically ambitious rendering of an Old Syriac reading ܐܡܪ ܪܒܪܒܬܐ ܥܠ ܢܦܫܗ (comp. Rom. ix. 3, 1 Cor. ix. 27). It may be added that the Syriac Vulgate represents λέγων εἶναί τινα ἑαυτόν (v. 36) thus: 'He-said about himself (ܥܠ ܪܒܐ) that-something great (was-)he'.

The Old Syriac reading preserved in the Bezan text of Acts xiv. 27 may be noticed here.

οca ο θc εποιηcεν αγτοιc[1]
μετα των ψγχων αγτων.

The true Greek text has ὅσα ὁ θεὸς ἐποίησεν μετ' αὐτῶν (comp. xv. 4). The Old Syriac no doubt rendered the μετ' αὐτῶν by the idiomatic phrase ܥܡ ܢܦܫܗܘܢ ; this was literally retranslated into Greek by the Bezan scribe. The Bezan αὐτοῖς probably represents an Old Syriac ܠܗܘܢ. Compare Ps. cxxv. 1 f. (ܥܡ ܢܦܫܢ ܠܡܥܒܕ = to-do with them.... ܠܡܥܒܕ ܠܢ = to-do to-us). Thus it appears that the original μετ' αὐτῶν is twice represented in the Bezan Greek, and probably was twice represented in the Old Syriac.

v. 38.   και τα νγν εicιν αδελφοι λεγω γμειν
αποcτητε απο των ανθρωπων τογτων
και εαcατε αγτογc
μη μιαινάντες τας χείρας.

The true text has καὶ [τὰ] νῦν λέγω ὑμῖν, ἀπόστητε ἀπὸ τῶν ἀνθρώπων τούτων καὶ ἄφετε αὐτούς.

There are three points here to be considered. (1) What of the interpolated words εἰσὶν ἀδελφοί? Their history is, I believe, somewhat as follows. (a) The introduction of 'brethren' is due to assimilation more or less conscious. Note in the Syriac

iii. 17.   Now, my-brethren, knowing (am) I.
v. 38.   Now   saying (am) I.

Hence in v. 38 the word 'brethren' would very easily intrude itself. (b) But the interpolated 'brethren' generated the

---

[1] Compare the gloss in xvi. 40 οca εποιηcεν κc αγτοιc.

further interpolation of ܐܢܘܢ (they (are)); compare vii. 26 'brethren (are) ye', Gen. xxxvii. 27 'our-brother (is) he'. Probably also dislike was felt of the apostolic 'brethren' put into the mouth of Gamaliel. (2) Cod. D, like Cod. E, has ἐάσατε in place of the true text ἄφετε. The ἐάσατε is probably an independent translation of the Syriac word; see on vi. 3. (3) Cod. E has the same gloss as Cod. D but in a different and somewhat fuller form—ΜΗ ΜΟΛΥΝΟΝΤΕC ΤΑC ΧΕΙΡΑC ΥΜΩΝ. The variation between these MSS. as to wording points here, as in other passages, to a common Syriac original. We shall later on (see on vii. 43, xix. 29, comp. iv. 24) find passages where beyond doubt the Old Syriac incorporated phrases from the O.T. Prophets. Such a passage, I believe, is the present. In Is. lix. 3 there occur the words: 'Your hands are defiled with blood (ܐܝܕܝܟܘܢ ܓܐܠܝܢ ܒܕܡܐ)'. From this verse came, I believe, an Old Syriac gloss

ܘܠܐ ܬܓܐܠܘܢ ܐܝܕܝܟܘܢ.

In Is. lix. 3 the word in the LXX. which corresponds to ܓܐܠܝܢ is μεμολυσμέναι. The equivalent to the verb in Jude 8 (cf. 1 Pet. i. 4) is μιαίνω[1]. Further, the Old Syriac text represented in Cod. D probably had ܐܝܕܝܢ (hands), that represented in Cod. E probably had ܐܝܕܝܟܘܢ (your-hands). This solution of the problem, it will be seen, satisfies the conditions imposed by the occurrence of the gloss in two Greek forms[2].

v. 39. ΕΙ ΔΕ ΕΚ ΘΥ ΕCΤΙΝ ΟΥ ΔΥΝΗCΕCΘΑΙ ΚΑΛΥCΑΙ ΑΥΤΟΥC ΟΥΤΕ ΥΜΕΙC ΟΥΤΕ ΒΑCΙΛΕΙC ΟΥΤΕ ΤΥΡΑΝΝΟΙ ΑΠΕΧΕCΘΑΙ ΟΥΝ ΑΠΟ ΤΩΝ ΑΝΘΡΩΠΩΝ ΤΟΥΤΩΝ.

[1] Perhaps the Bezan scribe (who knew his LXX., see on iii. 1) had in his mind the LXX. of Eccles. vii. 18 ἀπὸ τούτου μὴ μιάνῃς τὴν χεῖρά σου (where the Syriac agrees with the Hebrew—'withdraw not'), and this phrase suggested to him his rendering of the Syriac gloss.

[2] Compare *The Doctrine of Addai*, p. 41: 'Take heed therefore of those that crucified, that ye be not friends to them, that ye be not responsible with them whose hands are full of the blood of Christ' (comp. Is. i. 15).

The true text has nothing to correspond with the last two lines. Cod. E reads ου δυνηςεςθε καταλγςαι αυτογς ογτε γμειc ογτε οι αρχοντες γμων.

(1) We can trace, I believe, with some confidence the growth of the Bezan gloss in the second line. (*a*) In discussing iii. 17 we saw that there is reason to believe that the Old Syriac read '*Ye* (ܐܕܘܟ) in-ignorance did evil as also *your-rulers*'. We may then trace the form of the gloss in v. 39 preserved in Cod. E to the Old Syriac of iii. 17. (*b*) But the words 'nor your rulers' suggested a further amplification through assimilation to the Gospels—Lc. xxi. 12 ἐπὶ βασιλεῖς καὶ ἡγεμόνας, Matt. x. 18 ἐπὶ ἡγ. δὲ καὶ βασ., Mc. xiii. 9 ἐπὶ ἡγεμόνων καὶ βασιλέων. But I think it is clear that the Bezan gloss is not originally Greek but comes from the Old Syriac of the Acts, for (i) in the Syriac the order of the words in Mc. xiii. 9 is assimilated to that in Lc. xxi. 12 (ܡܠܟܐ ܘܗܓܡܘܢܐ), the latter passage having a place in the Diatessaron (Ciasca, p. 73): the order 'kings and rulers' is thus the familiar order in the Syriac N. T.; (ii) the gloss as it stands in Cod. D is explained at once if we regard it as an independent translation from the Syriac. The Bezan scribe in his rendering of Old Syriac glosses is fond of using somewhat unusual words, such as τύραννοι (a LXX. word, Prov. viii. 16, Hab. i. 10, Dan. iii. 2, 3, iv. 33) is here. If this theory as to the growth of the gloss is correct, we have this interesting and important result that the form of the Old Syriac text which can be recovered from Cod. E is (at least in this instance) earlier than that implied in Cod. D. (2) The interpolated words of the third line are a context-gloss from *v*. 38. The reason why the Bezan scribe wrote ἀπέχεσθε, not ἀπόστητε (*v*. 38), is that he is translating a Syriac gloss. It is indeed remarkable in how many authorities these glosses reappear and what various forms they take (see Tischendorf). A MS. of the Latin Vulgate (Cod. demidianus) has 'neque uos neque principes uiri'; Bede, 'neque uos neque principes uestri'.

One Greek cursive MS., viz. 33, reads (in the margin) ἐγκρατεύετε οὖν ἀπὸ τῶν ἀνθρώπων τούτων: another cursive, viz. 180, ἀπέχεσθε οὖν ἀπὸ τῶν ἀνδρῶν τούτων.

v. 40.   επειcτ εc δε αγτω.

The true text has ἐπείσθησαν δὲ αὐτῷ. The Bezan scribe hesitated, it would seem, between ἐπείσθησαν and πεισθέντες. Probably the Old Syriac text read here ܐܘܢ ܡܬܛܦܝܣܝܢ, as in viii. 6, xiv. 2, xxviii. 24. For similar cases of hybrid readings see i. 5 (probably), xiii. 29.

vi. 1.   οτι παρεθεωροyντο εν τη διακονια
         καθημερινη αι χηραι αγτων
         εν τη διακονια των εβραιων.

The true text has the article before καθημ., and has nothing to correspond to the third line.

(1) The omission of τῇ before καθημερίνῃ would be syntactically important, if we could apply the rules of syntax to Bezan Greek. But with our scribe syntax gives way to Syriac. The Syriac here has 'in-the-ministration of-every day'. It may be convenient to note once for all that the Syriac cannot (except by the addition of 'that', 'those'; see on vi. 5) express the definite article. Hence the Bezan scribe, who is a more or less independent translator from the Syriac, sometimes omits the article found in the true Greek text (see e.g. i. 14, 20, 26, ii. 38, iii. 4, 25), and sometimes inserts the article (see e.g. i. 14, 15, 16, 21, 25, iii. 4, 6, 21). One instance, as I believe, of the omission of the article is of special interest. When Cod. D in Lc. xi. 2 has αγιασθητω ονομα coy εφ ημας, the anarthrous ὄνομα probably indicates that the Bezan scribe is here following an Old Syriac text, and that therefore the ἐφ' ἡμᾶς is derived from a Syriac source[1]. For a discussion of other points connected with this petition see *The Lord's Prayer in the Early Church* (*Texts and Studies*, vol. i. no. 3),

---

[1] Compare Acts xv. 8 in Cod. D : δογ επ αγτογc το πνα το αγιον.

p. 31 ff. (2) I believe that the gloss contained in the third line may be explained by the simple supposition that the lines in an early Syriac MS. were thus divided:

ܒܫܡܫܬܐ ܕܥܒܪܝܐ܂ ܗܘܐ ܪܛܢܐ ܕܗܠܝܢ ܝܘܢܝܐ ܥܠ ܥܒܪܝܐ

The word ܥܒܪܝܐ (the-Hebrews) was written by a scribe in place of ܝܘܢܝܐ, and thus the gloss ܒܫܡܫܬܐ ܕܥܒܪܝܐ ('in-the-ministration of-the-Hebrews') arose, a gloss which in the Old Syriac MS. used by the Bezan scribe was added at the end of the sentence. We have here another indication that the Old Syriac text had already a history before that form of it was produced which is followed in the Bezan Greek text.

vi. 3. ΟΥϹ ΚΑΤΑϹΤΗϹΟΜΕΝ ΕΠΙ ΤΗϹ ΧΡΙΑϹ ΑΥΤΗϹ.

In place of αὐτῆς the true text has ταύτης. This is a simple case of what often occurs in the Bezan Greek. When there can be no special reason for the change, in place of the word which occurs in the true Greek text we find another Greek word substituted. The reason is that the Bezan scribe, as we have now seen abundant evidence for believing, is always liable to be as much a translator of the Old Syriac as a transcriber of the Greek text. It will be sufficient to give some instances of this phenomenon from the first three chapters: i. 11 ἐνβλέποντες (not βλέποντες), ii. 2 καθεζόμενοι (not καθήμενοι), ii. 12 διηπόρουν (not -οῦντο), ii. 14 ἐνωτίσατε (not -ασθε), ii. 20 μεταστρέφεται (not -στραφήσεται), ii. 22 [δεδοκιμ]ασμένον (not ἀποδεδειγμένον), ii. 29 μνημεῖον (not μνῆμα), ii. 33 καὶ τὴν ἐπαγγελίαν (not τήν τε ἐπαγγ.), ii. 37 τῇ καρδίᾳ (not τὴν καρδίαν), ii. 44 πάντα (not ἅπαντα), iii. 13 ἀπηρνήσασθε (not ἠρνήσασθε), iii. 14 ᾐτήσατε (not -ασθε), iii. 25 τῆς διαθήκης ἣν (not τῆς διαθ. ἧς), iii. 26 ἐξαπέστειλεν (not ἀπέστειλεν), ἐκ τῶν πονηρῶν (not ἀπὸ τῶν πονηριῶν). Sometimes it is possible to see that, though the true Greek word is rightly represented by a particular Syriac word, yet the Bezan word is a more exact equivalent of that Syriac word than is the Greek word which it translates. A single example will make my meaning clear. In iv. 18 the true Greek is καλέσαντες αὐτούς. The Syriac rightly enough has ܩܪܐ ܐܢܘܢ. But the Bezan text has φωνήσαντες αὐτούς. The reason is plain. The word ܩܠܐ suggests the idea of *voice, sound.* It is used, for example, of the cock crowing, Matt. xxvi. 34 (= φωνῆσαι); of the trumpet sounding, 1 Cor. xiv. 8 (= φωνὴν δῷ), xv. 52. Thus the word φωνῆσαι can be its equivalent where καλέσαι would be impossible, and φωνήσαντες is the word which is naturally suggested to the Bezan scribe by ܐܢܘܢ. But the Bezan scribe is not always so fortunate in his dealings with this word. ܩܠܐ is used to translate συνκαλεῖν in Acts v. 21, xxviii. 17. Hence our scribe has in xiii. 7 ΟΥΤΟϹ ϹΥΝΚΑΛΕϹΑΜΕΝΟϹ (Syr. ܩܠܐ; true Greek προσκαλ.) ΒΑΡΝΑΒΑΝ ΚΑΙ ϹΑΥΛΩ. A noteworthy instance of variation is found in xiii. 45 where τοὺς ὄχλους (true text) = ܟܢܫܐ (sing. or plur. according to vocalization) = ΤΟ ΠΛΗΘΟϹ (Cod. Bezae).

vi. 4.   ΗΜΕΙϹ ΔΕ ΕϹΟΜΕΘΑ ΤΗ ΠΡΟϹΕΥΧΗ ΚΑΙ ΤΗ ΔΙΑΚΟΝΙΑ
         ΤΟΥ ΛΟΓΟΥ ΠΡΟϹΚΑΡΤΕΡΟΥΝΤΕϹ.

The true text has ἡμεῖς δὲ τῇ προσ. καὶ τῇ διακ. τοῦ λ. προσκαρτερήσομεν.

The Syriac 'and-we will-be continuing (ܢܗܘܐ ܐܡܝܢܝܢ) &c.' is a perfectly natural translation of the true Greek. It is literally represented in Cod. D. Another instructive variation in the translation of verbs occurs below *v.* 15.

vi. 5.   ΚΑΙ ΗΡΕϹΕΝ Ο ΛΟΓΟϹ ΟΥΤΟϹ.

The true text has nothing answering to οὗτος. The Bezan Latin has 'sermo hic'. The Syriac explains the insertion, for it has ܡܠܬܐ ܗܕܐ (this word). The case is typical. The Syriac not unfrequently, as here, inserts 'this', 'that', 'these', 'those' to represent the definite article, which it can express in no other way. Examples will be found in Matt. ii. 7 (Curet., not Pesh.), 16 (Curet., not Pesh.), ix. 8 (Pesh., Curet.

wanting), Acts iii. 13, v. 10; comp. v. 20, Lc. xxiv. 8, 9 (Curet.). In none of these passages has the Bezan text a corresponding addition. The references given above will shew that Syriac Versions would differ from each other as to the insertion and non-insertion of these defining pronouns, and that it is never safe to argue from non-insertion in the Peshito rendering of a particular phrase that such a pronoun had no place in an Old Syriac text. On the Syriac representation of the Greek article see Duval, *Traité de Grammaire Syriaque*, p. 289.

It should be added that these pronouns are inserted in numberless instances as the antecedent to a relative, e.g. Matt. xv. 24 (Curet., Cod. D, not Pesh.), Acts i. 2, 7, 13, 16 (Cod. D), ii. 2, iii. 15, iv. 22, 32.

vi. 10. ΟΙΤΙΝΕϹ ΟΥΚ ΙϹΧΥΟΝ ΑΝΤΙϹΤΗΝΑΙ ΤΗ ϹΟΦΙΑ
ΤΗ ΟΥϹΗ ΕΝ ΑΥΤΩ ΚΑΙ ΤΩ ΠΝΕΥΜΑΤΙ ΤΩ ΑΓΙΩ Ω ΕΛΑΛΕΙ
ΔΙΑ ΤΟ ΕΛΕΓΧΕϹΘΑΙ ΑΥΤΟΥϹ ΕΠ ΑΥΤΟΥ
ΜΕΤΑ ΠΑϹΗϹ ΠΑΡΡΗϹΙΑϹ
ΜΗ ΔΥΝΑΜΕΝΟΙ ΟΥ ΑΝΤΟΦΘΑΛΜΕΙΝ ΤΗ ΑΛΗΘΕΙΑ
ΤΟΤΕ ΥΠΕΒΑΛΟΝ Κ.Τ.Λ.

The true Greek text has καὶ οὐκ ἴσχυον ἀντιστῆναι τῇ σοφίᾳ καὶ τῷ πνεύματι ᾧ ἐλάλει. τότε ὑπέβαλον κ.τ.λ.

It will be convenient to give at once the text of Cod. E and that of the Syriac Vulgate.

Cod. E has ΚΑΙ ΟΥΚ ΙϹΧΥΟΝ ΑΝΤΙϹΤΗΝΑΙ ΤΗ ϹΟΦΙΑ ΤΗ ΟΥϹΗ ΕΝ ΑΥΤΩ ΚΑΙ ΤΩ Π͞Ν͞Ι ΤΩ ΑΓΙΩ Ω ΕΛΑΛΕΙ ΔΙΟΤΙ ΗΛΕΓΧΟΝΤΟ ΥΠ ΑΥΤΟΥ ΜΕΤΑ ΠΑϹΗϹ ΠΑΡΡΗϹΙΑϹ ΕΠΙΔΗ ΟΥΚ ΗΔΥΝΑΝΤΟ ΑΝΤΙΛΕΓΙΝ ΤΗ ΑΛΗΘΕΙΑ ΤΟΤΕ Κ.Τ.Λ.

The Syriac Vulgate has: 'And-not able were-they to-stand against (ܠܡܩܡ ܠܘܩܒܠ) the-wisdom and-the-spirit which-speaking was in-him (ܕܡܡܠܠ ܗܘܐ ܒܗ).'

In this complicated passage we can separate three glosses. These we will consider separately.

(1) The stages in the history of the gloss in the second line are, I believe, these. (*a*) There first arose the evangelical gloss preserved in the Syriac Vulgate. Its source is Matt. x.

C. C. B. 5

20 οὐ γὰρ ὑμεῖς ἐστὲ οἱ λαλοῦντες ἀλλὰ τὸ πνεῦμα τοῦ πατρὸς ὑμῶν τὸ λαλοῦν ἐν ὑμῖν (ܐܒܐ ܕܡܠܠ). The parallel passage Mc. xiii. 11 (οὐ γάρ ἐστε ὑμεῖς οἱ λαλοῦντες ἀλλὰ τὸ πνεῦμα τὸ ἅγιον) suggested the epithet τῷ ἁγίῳ found in Codd. DE. The whole context in Acts vi., but especially (as we shall see more distinctly later on) the words 'they could not resist,' recalled the saying of our Lord. (*b*) In a previous passage (iii. 8) we found an instance of the love which the Old Syriac had for symmetry. It would appear that in the present verse this influence was operating. A further gloss is added to balance the clause already interpolated from the Gospel: thus we have the following text—

The-wisdom   which-was in-him (ܕܒܗ ܗܘܬ)
The Holy Ghost which-speaking was in-him.

For the words 'which-was in-him' compare 1 Cor. xv. 10 'His-grace which (was)-in-me (ܕܒܝ); Gr. ἡ εἰς ἐμέ),' Mc. vi. 2, Jn. xiv. 17. If the history of the gloss suggested above is true, we must account for the absence in Codd. DE of the phrase 'which-speaking was in-him' in one of two ways. *Either* these words fell out in the Old Syriac, the passage being heavy with glosses. *Or* the phrase of the true text (ᾧ ἐλάλει) was retained in Codd. DE as fairly resembling the Syriac gloss.

(2) We pass on to consider the interpolation in the third and fourth lines, which, it will be noticed, Cod. E preserves in another form, i.e., as we shall see reason to believe, in another Greek rendering of the Syriac. In the Bezan form ἐπ' αὐτοῦ is an *itacism* for ὑπ' αὐτοῦ (so Cod. E). But to whom does the word αὐτοῦ refer? Is the reference to the Holy Spirit—'they were convicted by the Holy Spirit'—and is the source of the gloss Jn. xvi. 8? A conclusive argument against this supposition lies in the words μετὰ πάσης παρρησίας. But these words just quoted have a positive as well as a negative value. For in the *first* place they shew that the Greek form of the gloss is a translation, inasmuch as the term 'with all boldness' must refer to the

attitude not of the listener but of the speaker. But, as there is no Syriac expression exactly equivalent to this Greek term, it is possible that the Bezan scribe may have used it to represent some Syriac phrase against which the objection just urged could not be brought. And in the *second* place the words 'with all boldness' give us this clue—that the source of the gloss must contain something to correspond to the two expressions—'convict' and 'with all boldness'.

A parallel was drawn then, I believe, between the preaching of St Stephen and his victory over Judaism at Jerusalem and the success of Apollos in his disputes with the Jews at Corinth—εὐτόνως γὰρ τοῖς Ἰουδαίοις διακατηλέγχετο δημοσίᾳ ἐπιδεικνὺς διὰ τῶν γραφῶν εἶναι τὸν χριστὸν Ἰησοῦν (xviii. 28). The first clause of this verse, as it stood in the Old Syriac, supplied, as I believe, the gloss under discussion. But how did the clause stand in the Old Syriac? What in particular were the equivalents which it used for (*a*) διακατηλέγχετο, (*b*) δημοσίᾳ? As to the former (*a*), the Vulgate Syriac does not afford us much help, for its rendering of the whole passage is: 'For strongly disputing was-he against the-Jews before the-crowds (ܩܕܡ ܟܢܫܐ).' But it is very probable that the Old Syriac used here the literal rendering of διακατηλέγχετο which the Philoxenian Version has, viz., ܡܟܣܣ ܗܘܐ. The Aphel of ܟܣܣ is the regular Syriac equivalent of ἐλέγχειν (see e.g. Jn. xvi. 8). That the Old Syriac had here a fuller text than that preserved in the Vulgate seems probable also from the reading of Cod. D in xviii. 28 ϵΥΤΟΝШС ΓΑΡ ΤΟΙC ΙΟΥΔΑΙΟΙC ΔΙΑΚΑΤΗΛΕΓΧΕΤΟ ΔΗΜΟCΙΑ ΔΙΑΛΕΓΟΜΕΝΟС. As to the latter point (*b*), viz. the Old Syriac rendering of δημοσίᾳ: the Syriac Vulgate translates δημοσίᾳ in xvi. 37 by 'before the whole world', in xx. 20 (where δημοσίᾳ is contrasted with κατ' οἴκους) by 'in-the-streets'. We saw above that in xviii. 28 it has 'before the-crowds'. Does this rendering go back to the Old Syriac? Probably, for Cod. E has ΔΗΜΟCΙΑ ΚΑΙ ΚΑΤ ΟΙΚΟΝ (cf. xx. 20). Now in vi. 10 a Greek scribe would very probably represent the Syriac phrase 'in-the-streets' or 'before the-crowds', occurring in such a context, by the Greek *μετὰ πάσης παρρησίας*, for *publicity* is the essential notion of all the Syriac phrases (ܒܓܠܝܐ, ܓܠܝܐܝܬ, ܥܡ ܒܓܠܝܐ) which answer to *ἐν παρρησίᾳ κ.τ.λ.* To sum up; we may with some probability restore the Old Syriac gloss in vi. 10 thus:

ܡܛܠ ܕܡܬܟܣܣܝܢ ܗܘܘ ܡܢܗ ܩܕܡ ܟܢܫܐ

because convicted were-they by-him before the-crowds

(3) But this well-glossed passage supplies us with yet another problem. What of the gloss which appears in Cod. D as *μὴ δυνάμενοι κ.τ.λ.* and in Cod. E as *ἐπειδὴ οὐκ ἠδύναντο κ.τ.λ.*? I believe it to be a conflate gloss made up of material supplied by two passages. (*a*) One source is Lc. xxi. 15 *ἐγὼ γὰρ δώσω ὑμῖν στόμα καὶ σοφίαν ᾗ οὐ δυνήσονται ἀντιστῆναι ἢ ἀντειπεῖν ἅπαντες οἱ ἀντικείμενοι ὑμῖν.* For the words *ᾗ οὐ κ.τ.λ.* the Old Syriac has ܕܠܐ ܡܫܟܚܝܢ ܕܢܩܘܡܘܢ ܠܘܩܒܠܗ (which they shall not be-able that-they-should-stand against). (*b*) The other source is 2 Tim. iii. 8 *οὗτοι ἀνθίστανται τῇ ἀληθείᾳ* (ܗܢܘܢ ܩܝܡܝܢ ܠܘܩܒܠ ܫܪܪܐ). One more passage must be quoted to explain the characteristically bombastic representation of 'to stand against' in the Bezan Greek. Acts xxvii. 15 *μὴ δυνάμενοι ἀντοφθαλμεῖν τῷ ἀνέμῳ* runs thus in the Syriac:

ܘܠܐ ܐܫܟܚܬ ܕܬܬܩܘܡ ܠܘܩܒܠ ܪܘܚܐ.

I think that it is clear that nothing but the supposition that the gloss was originally a Syriac gloss, and was translated by one who knew his Syriac N.T., can bring all the passages which seem to contribute each its quota to the gloss and its rendering in Cod. D, viz., Lc. xxi. 15, 2 Tim. iii. 8, Acts xxvii. 15, naturally and easily into line.

There still remain a few points which require a brief notice. (*a*) We may suppose that the two glosses just discussed ('because they were refuted by him publicly', 'because they were not able to stand against the truth')

vi. 11, 15] IN THE BEZAN TEXT OF THE ACTS. 69

were originally rival glosses, competing against each other for a place in the text, and that the Old Syriac impartially settled the dispute by incorporating them both in the text. We have an instance of alternative glosses both securing a place in the Bezan (i.e. an Old Syriac) text in xiii. 28 f. (see below) and in xiv. 2,

οι δε αρχιcυναγωγοι των ιογδαιων
και οι αρχοντες της cυναγωγης.

(*b*) The third gloss probably began (as Cod. E suggests) ܘܗܘܘ ܡܬܟܬܫܝܢ ܕܠܐ ܢܨܚܘܢ. Here, as in gloss (2), Cod. D is less literal, in this case adopting the μὴ δυνάμενοι of xxvii. 15. (*c*) The fact that Cod. E has ἀντιλέγειν (from Lc. xxi. 15) and Cod. D ἀντοφθαλμεῖν (= to resist) is another indication that the Old Syriac Version of the Acts existed in more than one form. (*d*) If I am right in connecting the present passage with 2 Tim. iii. 8, we find here, what we shall find again, a proof of the existence of an Old Syriac Version of St Paul's Epistles. (*e*) The fact that the margin of the Philoxenian Version gives an absurdly literal translation of ἀντοφθαλμεῖν—'that they should not look against the truth'—shews (i) that we can never *assume* that the glosses in the margin of that version are more than a rendering of the glosses in their Greek form; (ii) that the Bezan Greek text, or some very kindred text, was known either in E. Syria where the Philoxenian version was originally made, or in a monastery of Alexandria, where it was revised by one Thomas with the help of 'approved and accurate Greek MSS.'

vi. 11. ρηματα βλαcφημιας.

This a literal translation of the natural Syriac rendering of ῥήματα βλάσφημα. The Syriac adjective is in the Syriac Vulgate used only in the masculine (1 Tim. i. 13, 2 Tim. iii. 2).

vi. 15. ωcει προcωπον αγγελογ
εcτωτος εν μεcω αγτων.

This last line is an interpolation, due to assimilation to

xxiv. 21, where the Greek is ἐν αὐτοῖς ἑστώς, but the Syriac Vulgate has ܒܝܢܬܗܘܢ ܩܐܡ ܗܘܐ ܗܘ. The word ܒܝܢܬܗܘܢ is used to translate ἐν μέσῳ αὐτῶν in Matt. xviii. 2, 20, Lc. xxiv. 36. Note the order of words in the Bezan gloss and in the Syriac of xxiv. 21. The Greek gloss must therefore be the rendering of an Old Syriac gloss.

vii. 4. ΤΟΤΕ ΑΒΡΑΑΜ ΕΞΕΛΘΩΝ ΕΚ ΓΗС ΧΑΛΔΑΙΩΝ
ΚΑΙ ΚΑΤΩΚΙΙϹΕΝ ΕΝ ΧΑΡΡΑΝ
ΚΑΚΕΙ ΗΝ ΜΕΤΑ ΤΟ ΑΠΟΘΑΝΕΙΝ ΤΟΝ ΠΑΤΕΡΑ ΑΥΤΟΥ
ΚΑΙ ΜΕΤΩΚΗϹΕΝ ΑΥΤΟΝ ΕΙϹ ΤΗΝ ΓΗΝ ΤΑΥΤΗΝ
ΕΙϹ ΗΝ ΥΜΕΙϹ ΝΥΝ ΚΑΤΟΙΚΕΙΤΑΙ
ΚΑΙ ΟΙ ΠΑΤΕΡΕϹ ΗΜΩΝ ΟΙ ΠΡΟ ΗΜΩΝ.

The true text has τότε ἐξελθὼν ἐκ γῆς Χ. κατῴκησεν ἐν Χ., κἀκεῖθεν μετὰ τὸ ἀποθανεῖν τὸν π. αὐτοῦ μετῴκισεν αὐτὸν...... κατοικεῖτε. The Syriac Vulgate has as an equivalent of the first two lines: 'And then *Abraham* went-out from the-land of-the-Chaldeans, *and* he-came (and) dwelt in Haran.' The Bezan scribe imperfectly assimilated the Greek (ἐξελθ....καὶ κατῴκ.) to the Syriac. In the remaining lines we can discern an Old Syriac text, as I believe, in regard to three points. (1) The κἀκεῖθεν of the true text becomes in Syriac ܘܡܢ ܬܡܢ (and-from there). Through *homoeoteleuton* the reading ܘܬܡܢ (and-there) would easily be produced. To complete the sense (especially in view of a further change to be noted directly) either ܗܘܐ (comp. Jn. xii. 9) or ܗܘܐ (comp. Matt. x. 11, Jn. ii. 1; commonly in sentences of this type the verb comes first, e.g. Matt. ii. 15, xxvii. 61, Acts xvi. 1) was added. (2) μετῴκισεν αὐτόν became (see the Syriac Vulgate) ܫܢܝܗ. But ܫܢܝ (Pael), though sometimes used as a transitive verb (vii. 43, 1 Cor. xiii. 2, Hebr. xi. 5 *bis*), is commonly employed in an intransitive sense—'to pass from one place to another' —(e.g. xiv. 6, xvi. 39, Matt. iv. 12, xi. 1, xii. 9, xiii. 53, xiv. 13, xv. 29, xvii. 20, xxvii. 5). Hence the change of

ܡܢܝܬ into ܐܝܬ would be both slight and natural. This latter word the Bezan scribe correctly translated by μετῴκησεν, but carelessly left the αὐτόν of the true text remaining. Cod. E also has μετωκηcεν αγτον. No doubt these three alterations, by which the Old Syriac underlying the Bezan text was produced, worked, so to speak, into each other's hands, so that about the precise stages of change it is impossible to dogmatise. (3) The last line of the Bezan text is an interpolation, suggested doubtless by such passages as vii. 51, xv. 10. I am not aware however that there is any parallel in the Greek N.T. to the phrase 'Our fathers who were before us.' But it may have had its origin in the Old Syriac Version of Matt. v. 12 'For so persecuting were-they (even) your-fathers the-prophets who before-you were (ܐܒܗܝܟܘܢ ܠܢܒܝܐ ܕܡܢ̣ܩܕܡܝܟܘܢ ܗܘܘ),' where the repeated suffix ܟܘܢ-(*your*-fathers, before-*you*) would make it natural to take the words to mean 'your-fathers who were before-you.'

    vii. 16. μετηχθηcαν εις cγχεν.

The true Greek text has μετετέθησαν εἰς Συχέμ. The variation in the verb shews that the Bezan scribe is translating. The form συχέν (the common συχέμ remains unchanged later on in the verse) witnesses, I believe, to a vulgarism in the Old Syriac text. The Syriac form of the word is ܫܟܝܡ (שְׁכֶם). The temptation to make this a plural ܫܟܝܡ would be irresistible to popular ingenuity.

The form ιcακ (*vv*. 8, 32 is) doubtless an attempt to reproduce ܐܝܣܚܩ. In xiii. 6 Cod. D has ονοματι καλογμενον Βαρηcογα (where the true Greek text is ᾧ ὄνομα Βαριησοῦς). Here the name Βαρηcογα evidently represents the current pronunciation of ܒܪ ܝܫܘܿܥ. The Syriac Vulgate avoids the sacred name by reading ܒܪ ܫܘܡܐ (Barsuma).

    vii. 17. της επαγγελιας ης επηγγειλατο.

The true text has for the last word ὡμολόγησεν. Cod. E

agrees with Cod. D. The Vulgate Syriac text accounts for the change and affords also a good instance of assimilation. It runs thus: 'And-when there had come the-time of-the-thing which God had promised with-an-oath to-Abraham' (comp. Gen. xxvi. 3, Lc. i. 73, and Matt. xiv. 7 Gr. and Curet. Syr.).

vii. 24. ΚΑΙ ΙΔШΝ ΤΙΝΑ ΑΔΙΚΟΥΜΕΝΟΝ ΕΚ ΤΟΥ ΓΕΝΟΥC.

The last three words are not in the true text. Cod. E has εκ τογ γενογc αγτογ. This gloss is a shortened form of a phrase interpolated in the Syriac: 'and-he-saw one, from the-sons of-his-race (ܚܕ ܡܢ ܒܢܝ ܛܘܗܡܗ).' The gloss in the Syriac is a very natural one. The Syriac Version of Exod. ii. 11 (like the LXX.) expands the verse thus: 'He-saw an-Egyptian smiting a-Hebrew from his-brethren *the-sons-of Israel.*' The Syriac translator of the Acts recalled the addition *the-sons-of Israel* in Exod. ii. 11, and it suggested to him the interpolation of a phrase which occurs several times in the Syriac N.T.—Acts x. 28 'an-alien who is not a-son of-his-race (= ἀλλοφύλῳ),' xiii. 26 'Brethren, sons of-his-race of-Abraham (= υἱοὶ γένους 'Αβραάμ),' 1 Thess. ii. 14 'Thus did ye also endure from the-sons of-your-race (= τῶν ἰδίων συμφυλετῶν).' For similar Syriac phrases compare Rom. xi. 14; Lc. i. 58, Acts vii. 3, x. 24; Lc. vii. 12, Acts xiv. 20; Jn. xviii. 35, Acts xxiv. 17.

vii. 30. ΚΑΙ ΜΕΤΑ ΤΑΥΤΑ ΠΛΗCΘΕΝΤШΝ ΑΥΤШ ΕΤΗ M̄.

The true text has καὶ πληρωθέντων ἐτῶν τεσσεράκοντα.

The Syriac is fond of phrases of connexion, and the Old Syriac no doubt read here ܗܘܐ ܘܟܕ. The Vulgate Syriac has: 'And-when there-were-filled-up (ܡܠܝ) for-him there forty years.' For the added 'to-him (ܠܗ)' compare ix. 23, xxiv. 27. The Syriac then explains why (1) the Bezan scribe uses the simple verb πλησθῆναι not πληρωθῆναι; (2) αὐτῷ is inserted; (3) the nominative ἔτη slips in.

vii. 39. ΟΤΙ ΟΥΚ ΗΘΕΛΗϹΑΝ.

The true text has ᾧ. The ὅτι may have arisen from a confusion between *cui* and *quia* on the Latin side. But it is surely far more probable that the Old Syriac literally rendered the Greek by ܕ݁ܠܐ[1] (the Vulgate has ܠܐ...ܕ݁), and that the Bezan scribe mistranslated the ܕ by ὅτι.

vii. 43. ΚΑΙ ΜΕΤΟΙΚΙѠ ΥΜΑϹ ΕΠΙ [ΤΑ ΜΕ]ΡΗ ΒΑΒΥΛѠΝΟϹ.

The true Greek text has ἐπέκεινα Βαβυλῶνος. The lacuna must doubtless be filled up with the letters which I have printed in brackets, for the Bezan Latin has 'in illas partes' and the Latin of Cod. E has 'in partem' (the Greek being ΕΠΕΚΙΝΑ). The Sahidic Version has 'in illas partes'.

The Vulgate Syriac does not help us: it has the phrase used in the Syriac of Amos v. 27 (comp. Matt. viii. 30, 2 Cor. x. 16). It is however through the Syriac that a solution of the problem comes. The word ܐܬܪܐ (= the-place) is used to translate τὰ μέρη in Matt. ii. 22, xvi. 13 by the Old and the Vulgar Syriac, and by the latter version (the Curetonian fragments here failing us) in Mc. viii. 10. In Acts ii. 10, xix. 1, xx. 2 the same Greek phrase is represented by ܐܬܪܘܬܐ (= the-places). But this word 'places' takes us back to a series of passages in the Prophets: Jer. viii. 3 'all the residue...which remain in all the *places* whither I have driven them,' Jer. xxiv. 9, xxix. 14, xl. 12 'then all the Jews returned out of all *places* whither they were driven,' Ezek. xxxiv. 12 'I will deliver them out of all *places* whither they have been scattered in the cloudy and dark day.' Thus in the Prophets of the Captivity the phrase 'the places' is almost a technical expression meaning 'the foreign countries of exile'. The Syriac O.T. has ܐܬܪܘܬܐ in all these

---

[1] 'Auch das *Objectverhältniss* wird in der Mehrzahl der Fälle nicht durch die Rückweisung angedeutet' (Nöldeke, *Kurzgefasste Syr. Gram.*, p. 245).

passages (comp. Jer. xlv. 5, Amos iv. 6) except Jer. xxix. 14, where the Syriac is varied, possibly because the word in the singular occurs later in the verse ('I will bring you again unto *the place* whence I caused you to be carried away captive'). We may therefore with some confidence believe that the Old Syriac read in Acts vii. 43 ܠܐܬܪܘܬܐ ܕܒܒܠ (to-the-places of-Babylon), and we can see the rationale of the reading. The Old Syriac is *more suo* harmonising, embellishing a quotation from one Prophet with a characteristic expression of other Prophets, who deal with the same subject of the exile.

viii. 1 f. ...πλην των αποστολων
οι εμειναν εν ιερογοαλημ
cγνκομιcαντεc τον cτεφανον ανΔρεc εγλαΒειc
και εποιηcαν κ.τ.λ.

The true text has...πλὴν τῶν ἀποστόλων. συνεκόμισαν δὲ τὸν Σ. ἄνδρες εὐλ. καὶ ἐποίησαν κ.τ.λ.
There are two points to be noticed. (1) The second line is a gloss. Its source is doubtless Lc. xxiv. 49 (ὑμεῖς δὲ καθίσατε ἐν τῇ πόλει). It does not come however from the Greek, for (*a*) different Greek words (καθίσατε, ἔμειναν) are used; (*b*) when Ἰερουσαλήμ is added in the Greek text of Lc. xxiv. 49, it is always placed after ἐν τῇ πόλει. The Syriac Vulgate has: 'But ye remain-ye (ܩܘܘ) *in-Jerusalem the-city*.' Here *in-Jerusalem* comes before the word *thecity* (compare the Vulgate of Acts ix. 38, xiii. 51, xvi. 11, xvii. 1, 10, xx. 4, xxi. 7). The word ܩܘܐ is a very frequent equivalent of μένειν (e.g. Matt. xxvi. 38, Mc. xiv. 34, Lc. i. 56, xxiv. 29, Jn. i. 32, xv. 9). (2) In the last two lines the Bezan text is guilty, it seems, of mingling independent translation of the Syriac (συνκομίσαντες) and transcription of the Greek (καὶ ἐποίησαν), thus ruining the grammar (compare the Bezan text in e.g. xii. 14, 16, xiii. 7, 27, 29, xiv. 3, 6). The omission of καί before συνκομ. may be accounted for in two ways. (*a*) The Old Syriac perhaps translated the true Greek

text exactly—ܘܩܒܪܘܗܝ (and-they-buried-him). It is obvious that here the ܘ (and) would easily fall out[1]. (b) The Syriac Vulgate has: 'and-they-wrapped-(him-) round they-buried-him (ܘܟܪܟܘ ܩܒܪܘܗܝ) (even) Stephen.' This rendering very probably goes back to the Old Syriac text, for the assimilation to v. 10 in the word 'and-they-wrapped-(him-) round' is precisely in the manner of that text. But the similarity of ܩܒܪ and ܟܪܟ might well cause the first word to fall out. The sentence would then begin with 'they-buried-him'; hence the Bezan abruptness—συνκομίσαντες εἰς φυλακήν.

viii. 3. παρεΔιΔογc εic φγλακην.

The true text has παρεδίδου εἰς φυλακήν.
The Syriac Vulgate has ܡܫܠܡ ܗܘܐ. The Bezan scribe in the first part of his word παρεΔιΔογc conforms with the familiar Greek (παρεδιδ-): then his eye catches the Syriac participle and with characteristic fairness he conforms the termination of the word with that participle.

viii. 6. ωc Δε ηκογον παν οι οχλοι
προcειχον τοιc λεγομενοιc γπο φιλιππογ
οντ εν τω ακογειν αγτογc.

The true text has προσεῖχον δὲ οἱ ὄχλοι τοῖς λεγομένοις ὑπὸ τοῦ Φιλίππου ὁμοθυμαδὸν ἐν τῷ ἀκούειν αὐτούς. The Syriac Vulgate has: 'And-when hearing were-they his-word (even) the-men who-(were-)there, attending (ܨܝܬܝܢ) were-they to-him and-consenting were-they to-all that-saying was-he (ܗܘܐ ܕܐܡܪ ܠܟܠ ܗܘܘ ܘܡܬܛܦܝܣܝܢ).'

Let us begin our treatment of the problem here presented to us by a restoration of the Bezan text itself. That there is

---

[1] The Bezan text in xiii. 1 (ηρωΔογ και τετραρχογ) seems to bear witness to the converse process. The Syriac is ܪܒܝܬܐ ܕܗܪܘܕܣ. I would suggest that the second loop of the ܡ was read as ܘ (and) and that this 'and' had a place in the form of the Old Syriac which the Bezan scribe is here following.

some connexion between that text and the Syriac Vulgate seems clear even to a superficial observer. The two verbs ἤκουον and προσεῖχον of Cod. D have verbs answering to them in the Syriac Vulgate. We may then reasonably expect that the third verb in the Syriac will correspond with the third verb of the Bezan text, of which only three letters are preserved. Now the Syriac verb ܡܬܛܦܝܣ translates πείθεσθαι in Acts v. 40, xxi. 14, xxviii. 24 (the last passage has points of likeness to that under discussion). We may then with something like certainty restore ἐπείθοντο in the Bezan text.

It will be most convenient as the next step to render the true Greek text into Syriac (making use of any suggestion to be derived from the Syriac Vulgate), and then to see if the Bezan text (i.e. an Old Syriac text underlying the Bezan Greek) and the Syriac Vulgate can be derived from it.

The following then would be a Syriac translation of the true Greek text:

ܟܠܗܘܢ	ܟܢܫܐ	ܠܡܠܬܗ	ܗܘܘ	ܘܨܝܬܝܢ
all-of-them	the-crowds	to-his-word	were-they	attending

ܟܕ	ܫܡܥܝܢ	ܗܘܘ
while	hearing	were-they

As to this rendering three remarks. (1) I have left out the word *of-Philip*, because (*a*) it would make the line longer than we shall see reason for believing it was; (*b*) it has no place in the Vulgate; (*c*) in τοῖς λεγ. ὑπὸ Φ. the Bezan scribe seems to be simply incorporating a phrase of the common Greek text. (2) The phrase τὰ λεγόμενα (λαλούμενα) occurs also in xiii. 45 (see below), xxvii. 11, xxviii. 24. In the two latter places it is rendered by ܡܠܘܗܝ (his-words). In viii. 6 the Syriac Vulgate seems to suggest that the singular (his-word) was used. (3) For ܟܠܗܘܢ as the rendering of ὁμοθυμαδόν see vii. 57.

From the above Syriac rendering of the common Greek

can we plausibly derive the Old Syriac text implied in the Bezan Greek, and the Syriac Vulgate?

The following are the probable stages of development. (1) It appears that the words ܟܕ ܫܡܥܝܢ ܗܘܘ slipped into the upper line; they stand in this position in the Vulgate and (literally rendered into Greek) in the Bezan text. The Bezan scribe when writing *ἐν τῷ ἀκούειν αὐτούς* relapses into following the common Greek text. (2) There were current, it would seem, two early Syriac translations of *προσεῖχον* viz. ܨܝܬܝܢ (cf. Jn. iii. 29, Acts ii. 14) and ܡܬܛܦܝܣܝܢ (compare Acts xxviii. 24 'consenting were-they to-his-words'). It is indeed not unlikely that assimilation to xxviii. 24 led to the introduction of the latter word in our present passage. (3) Besides the rendering of *τοῖς λεγομένοις* given above, there was, it appears, another Syriac equivalent of that phrase, viz. ܠܟܠ ܕܐܡܪ ܗܘܐ (to-all which-saying was-he); compare xiii. 45 *τοῖς ὑπὸ Παύλου λαλουμένοις* (*v. l.* *λεγομένοις*), Syr. ܠܡܠܐ ܕܐܡܪ ܗܘܐ ܦܘܠܘܣ (where note that Cod. D has ΤΟΙϹ ΛΟΓΟΙϹ ΥΠΟ ΤΟΥ ΠΑΥΛΟΥ ΛΕΓΟΜΕΝΟΙϹ). This latter phrase 'to-all which-saying was-he' appears as a whole in the Syriac Vulgate, and a fragment of it is found in the *πᾶν* of the Bezan text. (4) ܠܗܘܢ probably dropped out when brought into proximity with ܠܟܠ.

We may then suppose that the Old Syriac text represented by the Bezan Greek ran somewhat as follows:

ܘܟܕ ܫܡܥܝܢ ܗܘܘ ܟܢܫܐ ܠܟܠ ܕܐܡܪ ܗܘܐ

was-he that-saying all the-crowds were-they hearing and-when

ܨܝܬܝܢ ܗܘܘ ܠܡܠܬܗ ܘܡܬܛܦܝܣܝܢ ܗܘܘ.

were-they and-consenting to-his-word were-they attending

Thus starting with a Syriac translation of the common Greek text we can trace how there grew up on the one hand the Old Syriac text underlying the Bezan Greek, and on the other that represented by the Vulgate[1].

[1] What of the Vulgate phrase 'the-men who-(were-)there'? Is it possible that it is due to assimilation with some Old Syriac Version of Jn. iv. 28 *ἀπῆλθεν*

viii. 19. παρακαλωΝ καὶ λεΓωΝ.

Here παρακαλῶν καὶ is a gloss which, I believe, goes back to an Old Syriac text. The whole phrase (π. αὐτὸν καὶ λ.) is found in the true text of Matt. viii. 5, where the Old Syriac has 'was entreating of-him and-beseeching him and-saying'. It should be noticed also that just below (viii. 24) Cod. D interpolates παρακαλω in Simon's prayer for forgiveness.

Such double phrases as this are common in the Syriac N.T. In the Syriac Vulgate of the Acts the following may serve as examples: ii. 13 'These have drunk wine and are drunken': iii. 16 'He strengthened and healed (him)': iii. 26 'If ye turn and repent': iv. 31 'And when they had prayed and made supplication': viii. 13 'He was astonished and amazed': x. 28 'An alien who is not a son of his race': x. 45 'they were astonished and wondered': xxi. 36 'They were crying out and saying.' In none of these cases does Tischendorf give any other authority for the reading. A very interesting collection of 'double translations of the Greek text in the Old Latin and Old Syriac Versions' is given by Mr Rendel Harris, *A Study of Codex Bezae*, p. 254. He argues that they are 'Latinisms', and 'that the Syriac Versions owe them to Western bilingual influence'. I venture to think a further study of the phenomenon which he notices shews that these double translations are characteristic of the Syriac language in itself and of the Syriac translations of the N.T. They are due in the main to three causes. (1) Syriac is an essentially pleonastic language. This characteristic is most marked in expressions denoting *going and coming* and *speaking*. (2) It could render Greek compound verbs only by some kind of periphrasis (see above on i. 4). Thus, for example, the προ- of compound verbs is represented by the verb ܩܕܡ ; προεῖπεν becomes ܩܕܡ ܐܡܪ Acts i. 16,

εἰς τὴν πόλιν καὶ λέγει τοῖς ἀνθρώποις? The scene of Jn. iv. and of Acts viii. is laid at Samaria. Did an Old Syriac text read 'and-said to-the-men who-(were-)there'? The Syriac Vulgate has simply 'And-she-said', as though the following phrase had come under suspicion as a gloss and been omitted. The Curetonian has 'to-the-men'.

viii. 24]   IN THE BEZAN TEXT OF THE ACTS.   79

compare e.g. Rom. xi. 35, Gal. iii. 8, Eph. i. 5, 9, Hebr. xi. 40. On this principle the Old Syriac renders ἀπαγγείλατε (Matt. ii. 8) 'come, shew-me'; παρακαθεσθεῖσα (Lc. x. 39) 'she-came, sat'; the Syriac Vulgate ἐξῆλθεν σὺν αὐτοῖς (Acts x. 23) 'he went-out and-went with-them.' Compare the Old Syriac renderings—'She-crieth and-cometh after-us' for κράζει ὄπισθεν ἡμῶν (Matt. xv. 23) and 'He-goeth, seeketh that which-was-lost' for πορεύεται ἐπὶ τὸ ἀπολωλός (Lc. xv. 4). (3) Such renderings are sometimes, I believe, due to the influence of assimilation, which we have seen to be so potent a factor in the Syriac Versions of the N.T. A simple example is found in the Old Syriac of Lc. viii. 8. To quote the passage is, I think, to show how the double rendering arose. It is a case of context-assimilation. The words are: 'And-other fell on-ground good and-giving fruit (ܐܒܥܠܐ ܘܝܗܒ) and-sprang-up and-gave fruit (ܝܗܒ ܘܐܥܠܐ) a hundredfold.' The gloss *and-giving fruit* emphasises the correspondence between the fate of the seed and the character of the soil.

viii. 24.   ΟΠⲰⲤ ΜΗΔΕΝ ΕΠΕΛΘΗ ΜΟΙ
ΤΟΥΤⲰΝ ΤⲰΝ ΚΑΚⲰΝ ΟΝ ΕΙΡΗΚΑΤΕ ΜΟΙ
ΟΣ ΠΟΛΛΑ ΚΛΑΙⲰΝ ΟΥ ΔΙΕΛΥΜΠΑΝΕΝ.

The true text has ὅπως μηδὲν ἐπέλθῃ ἐπ' ἐμὲ ὧν εἰρήκατε[1].

(1) The Syriac Vulgate has: 'That there-come not upon-me any of these-things which-ye-have-spoken-of (ܡܢ ܗܠܝܢ ܕܐܡܪܬܘܢ).' The Old Syriac therefore implied by the Bezan text inserted ܒܝܫܬܐ (evils) after ܡܢ. (2) The third line is a gloss. The tears of Simon have a place in the story of the Clementines (*Clem. Hom.* xx. 21, *Recog.* x. 63 and perhaps elsewhere). There his tears are tears of rage and disappointment; here of repentance. It is possible therefore that this gloss is connected, either as cause or as effect, with some detail in some of the many Simonian legends.

But I think that there is reasonable ground for saying that

[1] Codex E reads ⲰΝ ΕΙΡΗΚΑΤΕ ΚΑΚⲰΝ.

the gloss is Syriac. In the Bezan text of xvii. 13 we read
κακει cαλεγοντες και ταccοντες (= ταράσσοντες) τογc οχλογc ογ
διελιμπανο [1]. In that passage and its context there are, I
think, several signs of Syriac influence; the Syriac Vulgate
has ܘܠܐ ܫܠܝ (and they did not cease), which the Bezan
text accurately represents. We may reasonably conclude
therefore that our present gloss is in its origin Syriac and
that an Old Syriac Version had the interpolated words in the
following form (comp. Apoc. v. 4) :

ܕܠܐ ܫܠܝ ܡܢ ܒܟܝܐ

Is this gloss due to the principle of assimilation, the
activity of which in generating glosses we have often noted? It
is with the hesitation which should always be the feeling of one
venturing on a flight into the region of the unverifiable that I
ask, and endeavour to answer, this question. The two actors
in the scene are Simon Magus and Simon Peter. Simon's
tears are tears of repentance. Is the gloss to be traced back
to the Gospel account of St Peter's weeping on the night of
the betrayal?

St Mark (xiv. 72) uses the enigmatical phrase καὶ ἐπι-
βαλὼν ἔκλαιεν. Is it possible that some Old Syriac Version
(the Curetonian fragments fail us here) translated it in the
words adopted as a gloss in our passage of the Acts? I offer
the suggestion for the following reasons. (*a*) There is some
slight external evidence for an Old Syriac text having read
ܒܟܝܐ in Mc. xiv. 72 in a passage in Aphrahat *Homily* vii.
(Dr Wright's ed. p. ܣܓܝ ; Bert, *Texte u. Untersuchungen*, iii.
3, p. 121). After speaking of St Peter's denial with oaths and
curses Aphrahat continues ' And when repentance came over
him and he wept much (ܘܐܣܓܝ ܕܡܥܐ ܕܒܟܝܗ, lit. he-
made-much the-tears-of his-weeping)[2].' (*b*) It may be thought

---

[1] The Greek word, with which, if I am right, the Bezan scribe renders the
Syriac, may have been suggested by Tobit x. 7 οἱ διελίμπανεν θρηνοῦσα Τωβείαν
τὸν υἱὸν αὐτῆς.

[2] Cod. A has another reading ܘܐܫܝܓ ܚܛܗܘܗܝ ܒܕܡܥܐ ܕܒܟܝܗ
(He washed away his sins by the tears of his weeping).

(if my suggestion is worth consideration) that in Mc. *l. c.* the Syriac phrase as a whole was designed to express the contents of the Greek phrase as a whole. On the other hand as the phrase 'they ceased not' in Acts xvii. 13 is apparently used to bring out the continuousness of the action described by the present participles, so we may suppose that the phrase 'he ceased not' was designed to represent the imperfect ἔκλαιεν as contrasted with ἔκλαυσεν (Matt. xxvi. 75, Lc. xxii. 62 (?)), and that the word *much* was intended to express the idea of *accession* conveyed by ἐπιβαλών[1].

viii. 27. ΟC ΗΝ ΕΠΙ ΠΑCΗC ΤΗC ΓΑΖΗC ΑΥΤΟΥ.

The true text has αὐτῆς. The Syriac has ܓܙܗ ܕܝܠܗ ܗܘ. The last word may mean 'his-treasure' or 'her-treasure' according to the way in which it is vocalized. The sense shews that it should be pointed ܗܘ (her-treasure): but the proximity of ܓܙܐ where the suffix is masculine (ܓܙܐ being masculine) made a mistake here peculiarly easy. The blunder of the Bezan scribe here is important, for it is typical. In unpointed Syriac the suffix of the third person, except in the case of the plural of masculine nouns, is as indeterminate as *eius, ei* in Latin. A similar explanation, to take a single example, may be given of the Bezan reading in Mc. xvi. 11 (the reference is to Mary Magdalene) καὶ οὐκ ἐπίστευσαν αὐτῷ. The Vulgate Syriac

[1] Has the Peshito rendering of Mc. xiv. 72 any bearing on this suggestion? The rendering is ܫܪܝ ܕܢܒܟܐ (and-he-began that-he-should-weep). But in the suggested Old Syriac reading of Mc. xiv. 72 it would not be impossible for ܘܫܪܝ to fall out before ܒܟܐ, and by no means improbable that it would fall out if (as might well be the case) the participle ܒܟܐ, not the perfect ܒܟܐ, were used. If the ܘܫܪܝ fell out, the text would read 'he ceased to weep'. Sense and sound (ܒܟܐ, ܒܟܐ) would then alike suggest the reading which is that of the Syriac Vulgate, with which Cod. D (ἤρξατο κλαίειν) agrees. This Syriac rendering, in itself singularly feeble and but ill corresponding with the Greek original, spread widely. If my theory, which I have hazarded with the full sense of the precariousness of conjecture, be true, we have yet another instance of the smallness of our knowledge as to the early history of the Syriac text.

(harmonizing with Matt. xxviii. 10, Lc. xxiv. 22) throughout the verse changes the feminine singular into the feminine plural and has here 'they did not believe them'. But doubtless the Old Syriac which lies behind the Bezan text at this point read 'And they did not believe her (ܠܗ).' This ܠܗ could be vocalized either as masculine or feminine[1].

x. 27. ΚΑΙ ΕΙCΕΛΘωΝ ΤΕ ΚΑΙ ΕΥΡΕΝ CΥΝΕΛΗΛΥΘΟΤΑC ΠΟΛΛΟΥC
ΕΦΗ ΤΕ ΠΡΟC ΑΥΤΟΥC ΥΜΕΙC ΒΕΛΤΙΟΝ ΕΦΙCΤΑCΘΑΙ.

The true Greek text is καὶ συνομιλῶν αὐτῷ εἰσῆλθεν, καὶ εὑρίσκει συνεληλυθότας πολλούς, ἔφη τε πρὸς αὐτοὺς Ὑμεῖς ἐπίστασθε.
The Syriac Vulgate has: 'And-while speaking with-him, he-entered and-found many who-had-come thither, and-he-said to-them Ye know (ܐܢܬܘܢ ܝܕܥܝܢ ܐܢܬܘܢ).'
What of the words βέλτιον ἐπίστασθε? The first ܐܢܬܘܢ of the Syriac gave place in the Old Syriac, I believe, to the common adverb ܕܝܢ ܫܦܝܪ (well). This word is found in the same connexion in 2 Tim. i. 18 (βέλτιον σὺ γινώσκεις), and it intrudes itself into the Syriac Vulgate of Acts xxvi. 26 (ἐπίσταται). In these three passages two different Greek words meaning *to know* are used: in the Syriac it is the same word in each case.

xi. 2. Ο ΜΕΝ ΟΥΝ ΠΕΤΡΟC ΔΙΑ ΙΚΑΝΟΥ ΧΡΟΝΟΥ
ΗΘΕΛΗCΑΙ ΠΟΡΕΥΘΗΝΑΙ ΕΙC ΙΕΡΟCΟΛΥΜΑ
ΚΑΙ ΠΡΟCΦωΝΗCΑC ΤΟΥC ΑΔΕΛΦΟΥC
ΚΑΙ ΕΠΙCΤΗΡΙΖΑC ΑΥΤΟΥC ΠΟΛΥΝ ΛΟΓΟΝ
ΠΟΙΟΥΜΕΝΟC ΔΙΑ ΤωΝ ΧωΡωΝ
ΔΙΔΑCΚωΝ ΑΥΤΟΥC ΟC ΚΑΙ ΚΑΤΗΝΤΗCΕΝ ΑΥΤΟΙC
ΚΑΙ ΑΠΗΓΓΙΛΕΝ ΑΥΤΟΙC ΤΗΝ ΧΑΡΙΝ ΤΟΥ ΘΫ
ΟΙ ΔΕ ΕΚ ΠΕΡΙΤΟΜΗC ΑΔΕΛΦΟΙ ΔΙΕΚΡΙΝΟΝΤΟ
ΠΡΟC ΑΥΤΟΝ ΛΕΓΟΝΤΕC.

[1] Similarly in Ign. Eph. xix. ܘܡܘܠܕܗ (=and-her-child-bearing) becomes in the MSS., through omission of the dot over the ܗ, *his-birth* (Bp. Lightfoot's *Ignatius*, Vol. ii. Sect. ii. p. 674 n.).

The true text has ὅτε δὲ ἀνέβη Πέτρος εἰς 'Ιερουσαλήμ, διεκρίνοντο πρὸς αὐτὸν οἱ ἐκ περιτομῆς λέγοντες. This long interpolation, a miniature περίοδοι Πέτρου, is a striking example of the desire to assimilate the history of St Peter to that of St Paul. It is in fact a mosaic of phrases describing the movements of St Paul. I believe that this, like other Bezan glosses, came from the Syriac. I append a literal translation of the Syriac Vulgate of those passages which, as it seems to me, the *glossator* used, leaving it to the student to compare the Greek in each case. (*a*) Rom. i. 13 'Times many I-wished that-I-should-come to-you.' Compare Acts xix. 21 ('Paul purposed in-his-mind...that-he-should-go to-Jerusalem'), xxv. 20. (*b*) Acts xx. 1 'Paul called (ܠܬ) the-disciples.' Compare *v*. 17. (*c*) xx. 2 'And-when he-had-gone-round these places, and-comforted them with-words many.' xv. 32 'And-with-speech abundant they-strengthened the-brethren.' Compare the Bezan gloss in xiii. 44 ακογcαι παγλογ πολγν τε λογον ποιηcαμενογ περι τογ κγ̄. (*d*) xviii. 11 'Teaching was-he them the-word of-God.' (*e*) xi. 23 'And-when he-came [i.e. Barnabas] thither and-saw the-grace of-God.' xv. 3 'Telling (Gr. ἐκδιηγούμενοι) were-they about the-conversion of-the-peoples.' xv. 4 'And-they-told (Gr. ἀνήγγειλαν) them all-which God wrought with-them.' Compare the Bezan gloss in xvi. 40 διηγηcαντο οcα εποιηcεν κ̄c αγτοιc. A more careful search might disinter other phrases in the Pauline history which the interpolator worked up. But those quoted above make the character of the gloss clear.

xi. 25. ακογcαc δε οτι cαγλοc εcτιν ειc θαρcον
εξηλθεν αναζητων αγτον
26. και ωc cγντγχων παρεκαλεcεν
ελθειν ειc αντιοχειαν
οιτινεc παραγενομενοι ενιαγτον ολον
cγνεχγθηcαν οχλον ικανον
και τοτε πρωτον εχρηματιcεν εν αντιοχεια
οι μαθηται χρειcτιανοι.

The true text has ἐξῆλθεν δὲ εἰς Ταρσὸν ἀναζητῆσαι Σαῦλον, καὶ εὑρὼν ἤγαγεν εἰς Ἀντιόχειαν. ἐγένετο δὲ αὐτοῖς καὶ ἐνιαυτὸν ὅλον συναχθῆναι ἐν τῇ ἐκκλησίᾳ καὶ διδάξαι ὄχλον ἱκανόν, χρηματίσαι τε πρώτως ἐν Ἀντιοχείᾳ τοὺς μαθητὰς Χριστιανούς. I briefly notice three points. (1) The last two lines are, as a reference to the Vulgate shews, a literal translation from Syriac[1]. (2) The first five lines are likewise, I believe, a close representation of a Syriac Version (note e.g. καὶ ὡς = ܘܟܕ), glossed from the Petrine history ix. 38, 39. (3) But what of the strange reading συνεχύθησαν ὄχλον ἱκανόν? I believe that it is to be traced to a desire to assimilate the account of the early preaching of St Paul to that of the early preaching of St Peter. The Syriac Vulgate reads here: 'And-a-year all-of-it together assembled (ܘܐܠܦܘ) were-they in-the-church and-they-taught much people.' In Acts ii. 6 the Syriac Vulgate has: 'There-assembled (ܟܢܫ) all-of-it (even) the-people and-was-confounded (ܘܐܬܬܙܝܥ).' Between the two passages there are links in the words 'assembled', 'much people', 'all the people'. I venture to conjecture that in an Old Syriac text our passage was assimilated to ii. 6, and took a form somewhat as follows:

ܫܢܬܐ	ܟܠܗ	ܥܡܐ	ܟܢܫ	ܐܬܐ	ܘܟܕ
a-year	all-of-it	the-people	there-assembled	they-came	and-when

ܣܓܝܐܐ	ܥܡܐ	ܘܐܠܦܘ	ܘܐܬܬܙܝܥܘ	ܟܠܗ
much	people	and-they-taught	and-they-were-confounded	all-of-it

About this suggested restoration of an Old Syriac text, I make the following remarks. (*a*) The first two words probably come from ix. 39 (see above). They, unlike the Greek οἵτινες παραγενόμενοι, are independent of the following words as far as the construction is concerned. (*b*) There is nothing in the Bezan Greek to answer to the words συναχθῆναι ἐν τῇ ἐκκλησίᾳ. I believe that their place was taken

---

[1] Except that the Vulgate has 'from then' = ἀπὸ τότε.

in an Old Syriac text by the words from ii. 6 ('there assembled the-people all-of-it'). We can see that in the Syriac text as given above these words would easily drop out before the Syriac words 'a-year all-of-it', which, in their Greek equivalent, have a place in the Bezan text. (*c*) The two words ܐܬܒܠܒܠܘ (and-they-were-confounded) and ܐܠܦܘ (and-they-taught) resemble each other in their beginning and their ending, and the eye of a careless scribe might easily pass straight from the former to the words which succeed the latter[1]. It may be added (i) that another link between Acts xi. and Acts ii. may be found in xi. 24 'much people was-added to-our-Lord' when compared with ii. 47 'Our-Lord added to-the-church, etc.': (ii) that in the gloss which we have been considering *c*. ii. is paying back a debt to *c*. xi.; for we have already seen that ii. 47 in the Old Syriac appropriated from xi. 26 the word 'in-the-church'.

xi. 27 f. ΗΝ ΔΕ ΠΟΛΛΗ ΑΓΑΛΛΙΑϹΙϹ
ϹΥΝΕϹΤΡΑΜΜΕΝΩΝ ΔΕ ΗΜΩΝ
ΕΦΗ ΕΙϹ ΕΞ ΑΥΤΩΝ ΟΝΟΜΑΤΙ ΑΓΑΒΟϹ.

The true text is ἀναστὰς δὲ εἷς κ.τ.λ.

There are two glosses here due to assimilation. (1) The gloss in the first line comes from Acts viii. 8, where the Syriac renders χαρά by the word used to represent ἀγαλλίασις in Lc. i. 44, Hebr. i. 9, Jude 24. Note ἐγένετο (viii. 8) = ܗܘܐ ܟܕ ܗܘܐ = ἦν (xi. 27), comp. note on iii. 10. (2) The gloss in the second line is from xx. 7 ܟܕ ܟܢܝܫܝܢ (= συνηγμένων ἡμῶν, comp. *v*. 8). This latter gloss is of special interest because the Bezan reading has been some-

---

[1] In view of this and of other suggestions which I have made in regard to possible cases of confusion between Syriac words, whether in the Old Syriac itself or as it was read by the Bezan scribe, I may be allowed to refer to the long series of confusions which Bp. Lightfoot (Ignatius i. p. 86—p. 97) points out as implied in the readings of the Syriac fragments of Ignatius and in the Armenian version, itself (like portions of the Bezan text) a translation of a Syriac translation. In the particular case considered above the confusion may have arisen from the dropping out of καὶ ἐδίδαξαν in the Bezan Greek.

times thought to supply what might conceivably be authentic information as to a connexion of St Luke with St Paul at an earlier date than that indicated by the common text of the Acts (xvi. 10). Compare x. 41 συνεφάγομεν[1] καὶ συνεπίομεν αὐτῶ καὶ συνεστράφημεν. The last two words are a gloss, due to assimilation to Lc. xxiv. 33 (ἠθροισμένους, see v. 41), Acts i. 6 (συνελθόντες), in both which passages the Syriac is ܟܢܝܫܝܢ. See also below xvii. 5.

xii. 10.   καὶ ἐξελθόντες κατέβησαν τοὺς z̄ βαθμοὺς
           καὶ προσῆλθαν ῥύμην μίαν.

The true text has καὶ ἐξελθόντες προῆλθον ῥύμην μίαν.

On more than one occasion we have been able to trace to the O.T. what we have had reason to hold an Old Syriac reading (see on iv. 24, v. 38, vii. 43). In this connexion it is instructive to notice how frequently Aphrahat quotes from the O.T. There are in his Homilies, according to Dr Bert's *Verzeichniss der Schriftcitate*, 99 references to Isaiah, 65 to Jeremiah, 54 to Ezekiel, 50 to St John's Gospel, 5 to the Acts. I believe that this mysterious gloss, 'they went down the seven steps,' comes from the O.T.

It would seem that the appearance of the angel and St Peter's guidance by the angel through the precincts of the prison recalled Ezekiel's vision (Ezek. xl.) of the man 'whose appearance was like the appearance of brass' (*v.* 3) and the guidance of the prophet by him through the precincts of the temple (*vv.* 5 ff.). 'After measuring the surrounding wall', says Dr Davidson in his summary of the vision (*Ezekiel*, in *The Cambridge Bible for Schools*, p. 293), 'the man entered the gateway. On the outside of the entrance, ascending to it were steps, seven in number, as is stated in connexion with

---

[1] Is not the remarkable gloss in the Old Syriac (Curetonian) text of Lc. xxiv. 42 ff. (And they gave to Him a piece of fish that was boiled, and of a honey-comb. And when He took it He ate before their eyes. *And He took up that which remained* [cf. Lc. ix. 17] *and gave to them*) due to a remembrance of this passage?

N. and S. gateways (xl. 22, 26).' Let us place the passages in Ezekiel and the Bezan text of the Acts side by side:—

Ezek. xl. 6.	Acts xii. 10.
Then came he unto the gate which looketh towards the east, and went up the steps thereof And they went up unto it by seven steps (v. 22)	They came unto the iron gate that leadeth into the city... and they went out and went down the seven steps.

Thus in Ezekiel we have, it seems, the picture of the prophet guided by the angel ascending seven steps to the gate which led into the building. In the Bezan text of the Acts we have the picture of the apostle guided by the angel passing out of the building through the gate and descending the seven steps.

It remains that I should state the reasons which lead me to the conclusion that this gloss 'the seven steps' comes into the Bezan text from an Old Syriac text. (1) I noticed above that in many other passages the Old Syriac text of the Acts incorporated, as it seems, phrases from the O.T. (2) It is not likely that the gloss was originally Greek. For Ezek. xl. in the LXX. has no special points of similarity to Acts xii. 10. In Ezek. xl. 6 the LXX. (which introduces at this point 'the seven steps'[1]) has καὶ εἰσῆλθεν εἰς τὴν πύλην... ἐν ἑπτὰ ἀναβαθμοῖς. In vv. 22, 26 it has κλιμακτῆρες for 'steps'. (3) When we place side by side the Syriac of the opening words of Ezek. xl. 6 and the Vulgate Syriac of Acts xii. 10,

ܐܪܥܐ ܬܪܥܐ Ezek.

ܐܪܥܐ ܕܦܪܙܠܐ ܬܪܥܐ Acts

though the words are simple, the correspondence is close. As to the words which follow—'which looketh towards the east' (Ezek.), 'that leadeth into the city' (Acts)—it is not improbable that in the Old Syriac of the Acts the correspondence was equally close, and that the phrase 'which

---

[1] As indeed it is very possible that some ancient Syriac text of Ezekiel did.

looketh' was used to represent the Greek phrase 'which leadeth'. For in the Syriac Vulgate the clause 'which leadeth into the city' has no place, as though these words, wearing the appearance of a gloss, had been, like 'the seven steps', deliberately expunged in that revised Syriac Version. (4) There are in the previous context indications of Syriac influence in the Bezan text. Of these I will notice two. (*a*) The true Greek text (*v.* 10) has διελθόντες δὲ πρώτην φυλακὴν καὶ δευτέραν. The Syriac Vulgate: 'And-when there-was-passed the-ward the-first and-the second.' With this order of the words 'the-first and-the-second' the Bezan text agrees—ΔΙΕΛΘΟΝΤΕC ΔΕ ΠΡΩΤΗΝ ΚΑΙ ΔΕΥΤΕΡΑΝ ΦΥΛΑΚΗΝ. (*b*) In *v.* 7 Cod. D has ΝΥΞΑC ΔΕ ΤΗΝ ΠΛΕΥΡΑΝ, the true text being πατάξας δὲ τὴν πλευράν. We have, it seems to me, a choice between two possible explanations of the Bezan νύξας. (i) The Old Syriac may have rendered πατάξας here by its almost invariable equivalent ܡܚܐ (see Matt. xxvi. 31, 51, Lc. xxii. 49, Acts xii. 23). But this Syriac verb is used to translate ἔνυξεν (Jn. xix. 34). The mind of the Bezan scribe, if he were following in Syriac, would be carried back to Jn. xix. 34, and his choice of the word νύξας is seen to be natural. (ii) The Syriac Vulgate may have preserved here the rendering of the Old Syriac. The former version, influenced by the desire for assimilation, renders πατάξας by the word used in Jn. xix. 37 (comp. Apoc. i. 7)—'they shall look on him whom they *pierced*.' The Bezan scribe retranslated this Old Syriac translation by a Greek word used in the same connexion—νύξας δὲ τὴν πλευράν (Jn. xix. 34)[1]. Of these two explanations I decidedly prefer the former; for to the Bezan νύξας, if thus

---

[1] Two further points may be noticed. (*a*) The word νύσσειν does not always mean *to prick with a sharp point*. Liddell and Scott refer, for example, to Hom. *Od.* XIV. 485 προσηύδων ἐγγὺς ἐόντα | ἀγκῶνι νύξας. Some might justify the word by the fact that Ezekiel's guide had 'a measuring reed' in his hand (xl. 3). (*b*) The Bezan Latin has: 'descenderunt septem grados et processerunt gradum unum.' My study of the Bezan Latin convinces me that in the last words we have a blundering translation of the Bezan Greek. Anyone who is able to form a higher estimate of the Latin than I have been able to do may point to the fact that in Ezek. xl. 37 there is mention of 'eight steps'.

xiii. 15, 27 ff.] IN THE BEZAN TEXT OF THE ACTS. 89

generated, I shall in the next chapter (p. 122) point out a
parallel in 'the Gospel according to Peter'.

xiii. 15.   ΕΙ ΤΙC ΕCΤΙΝ ΛΟΓΟΥ CΟΦΙΑC
ΕΝ ΥΜΕΙΝ ΠΑΡΑΚΛΗCΕΩC
ΠΡΟC ΤΟΝ ΛΑΟΝ ΛΕΓΕΤΑΙ.

The true text is εἴ τις ἔστιν ἐν ὑμῖν λόγος παρακλήσεως
πρὸς τὸν λαόν, λέγετε. The interpolated σοφίας clearly comes
from 1 Cor. xii. 8. If we place the Syriac of the two passages
side by side, the likeness in the Syriac is a strong argument
that the interpolated word had a place in the Old Syriac of
the Acts.

ܐܬܠܐ ܠܥܡ   ܐܝܬ݂ ܐܢܫ Acts
ܐܬܪܥܝܬܐ ܐܬܠܐ... ܥܠ ܠܥܡܐ ܐܝܬ   1 Cor.

The Bezan λόγου is probably simply a slip in the transcription of the Greek, possibly due to a remembrance of
ἐν σοφίᾳ λόγου (1 Cor. i. 17).

xiii. 27 ff. 27. ΟΙ ΓΑΡ ΚΑΤΟΙΚΟΥΝΤΕC ΕΝ ΙΕΡΟΥCΑΛΗΜ
ΚΑΙ ΟΙ ΑΡΧΟΝΤΕC ΑΥΤ C
ΤΑΙC ΤΑC ΓΡ ΑC ΤΩΝ ΠΡΟΦΗΤΩΝ
ΤΑC ΚΑΤΑ ΠΑΝ CΑΒΒΑΤΟΝ ΑΝΑΓΕΙΝΩCΚΟΜΕΝΑC
ΚΑΙ ΚΡΕΙΝΑΝΤΕC ΕΠΛΗΡΩCΑΝ
28. ΚΑΙ ΜΗΔΕΜΙΑΝ ΑΙΤΙΑΝ ΘΑΝΑΤΟΥ
ΕΥΡΟΝΤΕC ΕΝ ΑΥΤΩ
ΚΡΕΙΝΑΝΤΕC ΑΥΤΟΝ ΠΑΡΕΔΩΚΑΝ ΠΕΙΛΑΤΩ
29. ΙΝΑ ΕΙC ΑΝΑΙΡΕCΙΝ ΩC ΔΕ ΕΤΕΛΟΥΝ·
ΠΑΝΤΑ ΤΑ ΠΕΡΙ ΑΥΤΟΥ ΓΕΓΡΑΜΜΕΝΑ ΕΙCΙΝ
ΗΤΟΥΝΤΟ ΤΟΝ ΠΕΙΛΑΤΟΝ ΤΟΥΤΟΝ ΜΕΝ CΤΑΥΡΩCΑΙ
ΚΑΙ ΕΠΙΤΥΧΟΝΤΕC ΠΑΛΙΝ
ΚΑΙ ΚΑΘΕΛΟΝΤΕC ΑΠΟ ΤΟΥ ξύλου
ΚΑΙ ΕΘΗΚΑΝ ΕΙC ΜΝΗΜΕΙΟΝ.

The true text is οἱ γὰρ κατοικ. ἐν Ἱερουσ. καὶ οἱ ἄρχοντες
αὐτῶν τοῦτον ἀγνοήσαντες καὶ τὰς φωνὰς τῶν προφ. τὰς κατὰ

90   THE OLD SYRIAC ELEMENT   [xiii. 27 ff.

πᾶν σάββατον ἀναγιν. κρίναντες ἐπλήρωσαν, καὶ μηδεμίαν αἰτίαν θ. εὑρόντες ᾐτήσαντο (v. l. ᾔτησαν τὸν) Πειλᾶτον ἀναιρεθῆναι αὐτόν· ὡς δὲ ἐτέλεσαν πάντα τὰ περὶ αὐτοῦ γεγραμμένα, καθελόντες ἀπὸ τοῦ ξ. ἔθηκαν εἰς μνημεῖον.

I take the chief points of this somewhat tangled passage in order. (1) In the third line the ⲦⲀⲒⲤ is probably (see Scrivener, p. 444) a surviving fragment of ⲘⲎ ⲤⲨⲚⲒⲈⲚⲦⲀⲒⲤ. The words which follow are obviously ⲦⲀⲤ ⲄⲢⲀⲪⲀⲤ. In the Bezan text thus restored we notice these points. (i) The τοῦτον and καί of the true text are omitted. The following explanation seems not improbable. The Syriac Vulgate has ܐܠܐ ܐܦ ܠܐ ܟܬܒܐ ܕܝܠܗ. If the eye of the scribe after writing ܕܝܠܗ passed to ܟܬܒܐ, if, that is, the repeated preposition caught his attention, then, having passed over the ܐܦ ܠܐ (nor-yet), he would take the noun as singular (comp. vii. 42, Mc. xii. 26, Lc. iii. 4), and regard the ܕܝܠܗ as the anticipating pronoun[1]. (ii) Cod. D agrees with the Syriac in substituting 'writings (writing)' for 'voices'. (iii) μὴ συνιέντες is an independent translation of the Syriac, probably suggested by Lc. xxiv. 45 τοῦ συνιέναι τὰς γραφάς. (2) The καί before κρίναντες (v. 27) is doubtless due to an Old Syriac reading: 'They-knew not...and-they-judged.' The Vulgate has 'but'. Note in v. 29 the thrice repeated καί. In v. 28 the ἐν αὐτῷ is due to assimilation (Jn. xviii. 38, xix. 4, 6). (3) The κρίναντες of v. 28 is a gloss from the Syriac of Mc. xiv. 64, 'But they all-of-them judged (ܘܢ = κατέκριναν) that-guilty was-He of-death.' It will be noticed that in the Syriac Vulgate of Mc. l. c. there is nothing to answer to the αὐτόν of our gloss. In Mc. l. c. however Cod. D has ⲔⲀⲦⲈⲔⲢⲒⲚⲀⲚ ⲀⲨⲦⲰ ⲈⲚⲞⲬⲞⲚ ⲐⲀⲚⲀⲦⲞⲨ. This αὐτῷ is doubly instructive. It must surely be a literal translation of ܠܗ. If so, it shews that the Old Syriac in Mc. l. c. had the 'Him' which has fallen out

---

[1] In this case the plural (τὰς γραφάς) of the Bezan Greek is probably due to the influence of Lc. xxiv. 45, quoted above (iii). But it is just possible that the fact that the words ܐܦ ܠܐ ܕܝܠܗ begin and end with the same letters as ܟܬܒܐ led to the falling out of the two former words.

in the Vulgate. The words παρέδωκαν Πειλάτῳ are from Mc. xv. 1, Matt. xxvii. 2. (4) In *v*. 29 we come to the instructive words ἵνα εἰς ἀναίρεσιν. I venture to offer the following solution of the problem which they suggest. The Syriac Vulgate has an idiomatic rendering of the true Greek ἀναιρεθῆναι αὐτόν, viz. 'that-*they*-might-kill-Him.' The phrase seems to be an instance of the 'indeterminate third person' plural (see note on iv. 15, and (6) below). This phrase, which probably goes back to the Old Syriac, the Bezan scribe began to translate literally by ἵνα: he then was checked by the misunderstood 3rd person plural, and finally, leaving the ἵνα standing, he gave a translation (εἰς ἀναίρεσιν) which shirked the difficulty of the plural. (5) In the next line τὰ...γεγραμμένα εἰσιν is (except that the plural of the true Greek is retained) a literal rendering of ܕܟܬܒܝܢ ܐܢܘܢ. (6) In the next line we have incorporated in the text a phrase, which probably was once competing for that honour with the gloss inserted above κρίναντες...Πειλάτῳ (compare note on vi. 10). It seems to be derived from an Old Syriac reading in Lc. xxiii. 23 (αἰτούμενοι αὐτὸν σταυρωθῆναι). The Syriac Vulgate indeed uses, it seems, the idiom noticed just above, for it renders 'asking were they him that-*they*-should-crucify-Him.' The Old Syriac however, as the Curetonian fragments present it to us, reads 'And-saying to-him that-He-should-be-crucified (ܕܢܙܕܩܦ).' This *Ethpeel* form would easily pass into the Peal form ܕܢܙܩܘܦ (that-he-should-crucify). Such an Old Syriac reading in Lc. *l. c.* is, I believe, implied in our gloss σταυρῶσαι. (7) The request which Christ's enemies addressed to Pilate suggested, it would seem, to the mind of the *glossator* the request which Christ's friend addressed to Pilate. The καὶ ἐπιτυχόντες represents, I believe, the ܘܫܐܠܘܗܝ (= ἔλαβον) of Jn. xix. 40. The passage had a place in the Diatessaron (Ciasca, p. 93). The verb ܫܐܠ in the same connexion is used in Jn. xix. 38 (*bis*), Matt. xxvii. 59 (comp. Mc. vi. 29). The Curetonian fragments fail us at this part of the Gospel history (except in

St Luke), and I have no evidence to produce for an Old Syriac equivalent to πάλιν in the passages from St Matthew and St John.

xv. 14—29.

The Apostolic decree (*vv.* 23—29) in the text of our Codex has some points of special interest. It is necessary to consider it in connexion with the speech of St James. Very briefly I will deal *seriatim* with the points in the whole passage. (1) *v.* 15 ΚΑΙ ΟΥΤѠC CΥΜΦѠΝΗCΟΥCΙΝ ΟΙ ΛΟΓΟΙ. True text καὶ τούτῳ συμφωνοῦσιν οἱ λόγοι. Did an early Syriac translator take τούτῳ as masculine, i.e. as referring to St Peter, and render it ܠܗܢܐ (to-him)? If so, οὕτως might be generated as in Jn. xxi. 22 (see above on i. 5). The Syriac Vulgate has ܠܗܕܐ (to-this-thing). (2) *v.* 16 ΜΕΤΑ ΔΕ ΤΑΥΤΑ. The true text has no δέ. The Syriac Vulgate begins the sentence ܡܢܒ. The δέ may be due to a confusion between ܕ and ܘ. Comp. Hebr. iv. 4 (καὶ κατέπαυσεν = ܘܐܬܬܢܝܚ).

(3) *vv.* 17 f.
ΛΕΓΕΙ K̄C̄ ΠΟΙΗCΕΙ ΤΑΥΤΑ
ΓΝѠCΤΟΝ ΑΠ ΑΙѠΝΟC ΕCΤΙΝ ΤѠ K̄Ѡ̄ ΤΟ ΕΡΓΟΝ ΑΥΤΟΥ.

The true text is λέγει κύριος ποιῶν ταῦτα γνωστὰ ἀπ' αἰῶνος. (*a*) The Syriac Vulgate has: 'Saith the-Lord who-made (ܕܥܒܕ) these-things all-of-them.' The Bezan scribe took ܥܒܕ as a participle referring to the future; the ܕ as introducing the divine words; the 'saith the Lord' as referring to the succeeding, not the preceding, context. (*b*) The Syriac Vulgate has: 'known are-they from eternity his-works of-God.' The words, I venture to conjecture, are due to assimilation to some passage of the prophets, which I have not traced. The gloss probably took slightly different forms, of which one is preserved in the Syriac Vulgate, another in the Syriac text implied in Cod. D. (4) *v.* 20 ΚΑΙ ΤΗC ΠΟΡΝΕΙΑC ΚΑΙ ΤΟΥ ΑΙΜΑΤΟC. Here the καὶ πνικτοῦ which the true text has after τῆς πορνείας is omitted. Compare v. 29 καὶ αἵματος καὶ πορνείας, where the true text has καὶ πνικτῶν after αἵματος. In v. 29 (where the omission was probably first made, since there it is most easily explained as due to transcriptional causes) the Syriac Vulgate reads 'and-from blood and-from what-is-strangled (ܡܢ ܚܢܝܩܐ) and-from fornication (ܡܢ ܙܢܝܘܬܐ).' The Syriac phrase 'and-from what-is-strangled' would easily fall out before the Syriac phrase 'and-from fornication'[1]. (5) There is a remarkable gloss in vv. 20, 29[2].

v. 20.	v. 29.
καὶ ὅσα μὴ θέλουσιν ἑαυτοῖς γείνεσθαι ἑτέροις μὴ ποιεῖτε.	καὶ ὅσα μὴ θέλετε ἑαυτοῖς γείνεσθαι ἑτέρῳ μὴ ποιεῖν.

This gloss, a negative version of the golden rule, was first, I believe, inserted in v. 29 (for it will appear that it is only partially adapted to its context in v. 20), and goes back to the Syriac. My reasons for this latter opinion are two. (a) We have in v. 20 ἑτέροις, in v. 29 ἑτέρῳ. The difference is very slight between ܐܚܪܝܢ (another) and ܐܚܪܢܝܢ (others). The diversity may *either* have arisen in an Old Syriac MS., *or* be due to the Bezan scribe. (b) In v. 20 μὴ ποιεῖτε is alien to the context ('that *they* abstain'). We turn to v. 29. There the Bezan scribe has μὴ ποιεῖν correctly following after the infinitive ἀπέχεσθαι. But in Syriac this ἀπέχεσθαι becomes ܕܢܬܪܚܩܘܢ (that-ye-should-abstain). The μὴ ποιεῖν therefore of the gloss represents ܠܐ ܬܥܒܕܘܢ (ye shall not do). This was transferred to v. 20 despite the context there, and was literally translated by the Bezan scribe.

(6) v. 26.   ἀνθρώποις
παραδεδωκάσιν τὴν ψυχὴν αὐτῶν
ὑπὲρ τοῦ ὀνόματος τοῦ κυ ἡμῶν ιηυ χρυ
εἰς πάντα πειρασμόν.

[1] See also below, pp. 104, 108, 114.
[2] For a further discussion of this gloss and its source see below, p. 114, cf. p. 108.

The true text has ἀνθρ. παραδεδωκόσιν τὰς ψυχὰς αὐτῶν ὑπέρ...χριστοῦ. The fourth line of the Bezan text is a gloss. The points are these. (*a*) The Syriac Vulgate has ܐܢܫܐ ܐܫܠܡܘ ܢܦܫܗܘܢ (men who-surrendered). The παραδεδώκασιν then follows the Syriac. It is possible that in the Old Syriac copy used by the Bezan scribe the relative ܕ fell out between the two Olaphs. (*b*) As to the singular τὴν ψυχὴν αὐτῶν, ܢܦܫܬܗܘܢ (their-souls) would easily pass into ܢܦܫܗܘܢ (their-soul). (*c*) What of the gloss εἰς πάντα πειρασμόν, which is also found in Cod. E? The only other passage in the N. T. where the expression 'every temptation' occurs is Lc. iv. 13 συντελέσας πάντα πειρασμόν. In this latter passage the Syriac Vulgate indeed has 'all-of-them his-temptations', but the Arabic Tatian 'Cum consummasset diabolus *omnem tentationem*' (Ciasca, p. 8) is good evidence that the Old Syriac had a literal translation of the Greek—ܠܟܠ ܢܣܝܘܢܐ (every temptation)[1]. In the Greek there is no point of contact between Lc. iv. 13 and Acts xv. 26. But in the Syriac it will be noticed that in Lc. ܫܠܡ = συντελέσας, in Acts ܐܫܠܡ = παραδεδώκασι; the same verb, that is, is used in the two passages though not in the same sense. I would suggest therefore that, when some Syriac scribe wished to qualify the words 'men who-surrendered their-soul', the sound of the verb carried his thoughts to Lc. iv. 13 and therefore he appended the phrase 'to (ܠ) -every temptation'.

(7) *v.* 27 ΑΠΑΓΓΕΛΟΥΝΤΑC ΤΑΥΤΑ. The true text has ἀπαγγέλλοντας τὰ αὐτά. The Syriac Vulgate has: 'Who-*shall*-tell to-you these very-things.' (8) *v.* 29. (*a*) ΑΦ ωΝ, in place of the true text ἐξ ὧν, is an independent translation of the Syriac. (*b*) ΕΥ ΠΡΑΖΑΤΕ ΦΕΡΟΜΕΝΟΙ ΕΝ Τω ΑΓΙω ΠΝΕΥΜΑΤΙ ΕΡΡωCΘΕ. The Old Syriac has: 'well ye-shall-be (ܬܗܘܘܢ), be strong (ܒܡܪܢ ܗܘܘ) in-our-Lord.' Probably the Bezan εὖ πράξατε (true text εὖ πράξετε) represents an Old Syriac reading 'well

---

[1] The word ܢܣܝܘܢܐ could of course be vocalized as plural: the word thus vocalized is the connecting link between the Old and the Vulgate Syriac.

be-ye'. But what of the Bezan interpolation? I believe that the desire to make the Apostolic decree more spiritual[1] led to the introduction into the Old Syriac text of a phrase from a Pauline epistle, which deals with the Judaistic controversy. See Gal. v. 18 'But if in-the-Spirit led (ܡܬܕܒܪܝܢ) (are) ye, ye are not under the-law'; and compare Rom. viii. 14, Jn. xvi. 13, Lc. iv. 1 'There-led-Him (ܕܒܪܬܗ) the-Spirit into-the-wilderness[2]'; it will be remembered that we saw reason to think that the context of this last passage suggested the gloss in v. 26. The rendering of the Syriac 'led' by φερόμενοι is quite natural (see the use of the Greek word in Mc. xv. 22, Jn. xxi. 18, Acts xiv. 13), especially as the Bezan scribe in translating Syriac glosses frequently avoids the most obvious Greek word. The choice of the word was *possibly* influenced by 2 Pet. i. 21 (where the Syriac has another word)[3]. This suggestion as to the source of the gloss is strongly confirmed by the fact that Irenaeus (iii. 17, ed. Harvey) preserves another Pauline form of the gloss—'ambulantes in Spiritu Sancto' (Gal. v. 16). It would appear that in this passage Irenaeus, like Cod. E in v. 39, vi. 10, preserves an Old Syriac reading different from that implied in Cod. D. (9) My position that these are *Syriac* glosses

---

[1] Compare xvi. 4 ΕΚΗΡΥCCON ΚΑΙ ΠΑΡΕΔΙΔΟCΑΝ ΑΥΤΟΙC ΜΕΤΑ ΠΑCΗC ΠΑΡΡΗCΙΑC ΤΟΝ ΚΝ ΙΗΝ ΧΡΝ ΑΜΑ ΠΑΡΑΔΙΔΟΝΤΕC ΚΑΙ ΤΑC ΕΝΤΟΛΑC ΑΠΟCΤΟΛωΝ ΚΑΙ ΠΡΕCΒΥΤΕΡω. The true text is παρεδίδοσαν αὐτοῖς φυλάσσειν τὰ δόγματα τὰ κεκριμένα ὑπὸ τῶν ἀποστ. κ. πρεσβ. The Syriac Vulgate has 'Preaching were-they and-teaching them that-they-should-be keeping the-commands those which-they-wrote (even) the-Apostles and the-Elders.' The interpolated words in Cod. D come from Acts xxviii. 31 through the Syriac, the link being ܡܠܦ (=παρεδίδοσαν xvi. 4) and ܐܠܦ (=διδάσκων xxviii. 31). Note too τὰ δόγματα (true text)=ܦܘܩܕܢܐ (Syr. Vulg., comp. Lc. ii. 1, Acts xvii. 7, Eph. ii. 15, Col. ii. 14)=τὰς ἐντολάς (Cod. D, comp. e.g. Matt. xix. 17, xxii. 40, Lc. i. 6, Jn. xv. 10).

[2] Tert., *de Pudicitia*, xii. gives the gloss in this form: 'uectante uos Spiritu Sancto.' It is quite possible that this is to be traced to a Syriac gloss derived directly from Lc. iv. 1, viz. ܒܪܘܚܐ ܩܕܝܫܐ ܕܢܘܒܠܟܘܢ ܗܝ.

[3] The Bezan Latin scribe, taking φερόμενοι as middle, has '*ferentes* in santo spo'—a rendering which appears to be without meaning.

is confirmed by the fact that the Syriac Vulgate preserves yet another expedient for spiritualizing the decree. In place of the simple 'be strong (ἔρρωσθε)' it has the phrase (see above) 'be strong in-our-Lord.' With this compare Eph. iv. 15 ܐܬܚܝܠܘ ܒܡܪܢ[1]. (10) This Bezan gloss (see also i. 5, vi. 10, xi. 2 (probably), xiii. 15) together with that preserved in Irenaeus implies an Old Syriac Version of the Pauline Epistles.

xvii. 5. ΟΙ ΔΕ ΑΠΕΙΘΟΥΝΤΕϹ ΙΟΥΔΑΙΟΙ
ϹΥΝϹΤΡΕΨΑΝΤΕϹ ΤΙΝΑϹ ΑΝΔΡΑϹ
ΤΩΝ ΑΓΟΡΑΙΩΝ ΠΟΝΗΡΟΥϹ
ΕΘΟΡΥΒΟΥϹΑΝ ΤΗΝ ΠΟΛΙΝ.

The true text has ζηλώσαντες δὲ οἱ Ἰ. καὶ προσλαβόμενοι τῶν ἀγοραίων ἄνδρας τινὰς πονηροὺς καὶ ὀχλοποιήσαντες ἐθορύβουν τὴν πόλιν. The points in this passage are these. (1) The first line of the Bezan passage is due to assimilation to xiv. 2, where the Syriac Vulgate has: 'who-not obeying were'; hence the present participle (ἀπειθοῦντες) in this gloss. (2) The Old Syriac rendered προσλαβ. and ὀχλοποι. by a single phrase suggested by the latter Greek word— ܟܕ ܐܬܟܢܫܘ (when they-had-assembled; cf. xix. 25). This Syriac phrase the Bezan scribe rendered by the word which he had used to translate the same Syriac verb in x. 41, xi. 27 (see note). (3) ΕΘΟΡΥΒΟΥϹΑΝ = ἐθορύβουν ἦσαν (comp. ΚΑΤΟΙΚΟΥϹΑΝ, ii. 46) = ܗܘܘ ܕܥܡܪܝܢ (Syriac Vulgate). Here we have a mechanical reproduction in the Bezan Greek of a Syriac idiom.

xvii. 34. ΕΝ ΟΙϹ ΚΑΙ ΔΙΟΝΥϹΙΟϹ ΤΙϹ ΑΡΕΟΠΑΓΕΙΤΗϹ
ΕΥϹΧΗΜΩΝ ΚΑΙ ΕΤΕΡΟΙ ϹΥΝ ΑΥΤΟΙϹ.

The true text is ἐν οἷς καὶ Διονύσιος [ὁ] Ἀρεοπαγίτης καὶ γυνὴ ὀνόματι Δάμαρις καὶ ἕτεροι σὺν αὐτοῖς. There are three

---

[1] Here the adjective has its common meaning 'true'. For this use of the perfect comp. 1 Cor. iv. 1 (Nöldeke, *Syr. Gram.*, p. 181, § 260).

points to be considered. (1) The Bezan text inserts τις after Διονύσιος. The Syriac Vulgate has: 'But *a-certain-one* ([Syriac]) from-them was Dionysius from the-judges of-Arius Pagus and-a-woman *a-certain-one* ([Syriac]) whose-name (was) Damaris.' The word *a-certain* is also inserted in vii. 58 (Cod. D and Syr. Vulg.), viii. 27 (Syr. Vulg. '*a-certain* ([Syriac]) eunuch'; Cod. D ΚΑΝΔΑΚΗC ΒΑCΙΛΕΙCCΗC ΤΙΝΟC), x. 22 (Cod. D and Syr. Vulg.) (2) The gloss εὐσχήμων represents, I believe, an Old Syriac gloss [Syriac] (= honoured). The Syriac Vulgate uses this word to translate εὐσχήμων (Mc. xv. 43, the epithet applied to Joseph of Arimathea), τίμιος (Acts v. 34, the epithet applied to Gamaliel). Thus the intention of the gloss here is to assimilate the description of the Areopagite to that of the two other councillors in the N.T. who favoured the cause of Christ. Compare the note on the gloss in iv. 18. It must be noticed that in the next clause Codex E after καὶ γυνή has the gloss ΤΙΜΙΑ. This represents, I believe, an Old Syriac gloss [Syriac] (= known). This gloss also is due to assimilation; for this Syriac word is used in the Syriac Vulgate to render two epithets applied to *women*—τῶν πρώτων (xvii. 4), τῶν εὐσχημόνων (xvii. 12); probably in the Old Syriac it was used as the equivalent of the latter Greek word in xiii. 50, though there the Syriac Vulgate has [Syriac] (= rich, comp. Syr. Vulg. of ix. 36). This Syriac word (= known) might well be rendered by τιμία, for in xxi. 39 it is the equivalent of οὐκ ἄσημος, in Matt. xvii. 16, Rom. xvi. 7 of ἐπίσημος. (3) The omission of the words καὶ γ. ὄν. Δάμ. in Codex D is due, I venture to suggest, to the falling out of a line in the Old Syriac. The last two lines of the chapter probably stood thus.

[Syriac] [Syriac] [Syriac] [Syriac]
Damaris whose-name a-certain-one and-a-woman

[Syriac] [Syriac]
with-them and-others

The resemblance between the two words which begin the

two lines is sufficient to explain how the scribe may have accidentally omitted the former line.

xix. 1. ΘΕΛΟΝΤΟC ΔΕ ΤΟΥ ΠΑΥΛΟΥ
ΚΑΤΑ ΤΗΝ ΙΔΙΑΝ ΒΟΥΛΗΝ
ΠΟΡΕΥΕCΘΑΙ ΕΙC ΙΕΡΟCΟΛΥΜΑ
ΕΙΠΕΝ ΑΥΤω ΤΟ Π͞ΝΑ ΥΠΟCΤΡΕΦΕΙΝ ΕΙC ΤΗΝ ΑCΙΑ͞
ΔΙΕΛΘωΝ ΔΕ ΤΑ ΑΝωΤΕΡΙΚΑ ΜΕΡΗ
ΕΡΧΕΤΑΙ Κ.Τ.Λ.

The true text is ἐγένετο δὲ ἐν τῷ τὸν Ἀπολλὼ εἶναι ἐν Κορίνθῳ Παῦλον διελθόντα τὰ ἀνωτερικὰ μέρη ἐλθεῖν κ.τ.λ. I take the points in order. (1) In the last two lines the Bezan verbs διελθών...ἔρχεται reproduce a Syriac construction; for the Syriac text here at no stage of its history can have exactly represented the Greek 'accusative and infinitive' (see e.g. iii. 1, ix. 32). The earlier part of the paragraph however is remoulded. (2) The gloss of the first three lines can only have come from the Old Syriac, for it is derived from the Syriac of xix. 21, where the Syriac Vulgate has: 'Paul purposed in-his-mind (ܣܡ ܦܘܠܘܣ ܒܪܥܝܢܗ) = ἔθετο ὁ Παῦλος ἐν τῷ πνεύματι) that-he-should-go-round all Macedonia and-Achaia and-should-go to-Jerusalem.' It must be noticed that the Syriac word ܪܥܝܢܐ (mind) is used to translate not only νοῦς (1 Cor. ii. 16, Rom. xi. 34) and kindred words, but also γνώμη (1 Cor. i. 10, vii. 40), ἔννοια (1 Pet. iv. 1), ὑπόνοια (1 Tim. vi. 4). The βουλή therefore of the Bezan gloss is quite a natural rendering of this Syriac word. Further, we can understand why ἰδίαν is used when we note, for example, that ἀφ' ἑαυτοῦ (Jn. xvi. 13) becomes in the Syriac 'from the-thought (mind) (of) his-soul (ܡܢ ܪܥܝܢܐ ܕܢܦܫܗ)'. (3) The fourth line of the Bezan text is a gloss derived from a gloss; for in xx. 3 f. (Cod. D) we read—

3. ΕΙΠΕΝ ΔΕ ΤΟ Π͞ΝΑ ΑΥΤω ΥΠΟCΤΡΕΦΕΙΝ
ΔΙΑ ΤΗC ΜΑΚΕΔΟΝΙΑC
4. ΜΕΛΛΟΝΤΟC ΟΥΝ ΕΞΕΙΕΝΑΙ ΑΥΤΟΥ ΜΕΧΡΙ ΤΗC ΑCΙΑC.

Here the true text is ἐγένετο γνώμης τοῦ ὑποστρέφειν διὰ Μακεδ. As to this passage (xx. 3) we notice (*a*) the gloss εἶπεν...αὐτῷ is based on a remembrance of x. 19, xi. 12, xx. 23 (Syr. adds 'and-said'), xxi. 11; (*b*) the Syriac Vulgate has 'into(ܠ)-Macedonia', and this was probably the reading of the Old Syriac, though Cod. D retains the διά of the true text: we have therefore a Syriac basis for the ὑποστρ. εἰς of the Bezan gloss in xix. 1; (*c*) μέλλοντος οὖν ἐξιέναι αὐτοῦ has a curious history. μέλλοντι ἀνάγεσθαι εἰς τὴν Συρίαν (xx. 3, true text) = 'when he-was about to-go-away to-Syria (ܟܕ ܨܒܐ ܕܢܐܙܠ ܠܣܘܪܝܐ)'. This phrase, differently rendered in *v*. 3 of the Bezan text[1], was repeated ('Asia' taking the place of 'Syria') in *v*. 4. That the Bezan text in *v*. 4 represents an Old Syriac text is clear (among other reasons) because we find ἀνάγεσθαι (*v*. 3, true text) = ܕܢܐܙܠ = ἐξιέναι (*v*. 4, Cod. D). In xx. 3 f. therefore there was this Old Syriac gloss: 'And-there-said the-Spirit to-him that-he-should-return to-[Macedonia. When therefore about was-he to-go as-far-as] Asia.' The gloss was then transferred, the words enclosed in brackets above being omitted, to xix. 1.

It must suffice simply to refer to two glosses similar to the last one considered, viz. (1) xvii. 15 ΠΑΡΗΛΘΕΝ...ΛΟΓΟΝ derived from xvi. 8, 6; (2) xvi. 10 ΔΙΕΓΕΡΘΕΙΣ...ΗΜΙΝ based on x. 8 Syr. Vulg. and Cod. D (represented by the Latin).

xix. 9. ΤΟ ΚΑΘΗΜΕΡΑΝ ΔΙΑΛΕΓΟΜΕΝΟΣ ΕΝ ΤΗ ΣΧΟΛΗ
ΤΥΡΑΝΝΙΟΥ ΤΙΝΟΣ ΑΠΟ ΩΡΑΣ Ε ΕΩΣ ΔΕΚΑΤΗΣ.

The true text stops with the name. What account can be given of the gloss which tells us how many hours St Paul's working day lasted? It is due, I believe, to assimilation. The Apostle's position in the metropolis of Asiatic Paganism recalled his position at the centre of the world's life. St Luke's picture of the disputant in the school of Tyrannus in several points resembles his picture of the disputant in his lodging in one of the *insulae* of Rome. In the latter case the

[1] ΗΘΕΛΗΣΕΝ ΑΝΑΧΘΗΝΑΙ ΕΙΣ ΣΥΡΙΑΝ.

disputation of the one memorable day lasted ἀπὸ πρωὶ ἕως ἑσπέρας (xxviii. 23). Taking this phrase, and translating into a more picturesque form, the *glossator* tells us that the daily disputation at Ephesus lasted 'from the fifth hour till the tenth.' The number of the hours is, I believe, modelled on Matt. xxvii. 45 'From the sixth hour...unto the ninth hour[1]'. An hour is added at either end, so as to place the one limit well before noon and the other limit in the late afternoon or early evening. There is nothing in the gloss itself to decide what its original language was. But on both sides of it there are clear signs of Syriac influence.—In *v.* 9 (*a*) ΤΙΝΕϹ...ΑΥΤΩΝ : so Syriac Vulgate ܐܢܫܝܢ ܡܢܗܘܢ. (*b*) ΤΟΥ ΠΛΗΘΟΥϹ ΤΩΝ ΕΘΝΩ͂Ν : so Syr. Vulg. ܣܓܝܐܐ܂ ܡܢܗ (comp. Lc. i. 10). (*c*) ΤΟΤΕ. Comp. note on ii. 14. In *v.* 10 ΕΩϹ ΠΑΝΤΕϹ...ΗΚΟΥϹΑΝ ΤΟΥϹ ΛΟΓΟΥϹ ΤΟΥ ΚΥ͂ (true text ὥστε πάντας...ἀκοῦσαι τὸν λόγον τοῦ κυρίου): so (as far as regards the construction) Syr. Vulg. ܕܡܠܬܗ ܕܡܪܢ. For ܐ ܕܡܪܢ (until) = ὥστε, see Mc. iii. 10, 1 Cor. v. 1, 2 Cor. i. 8. The Old Syriac here probably read ܡܠܐ (words). There is every reason therefore to refer the gloss under discussion to the Old Syriac of the Acts (comp. note on iii. 1).

xix. 28 f. ΔΡΑΜΟΝΤΕϹ ΕΙϹ ΤΟ ΑΜΦΟΔΟΝ ΕΚΡΑΖΟΝ ΛΕΓΟΝΤΕϹ
ΜΕΓΑΛΗ ΑΡΤΕΜΙϹ ΕΦΕϹΙΩΝ
ΚΑΙ ϹΥΝΕΧΥΘΗ ΟΛΗ Η ΠΟΛΙϹ ΑΙϹΧΥΝΗϹ
ΟΡΜΗϹΑΝ ΔΕ Κ.Τ.Λ.

The true text is ἔκραζον λέγοντες Μεγάλη ἡ Ἄρτεμις Ἐφεσίων. καὶ ἐπλήσθη ἡ πόλις τῆς συγχύσεως, ὥρμησάν τε κ.τ.λ.

(1) The opening words in the Bezan text are a gloss. The *glossator* felt that, though St Luke tells us of the rush into 'the theatre' (*v.* 29), there is no notice of place in the

---

[1] It is to be especially noted that Matt. *l. c.* supplies a gloss in Acts x. 30 found in Cod. E: ΗΜΗΝ ΝΗϹΤΕΥΩΝ ΚΑΙ ΠΡΟϹΕΥΧΟΜΕΝΟϹ ΑΠΟ ΕΚΤΗϹ ΩΡΑϹ ΕΩϹ ΕΝΑΤΗϹ.

earlier part of the history. The information, which St Luke does not give, he supplies in his gloss. The word δραμόντες is the translation of a context-supplement in the Old Syriac. The word used to describe the rush into the theatre (v. 29) is here used to describe the rush into the market place: ὥρμησαν = ܐܠܗܘܢ = δραμόντες. Further, in Mc. xi. 4 ἄμφοδον is rendered in the Syriac Vulgate by ܫܘܩܐ (= πλατεῖα, e.g. Matt. xii. 19, ἀγορά, e.g. Matt. xi. 16). In xvi. 19 (Syriac Vulgate) we read: 'Her-masters...seized Paul and-Silas and-took (and) brought them into-the-market-place (ܠܫܘܩܐ = εἰς τὴν ἀγοράν)'. Comp. xvii. 5, 17, xxviii. 15. The *glossator* held that, as at Philippi, so at Ephesus the place of concourse was the market place. The Bezan scribe *more suo* employs an unusual equivalent of the Syriac word (Mc. xi. 4)[1]. (2) The addition of ὅλη is due to assimilation to xxi. 30 (ἡ πόλις ὅλη = ܟܠܗ ܡܕܝܢܬܐ = ὅλη ἡ πόλις). (3) What of the extraordinary reading συνεχύθη...αἰσχύνης? Once more we look to the Syriac for help. The Syriac word for 'of-shame' is ܕܒܗܬܬܐ. But this word bears a very strong resemblance to ܒܗܬܬ ܘ (and-she-was-ashamed); for confusion between ܘ and ܪ, see on i. 5, ii. 6; also p. 127. We have then obtained a probable restoration of the Old Syriac text through a meaningless corruption of the Bezan text. But probability becomes, I venture to think, certainty, when we recall the familiar O.T. phrase 'ashamed and confounded'. The pair of Syriac words answering to 'ashamed and confounded' occurs in the following passages: Is. xlv. 16 ('They shall be ashamed, yea, confounded (ܘܢܒܗܬܘܢ ܢܚܦܪܘܢ), all of them: they shall go into confusion (ܒܚܦܪܐ) together that are makers of idols'), Is. xxiv. 23[2], xli. 11, liv. 4, Jer. xv. 9, Mic. iii. 7, Ps. xl. 14. We may conclude that this is one of several passages (e.g. v. 38, vii. 43) in which there is good evidence

---

[1] The true text has ἡ Ἄρτεμις. For the omission of the article see note on vi. 1.
[2] Here the order is 'confounded...ashamed'.

that the Old Syriac text of the Acts was assimilated to a passage or phrase of the O.T. Here probably Is. xlv. 16 (cf. Mic. iii. 7) was in the *glossator's* mind. The clause then probably stood thus in the Old Syriac text:

ܘܒܗܬܬ݂   ܡܕܝܢܬܐ   ܟܠܗ   ܘܐܫܬܓܫܬ݂
and-was-ashamed   the-city   all-of-it   it-was-confounded

In the Syriac Vulgate we have here, it appears, a revised text. With the double purpose of avoiding the word ܐܫܬܓܫ, which does not occur in this sense in the Syriac Vulgate of the N.T., and of assimilating the passage to xxi. 30, that version replaces the 'was confounded and ashamed' of the Old Syriac by a single word ܐܬܕܠܚ (comp. vv. 32, 40, ii. 6, vi. 12, xiv. 18).

2.

THE BEZAN TEXT OF THE ACTS.
DATE. BIRTHPLACE. AFFINITIES.

THERE are three questions in regard to the Bezan text to which I shall endeavour to give some answer in the following chapter. If the theory which I have maintained as to a Syriac basis of the Bezan text finds acceptance with scholars, they will admit that it touches many subjects at many points, and that many problems call anew for careful investigation. I would disclaim therefore any attempt at finality in my treatment of those three questions, which yet claim some consideration, however tentative and provisional. The questions are these. (1) What *external* evidence is there as to the *date* of the Bezan text of the Acts and consequently as to that of the Old Syriac text which lies behind it? (2) What evidence is there as to the *birthplace* of the Bezan text? (3) What is the probable account of, and what the probable deductions from, its *affinity* to other texts?

(1) The date of the Bezan text and of the underlying Syriac text.
(i) The first witness whom we examine is Tertullian. This Father's references to the Acts are collected in Rönsch, *Das Neue Test. Tertullian's*. I have not made any effort to add to this collection. I have *italicised* those words and phrases which seem to agree with the Bezan text, or on

which I have for some reason added a brief note. It is sufficient to give a general reference to the notes in the previous chapter on the several passages.

Acts ii. 17 Et prophetabunt filii filiaeque *eorum* (*Adv. Marc.* v. 8). The same reading is found in *Passio S. Perpetuae, c.* 1. Professor Robinson adduces strong, if not conclusive, reasons for thinking that this Martyrdom (except the Visions) is the work of Tertullian (*Texts and Studies*, vol. i. No. 2, p. 47 ff.).

This passage is of special importance, inasmuch as it cannot, I think, be reasonably doubted that the Bezan reading is due to Syriac influence.

iii. 19 ff. Vti tempora *uobis superueniant* refrigerii ex persona dei...tempora exhibitionis omnium quae locutus est deus ore sanctorum prophetarum (*De Resurr. Carnis* 23).

Here, as in the Bezan text, there is nothing to answer to the words ἀπ' αἰῶνος. The word *exhibitionis* is at first sight puzzling. Its meaning here, however, is decided by *c.* 17, where *exhibitio carnis* is synonymous with *repraesentatio carnis*.

iv. 32 Itaque qui animo animaque miscemur, nihil de rei communicatione dubitamus. *Omnia indiscreta* sunt apud nos praeter uxores (*Apol.* 39).

The Bezan Greek is ἦν καρδία καὶ ψυχὴ μία καὶ οὐκ ἦν διάκρισις ἐν αὐτοῖς οὐδεμία...ἦν αὐτοῖς πάντα κοινά. Tertullian's *indiscreta* seems to be based upon the Bezan οὐκ ἦν διάκρισις. If this be so, it follows that the Syriacised Latin readings of Tertullian come through the medium of a Syriacised *Greek* text—either the Bezan text or some text closely akin to it.

viii. 24 Simon Samarites...frustra *fleuit* (*De Anima* 34).

xv. 28 f. Visum est Spiritui Sancto et nobis, nullum amplius uobis adicere pondus, quam eorum a quibus necesse est abstineri, *a sacrificiis et a fornicationibus et sanguine.* A quibus obseruando recte agitis, *uectante uos Spiritu Sancto* (*De Pudic.* 12).

As to the words *a sacrificiis et a fornicationibus*, note that the Syriac words ܪܒܚܐ, ܕܚܢܘܬܐ can be vocalised as singular or plural. The latter is vocalised as plural in Rom. i. 29 in some editions of the

DATE. BIRTHPLACE. AFFINITIES. 105

Syriac text (see Schaaf, *Lex. Syriacum*, sub voce). This reading of Tertullian's seems good additional evidence that behind his text there lies a Syriac text. The form of the gloss which follows, *uectante etc.*, as well as the plurals just considered, clearly indicate that the text on which Tertullian here depends is not identical with the Bezan text, and that it ultimately rests on a somewhat different form of Syriac text.

From these passages in Tertullian we learn that *very early in the third century* there was current in Carthage a Latin text of the Acts very closely allied to, though not absolutely identical with, the Bezan text and, like the Bezan text, ultimately based on a Syriac version. Between this Syriac version and Tertullian's Latin text, we have seen reason for believing that there intervened a Greek Syriacised text. This Syriac version therefore must go back a considerable distance in the *second century*.

(ii) From Tertullian we turn to Irenaeus. None of the passages in Irenaeus with which I have to deal, with one important exception, exist now in the original Greek. They are available only in the Latin translation. It will be a matter for argument whether the textual peculiarities in this Latin translation are due to the translator or go back to the Greek. The passages are all in Iren. III. xii. (ed. Harvey, whose text I have used). I shall use italics as before.

Acts i. 16 Viri fratres, oportebat impleri scripturam *hanc* quam praedixit &c.

ii. 33 Effudit *donationem* hanc quam uos nunc uidetis et auditis.

<small>Harvey notes that this reading is found in the Syriac Vulgate. It is due to assimilation to ii. 38. Cod. D reads εζεχεεν υμειν ο και κ.τ.λ.</small>

iii. 13 ff. Quem uos quidem *tradidistis in iudicium*, et negastis ante faciem Pilati, cum *remittere eum uellet*. Vos autem sanctum et iustum *aggrauastis*...17 Et nunc, fratres, scio quoniam secundum ignorantiam *fecistis nequam*....20 et ueniant *uobis* tempora refrigerii a facie Domini...21 quae locutus est Deus per sanctos prophetas suos. 22 Moyses quidem dicit *ad patres nostros*: Quoniam prophetam excitabit uobis Dominus Deus *uester* ex fratribus uestris quemadmodum me ipsum audietis.

In *v.* 20 the *uobis* corresponds with the reading of the Syriac Vulgate and Cod. E (see also Tertullian). In *v.* 21 there is nothing to correspond to ἀπ' αἰῶνος. In *v.* 22 *Deus uester* answers to the Bezan ο θ͞c ym͞ω. The last words of the extract admit of the interpretation which *must* be given of the passage in the Bezan text.

iv. 8 f. Principes populi et seniores *Israelitae*, si nos hodie redarguimur *a uobis* in benefacto hominis infirmi.

Cod. D has καὶ πρεcβγτεροι τογ ιcραηλ. For its reading in the second clause see note *in loco*.

iv. 31 ἐλάλουν τὸν λόγον τοῦ θεοῦ μετὰ παρρησίας παντὶ τῷ θέλοντι πιστεύειν.

The Greek of Irenaeus is here preserved in Cramer's *Catena* (p. 79). The Latin is: Loquebantur uerbum Dei cum fiducia *omni uolenti credere*. The Bezan gloss will be noted.

v. 31 f. Hunc Deus principem et saluatorem exaltauit *gloria sua*, dare poenitentiam Israel, et remissionem peccatorum: et nos *in eo* testes sumus sermonum horum.

Two points claim attention. (1) *Gloria sua*. The Greek of Cod. D has τη δοξη αγτογ, the Latin *exaltauit caritate sua* (where *caritate* probably arose from *claritate*). Two explanations are possible. (*a*) Is τῇ δόξῃ αὐτοῦ an *itacism* for τῇ δεξιᾷ αὐτοῦ? In that case, as Irenaeus has a text not absolutely identical with, though closely akin to, that of Cod. D, this reading is not a slip of the Bezan scribe, but must belong to a Greek text behind the Bezan text. (*b*) I am inclined to think however that the reading is due to a characteristic assimilation of this passage to Rom. vi. 4, and that this assimilation goes back to a Syriac text of the Acts. In Rom. vi. 4 we read in the Syriac Vulgate 'There-rose (ܩܡ) Jesus Christ from among the-dead by-the-glory (ܒܫܘܒܚܐ) of-His-Father.' The Greek is διὰ τῆς δόξης. It is not improbable that an Old Syriac version read here idiomatically 'by-*His*-glory.' We have perhaps a trace of this assimilation in a word interpolated in the Syriac Vulgate of Acts v. 31 'Him Himself God *raised* (ܐܩܝܡ) a-prince-and-a-saviour and-exalted-Him (ܘܐܪܝܡܗ) by(ܒ)-His-right-hand.' Whichever explanation we adopt, we have in this reading, which the Sahidic Version

DATE. BIRTHPLACE. AFFINITIES.

alone of other authorities preserves, a proof how closely related are the text of Cod. D and the text found in (the Latin) Irenaeus. (2) The *in eo* arises, I think, from a misplacement in the Bezan (or kindred) text, or more probably in the Old Syriac text. The Bezan text has

ΚΑΙ ΑΦΕϹΙΝ ΑΜΑΡΤΙШΝ ΕΝ ΑΥΤШ
ΚΑΙ ΗΜΕΙϹ ΕϹΜΕΝ ΜΑΡΤΥΡΕϹ.

The position of ἐν αὐτῷ here is natural. It is a gloss probably due to assimilation (in the Syriac) to Col. i. 14 (ܒܗ ܕ ܒܗ=ἐν ᾧ), Eph. i. 7 (ܒܗ ܕ=ἐν ᾧ). The ἐν αὐτῷ, or the Syriac ܒܗ, slipped down into, or was repeated in, the second line.

v. 42 Omni quoque die in templo et *in domo* non cessabant docentes et euangelizantes Christum Iesum *Filium Dei.*

The *in domo*, as Harvey notes, seems to come from the Syriac ܒܒܝܬܐ. This is the Syriac rendering of κατ᾽ οἶκον in Acts ii. 46, Rom. xvi. 5, 1 Cor. xvi. 19, Col. iv. 15, Philem. 2 (cf. Acts xx. 20). The last words seem due to assimilation to ix. 20.

vii. 5 *Sed* promisit dare ei in possessionem eam.

Cod. D has ἀλλα.

xv. 11 Sed per gratiam Domini *nostri* Iesu Christi credimus nos *posse* saluari, quomodo et illi.

Note two points (1) *nostri:* so, as Harvey notes, the Syriac Vulgate. See above note on Acts ii. 25. (2) *Posse* seems due to assimilation to xv. 1—an assimilation quite in the manner of the Old Syriac.

xv. 15 Et *sic* conveniunt sermones prophetarum.

See p. 8 n.

xv. 18 ff. *Cognitum a seculo est Deo opus eius*...20 uti abstineant a *uanitatibus* idolorum, et a fornicatione, et a sanguine: *et quaecunque nolunt sibi fieri, aliis ne faciant.*

Here note (*a*) that *a uanitatibus* seems due, as Harvey hints in his note, to assimilation to xiv. 15; (*b*) there is nothing to represent καὶ πνικτοῦ.

xv. 24 ff. Quia ex nobis quidam *exeuntes* turbauerunt uos...27 Misimus igitur Iudam et Silam, et ipsos per sermonem annuntiantes *nostram sententiam.* 28 Placuit enim

Sancto Spiritui et nobis, nullum amplius uobis pondus imponere, quam haec quae sunt necessaria, ut abstineatis ab idolothytis, et sanguine, et fornicatione : 29 *et quaecunque non uoltis fieri uobis, aliis ne faciatis:* a quibus custodientes uos ipsos, bene agetis, *ambulantes in Spiritu Sancto.*

Note in *v.* 27 the reading *nostram sententiam*. This has, I think, the appearance of being a Syriac reading. In *v.* 28 the Syriac Vulgate has : ' For it-was the-pleasure (ܪܥܝܢܐ) to-the-Spirit of-Holiness and-also to-us (ܠܢ).' From this verse the gloss ܪܥܝܢܐ (our-pleasure) in *v.* 27 would easily be generated. On the other points see notes *in loco.*

The important question still remains whether this text goes back to Irenaeus himself or whether its peculiarities are due to the Latin translator.

A thorough discussion of this question would involve an examination of the text of Irenaeus as a whole. Such an investigation is probably a necessary preliminary to anything like a final discussion of the problems connected with the 'Western' text. But apart from any attempt at such an exhaustive treatment, there are three arguments which satisfy me that the text of the Acts given by the Latin translator is a faithful reflection, at least in all essential features, of the text which Irenaeus himself incorporated in his book. These three arguments are as follows.

(1) Though it is likely enough that a Latin translator would from time to time introduce Latin readings into his renderings of N.T. quotations, it is hardly likely that he would substitute, and that continuously, another text for that used by his author. At least we are justified in asking for some decisive arguments before we acquiesce in such a conclusion.

(2) There are two passages of Irenaeus, where the Greek is preserved, in which the Acts is quoted. (*a*) The quotation from Acts iv. 31 in one of these passages was given above (p. 106): it contains a characteristic Bezan reading. (*b*) In the other passage (Iren. III. xii. 11) Acts ix. 20 is quoted in

the following form: ἐν ταῖς συναγωγαῖς ἐν Δαμασκῷ ἐκήρυσσε μετὰ πάσης παρρησίας τὸν Ἰησοῦν, ὅτι οὗτός ἐστιν ὁ Υἱὸς τοῦ Θεοῦ ὁ χριστός[1]. We have not the Bezan text to compare with this quotation, since there is a *lacuna* in Codex D viii. 29 —x. 4. We must therefore examine Irenaeus' quotation to see if it presents any peculiarities which are Bezan in character. In these few words then there are no less than three glosses: (i) ἐν Δαμασκῷ, (ii) μετὰ π. παρρησίας, (iii) ὁ χριστός. Of these the *last* is obviously due to assimilation to *v.* 22 (συνέχυννεν Ἰουδαίους τοὺς κατοικοῦντας ἐν Δαμασκῷ, συνβιβάζων ὅτι οὗτός ἐστιν ὁ χριστός); the *second* (a gloss which occurs elsewhere in the Bezan text vi. 10 (see note), xvi. 4) to assimilation to *v.* 27, where the Greek is ἐν Δαμασκῷ ἐπαρρησιάσατο ἐν τῷ ὀνόματι Ἰησοῦ, but the Syriac Vulgate 'in-Damascus openly (ܓܠܝܐܝܬ ܒܕܪܡܣܘܩ, a regular Syriac equivalent of μετὰ παρρ., μετὰ πάσης παρρ.; see on vi. 10) he-spoke in-the-name of-Jesus'. As to the *first* gloss (ἐν Δαμασκῷ), the first impression is that *Irenaeus* inserted the words for the sake of clearness, and this explanation is possible. But on the other hand it may come from *v.* 22 and *v.* 27, and it is to be noticed that the Syriac Vulgate has a similar gloss, suggested apparently by *v.* 22, viz., 'in-the-synagogues *of-the-Jews*'. In this quotation in Irenaeus then we have certainly two, probably three, context-glosses—a phenomenon which we have seen to be characteristic of the Bezan text (i.e. of the Syriac text which lies behind the Bezan). If therefore the Bezan text at this point were ever discovered, we may feel very certain that it would coincide with this quotation in Irenaeus.

We may then without rashness conclude from these two quotations in passages of Irenaeus where the Greek text has been preserved, that elsewhere the Latin translation accurately reproduces the lost Greek of Irenaeus' quotations from the Acts.

[1] The Latin translator has: In synagogis *in Damasco* praedicabat *cum omni fiducia* Iesum, quoniam hic est *Christus* Filius Dei.

110   THE BEZAN TEXT OF THE ACTS.

(3) Again, there are passages in Irenaeus, where the Greek is preserved, in which occur quotations from the N.T. containing readings which must be due, it would seem, to Syriac influence.

'A point of some interest,' writes Harvey in the Preface to his edition, p. v, 'will be found of frequent recurrence in the notes; which is, the repeated instances that Scriptural quotations afford, of having been made by one who was as familiar with some Syriac version of the New Testament, as with the Greek originals. Strange *variae lectiones* occur, which can only be explained by referring to the Syriac version.' It is but just to emphasise the fact that Harvey was, as I believe, completely in the right when he insisted on the Syriac element in the N.T. quotations in Irenaeus. The grateful acknowledgment of the importance of his edition in this respect must not of course be understood to imply assent to his detailed treatment of particular readings. Nor can I think that the presence of a Syriac element in his N.T. text proves that Irenaeus 'was as familiar with some Syriac version of the N.T. as with the Greek originals'. The supposition that he used a Syriacised Greek text harmonises with the conclusions as to Codex Bezae at which we have arrived, and with the fact that Tertullian also employed a Syriacised text.

Of these apparently Syriacised readings a single specimen must suffice. The passage in question is Lc. x. 21 f. ‖ Matt. xi. 25 f. It will be convenient to print side by side the quotation in Irenaeus (I. xiii. 2) and the true text.

Irenaeus.	The true text.
ἐξομολογήσομαί σοι, πάτερ,	ἐξομολογοῦμαί σοι, πάτερ,
κύριε τῶν οὐρανῶν καὶ τῆς γῆς,	κύριε τοῦ οὐρανοῦ καὶ τῆς γῆς,
ὅτι ἀπέκρυψας ἀπὸ σοφῶν καὶ συνετῶν,	ὅτι ἀπέκρ. (Matt. ἔκρυψας) ταῦτα ἀπὸ σ. καὶ συν.,
καὶ ἀπεκάλυψας αὐτὰ νηπίοις·	καὶ ἀπεκάλυψας αὐτὰ νηπίοις·
οὐά, ὁ πατήρ μου,	ναί, ὁ πατήρ,
ὅτι ἔμπροσθέν σου εὐδοκία μοι ἐγένετο.	ὅτι οὕτως εὐδ. ἐγένετο ἔμπρ. σου.
πάντα μοι παρεδόθη ὑπὸ τοῦ πατρός μου,	πάντα μοι παρεδόθη ὑπὸ τοῦ πατρός μου,

καὶ οὐδεὶς ἔγνω τὸν πατέρα εἰ μὴ ὁ   καὶ οὐδεὶς γινώσκει τίς ἐστιν ὁ υἱ. εἰ
υἱός,   μὴ ὁ πατήρ[1],
καὶ τὸν υἱὸν εἰ μὴ ὁ πατήρ,   καὶ τίς ἐστιν ὁ πατὴρ εἰ μὴ ὁ υἱός,
καὶ ᾧ ἂν ὁ υἱὸς ἀποκαλύψῃ[2].   καὶ ᾧ ἐὰν βοίληται ὁ υἱὸς ἀποκαλύψαι.

Looking at Irenaeus' text we must, I think, make our choice between two alternatives. *Either* he is quoting from memory—a satisfactory explanation unless it should appear that some other consistent account can be given of all, or most of, his variations from the true text, and unless his text appears in other independent authorities (see p. 112 n.): *or* he is adopting a text which has passed through the medium of a version. Let us compare then Irenaeus' text with the Old Syriac text (Curetonian) and that of other Syriac authorities.

(i) ἐξομολογοῦμαι = ܐܢܐ ܡܘܕܐ (thanking (am) I). So Curet., Syr. Vulg. of Matt. Lc. But this Syriac participle is timeless, and might be well represented by the future. (ii) τῶν οὐρανῶν. The Syriac ܫܡܝܐ is the equivalent of, and consequently might be rendered by, either the singular or the plural of the Greek word. (iii) οὐά. This interjection occurs once in the N.T. in Mc. xv. 29 οὐὰ ὁ καταλύων τὸν ναόν. The Syriac Vulgate represents it by ܐܘܢ. Now the Syriac equivalent for ναί in our present passage is ܐܝܢ. This word would very easily give place to ܐܘܢ and ܐܘ. The latter word is, in some Syriac texts, the equivalent of (1) οὐά Mc. xv. 29; (2) ὦ e.g. Matt. xv. 28; (3) εὖ Matt. xxv. 21, 23 (see

---

[1] Matt. καὶ οὐδεὶς ἐπιγινώσκει τὸν υἱὸν εἰ μὴ ὁ πατήρ, οὐδὲ τὸν πατέρα τις ἐπιγινώσκει εἰ μὴ ὁ υἱός.

[2] The Latin translation is this: 'Confiteor tibi Pater Domine terrae et caelorum, quoniam abscondisti ea a sapientibus et prudentibus, et reuelasti ea paruolis. Ita Pater meus, quoniam in conspectu tuo placitum factum est. Omnia mihi tradita sunt a Patre, et nemo cognouit Patrem nisi Filius, et Filium nisi Pater, et cuicunque Filius reuelauerit.' The Latin, it will be noticed, has nothing to correspond to the μοι after εὐδοκία in the Greek. This μοι would seem to be the result of some transcriptional accident. It is due, I believe, to the 'to me' in the next clause having slipped up a line. The distance between this 'to me' and the word 'good-pleasure' in the Syriac, though not in the Greek, favours this explanation. Thus the μοι is due to Syriac influence. It is the original Greek of Irenaeus, not the Latin translation (comp. 'confiteor', 'ita'), which here preserves a Syriacised text.

Payne Smith, *Thes. Syr.*). Thus in Syriac this interjection would be appropriate as expressing thankful joy, and could be transliterated by οὐά, as in Irenaeus. (iv) ὁ πατήρ μου. The Old Syriac and the Syriac Vulgate both in Matt. and Lc. read '*My*-Father'. The latter version in both Gospels has 'I thank thee *My*-Father'. (v) ἔγνω would be a natural independent translation of ܝܕܥ. (vi) In the two lines καὶ οὐδεὶς...ὁ πατήρ the form of the clauses in Matt. is followed, but the order of the clauses is reversed. This order however was apparently that in the Diatessaron. See Ephrem, *Diat.* (ed. Moesinger), p. 117 'Nemo nouit Patrem nisi Filius, et nemo nouit Filium nisi Pater.' (vii) In the last line ἀποκαλύψῃ takes the place of βούληται...ἀποκαλύψαι. This omission is easily explained when we turn to the Old Syriac of Lc. x. 22 (Matt. xi. 27):

ܠܗ   ܕܢܓܠܐ   ܒܪܐ   ܕܢܨܒܐ   ܘܠܡܢ
Him *or* to-him that-He-should-reveal the-Son there-should-wish and-to-whom

In this Syriac phrase there are two verbs, each in the future and each with a prefixed ܕ (with the first verb, the relative; with the second, 'that'). It would be very easy for the first of these futures i.e. ܕܢܨܒܐ (there-should-wish) to fall out[1].

Some other explanation might be suggested for one or another of these seven points. But the explanation which suits each and all simply and naturally is the supposition that Irenaeus is using a Syriacised text.

It seemed the better course to discuss in detail one case of the use in Irenaeus of a Syriacised text. To other

---

[1] Justin, *Dial. c.* 100, has καὶ οὐδεὶς γινώσκει τὸν πατέρα εἰ μὴ ὁ υἱός, οὐδὲ τὸν υἱὸν εἰ μὴ ὁ πατὴρ καὶ οἷς ἂν ὁ υἱὸς ἀποκαλύψῃ (ἀποκαλ. ὁ υἱός, *Apol.* i. 63). Comp. Tert., *Adv. Marc.*, iv. 25 'Nemo scit qui sit pater nisi filius, et qui sit filius nisi pater et cuicunque filius reuelauerit.' See Bishop Westcott, *Canon*, pp. 136 ff., 290. The subject of early evangelical quotations, especially those in Justin and in the Clementines, needs reinvestigation. If my conclusions are correct, Justin used a Syriacised text of the Gospels. But if so, how early must the date of the primitive Syriac Version be pushed back?

quotations from such a text, in places where the Greek of Irenaeus is preserved, it must suffice to give references. (i) 1 Tim. i. 4 is quoted in Iren. i. Praef. (Harvey, i. p. 1). Irenaeus' reading is due, I think, to assimilation to Tit. iii. 9; see the Syriac. (ii) In Iren. I. i. 5 (Harvey, i. p. 28) the phrase καὶ αὐτός ἐστι τὰ πάντα is quoted as St Paul's. A reference to Col. i. 17 (Syriac) shews how through omission of two words this reading would arise. In the quotation which follows in Irenaeus πάντα εἰς αὐτὸν καὶ ἐξ αὐτοῦ τὰ πάντα (Rom. xi. 36), τὰ πάντα is repeated as in the Syriac. (iii) Lc. xiv. 27, Mc. x. 21 are quoted in Iren. I. i. 6 (Harvey, i. p. 29). We have found passages then in Irenaeus, where the Greek is preserved, in which occur N.T. readings due to Syriac influence.

We return now to the quotations from the Acts in the Third Book of Irenaeus. The combined result of the three arguments just considered frees us, unless I am greatly mistaken, from the duty of suspending judgment. We may consider it established that the Syriacised text of the Acts (closely akin to, though not without some divergence from, the Bezan text), which we find in the Latin translation of Irenaeus, is a faithful representation, in all essential points, of the Greek text quoted by Irenaeus himself.

But to what date are we thus brought? 'The third book,' writes Bp. Lightfoot, *Essays on Supernatural Religion*, p. 260, 'was published during the episcopate of Eleutherus, who was Bishop of Rome from about A.D. 175 to A.D. 190; for he is mentioned in it as still living (iii. 3. 3). It must therefore have been written before A.D. 190.'

Our consideration then of the evidence furnished by Irenaeus brings us to the conclusion that the Syriac text of the Acts must be placed far enough back in the second century to allow of its having been used in the formation of a Greek, substantially the Bezan, text before the year A.D. 190.

(iii) One more witness I shall examine. From Gaul in

the West we turn to Antioch in the East. In Theophilus, *ad Autolycum*, ii. 34 there occurs the following passage: οἱ [προφῆται ἅγιοι] καὶ ἐδίδαξαν ἀπέχεσθαι ἀπὸ τῆς ἀθεμίτου εἰδωλολατρείας καὶ μοιχείας καὶ φόνου, πορνείας, κλοπῆς, φιλαργυρίας, ὅρκου ψεύδους, ὀργῆς καὶ πάσης ἀσελγείας καὶ ἀκαθαρσίας, καὶ πάντα ὅσα ἂν μὴ βούληται ἄνθρωπος ἑαυτῷ γίνεσθαι ἵνα μηδὲ ἄλλῳ ποιῇ.

Here we have that negative form of the golden rule which we found in the Bezan text of Acts xv. 20, 29. The matter will repay further examination.

In the Didaché (i. 2) the description of 'the Way of Life' opens thus: πρῶτον, ἀγαπήσεις τὸν θεὸν τὸν ποιήσαντά σε· δεύτερον, τὸν πλησίον σου ὡς σεαυτόν, πάντα δὲ ὅσα ἐὰν θελήσῃς μὴ γίνεσθαί σοι, καὶ σὺ ἄλλῳ μὴ ποιεῖ[1]. If this saying had a place in some early forms of 'the Two Ways', it would naturally become something of an apologetic common-place. Thus Aristides, who refers to 'the Way of Truth' (xvi), embodies this saying in his Apology c. xv. οὐ μοιχεύουσιν, οὐ πορνεύουσιν, οὐ ψευδομαρτυροῦσιν, οὐκ ἐπιθυμοῦσι τὰ ἀλλότρια, τιμῶσι πατέρα καὶ μητέρα, καὶ τοὺς πλησίον φιλοῦσι, δίκαια κρίνουσιν, ὅσα οὐ θέλουσιν αὐτοῖς γίνεσθαι ἑτέρῳ οὐ ποιοῦσι. From such an Apologetic passage the saying naturally passed into a similar context in Acts xv. Otto in his note on Theophilus *l. c.* rightly remarks that several passages of the N.T.—1 Pet. iv. 3, Matt. xv. 19 (φόνοι, μοιχεῖαι, πορνεῖαι), Gal. v. 19—are in the writer's mind at this point. But should not Acts xv. 29 (20) be added to the list of those passages whose language Theophilus here reflects? Three arguments appear to me to demand an affirmative answer to this question. They are these. (1) With ἀπέχεσθαι τῆς ἀθ. εἰδωλολατρείας compare Acts xv. 20, 28, ἀπέχεσθαι τῶν ἀλισγημάτων τῶν εἰδώλων.... ἀπέχεσθαι εἰδωλοθύτων. (2) If in Acts xv. 28 πνικτῶν be omitted, as in the text of Codex D, Tertullian, and Irenaeus, we have the words εἰδωλοθύτων καὶ αἵματος καὶ πορνείας. The word πνικτῶν having gone, it would be most natural to take the term αἷμα to mean *murder*. The three vices *idolatry, murder, fornication* are thus mentioned in the same order in Acts and Theophilus, the latter adding *adultery* after *idolatry*. (3) Theophilus ends his list of moral requirements with the same ancient saying with which the moral requirements of the decree close, as read in the text which Irenaeus quotes a very few years after Theophilus wrote. These three considerations taken together fall but a little short of proof that Theo-

---

[1] Dr Taylor, *The Teaching of the Twelve Apostles*, p. 8 ff., gives illustrations from Jewish sources.

philus of Antioch about the year 180 A.D. knew and referred to a reading of a passage in the Acts which we find in the Bezan text.

We have now brought to an end our investigation as to the date of the Bezan text of the Acts and of the Syriac text which lies behind it. This Syriac text must have been in existence so far back in the second century that it could generate (*a*), apparently through the medium of a Greek text, a Latin text in use at Carthage in the opening years of the third century; (*b*) a Greek text quoted by Irenaeus in South Gaul in a treatise which cannot be later than 190 A.D.; (*c*) *apparently*, for the evidence is perhaps insufficient to warrant a positive statement, a Greek text known to Theophilus of Antioch about the year 180 A.D. It is not therefore unreasonable to conclude (1) that the Bezan text of the Acts existed at least as early as 180 A.D.; (2) that the implied Syriac text existed shortly after, perhaps even some time before, the middle of the second century. The verdict therefore based on *external* evidence coincides with that based on *internal* evidence. We are right in speaking of the Syriac text of the Acts which lies behind the Bezan text as an *Old* Syriac text.

(2) From the question of time it is a natural transition to the question of place.

I have shewn, unless I am wholly mistaken, that Codex Bezae of the Acts contains a text which is the result of an assimilation of a Greek text to a Syriac text, and that this Greek text came into existence not later than 180 A.D., probably some years earlier. Can we point to any Church where such a text as this would be likely to arise?

The Church of Antioch at once rises to the mind. It was, from the earliest days of the Gospel, a great centre of Christian life. Its martyr Bishop is the most striking personality which the history of the second century brings before us. Ignatius, with his vigour and his practical enthusiasm, reflected, we can hardly doubt, the character of the Church over which he presided, and the character of the Church was as certainly confirmed by the life and work of its great Bishop. Moreover the Church of Antioch, if it was a predominantly Greek Church, must have had within it a considerable Syrian element. Here, if anywhere, two streams, a Syriac-speaking and a Greek-speaking population, would meet and coalesce. It must suffice to quote a passage from Rénan's description of the great Syrian capital. 'Antioch', he says, 'from its foundation, had been altogether a Grecian city.... Beside the Greek population, indeed, which in no part of the East (with the exception of Alexandria) was as numerous as here, Antioch included in its population a considerable number of native Syrians, speaking Syriac. These natives composed a low class, inhabiting the suburbs (*les faubourgs*) of the great city, and the populous villages which formed vast outskirts (*une vaste banlieu*) all around it, Charandama, Ghisira, Gandigura, and Apate, names chiefly Syriac. Marriages between the Syrians and the Greeks were common, Seleucus having formerly made naturalization a legal obligation binding on every stranger establishing himself in the city, so that Antioch, at the end of three centuries and a half of its existence, became one of the places in the world where race was most intermingled with race' (*Les Apôtres*, p. 217 f.; English trans. p. 181 f.).

The probability then is strong that Antioch was the birth-place of the Bezan text of the Acts[1]. This probability will be greatly increased, it will indeed fall little short of certainty, if we can point to any other Syriacised Greek text which we can with certainty connect with Antioch. Such a text I believe that we have in the newly discovered fragment of 'the Gospel according to Peter'.

I am not aware that any doubt has been expressed in regard to the belief that our fragment is part of 'the Gospel according to Peter' which Serapion, Bishop of Antioch 190—203 A.D., found in circulation at Rhossus, a town a few

---

[1] I have already pointed out that probably the earliest reference to this text is found in the work of Theophilus, Bishop of Antioch in the last quarter of the second century.

miles north of Antioch. The Gospel was found then not far from Antioch, the greatest centre in the East of Christian activity and thought. It seems impossible to doubt that its birthplace was Antioch, or some place in its immediate vicinity. The date of this Gospel does not immediately concern us. It cannot however be separated by many years from the date which we have assigned to the Bezan text of the Acts. I hope to be able to shew that the Petrine fragment has important points of similarity to the Bezan text which we have examined.

The interest and importance of the fragment are so great that I make no apology for treating the question of the genesis of its text with some fulness.

The investigation falls under two heads. I shall endeavour to shew (i) that the influence of assimilation has been active here, as in the Bezan text: (ii) that behind considerable portions of our Greek fragment there lies a Syriac text.

I quote from what I believe is the *Editio Princeps* of the Fragment, viz. Dr Swete's edition of the text, which he has re-issued, incorporating some corrections which Professor Bensly supplied after inspecting the MS. itself[1].

(i) Passages from other parts of Scripture are woven into the fabric of this Petrine history of the Passion and the Resurrection.

P. 3, l. 13 f. γέγραπται γὰρ ἐν τῷ νόμῳ ἥλιον μὴ δῦναι ἐπὶ πεφονευμένῳ. Comp. p. 4, l. 18 f.

The thought is doubtless that of Deut. xxi. 22 f. But the language seems to be derived from two other passages in Deut., viz. (i) xxiv. 15 'Thou shalt give him his hire, *neither shall the sun go down upon it.*'

---

[1] In treating of the Petrine fragment I have had before me (1) Professor Robinson's Greek text and his lecture delivered 'three days after the text was first seen in Cambridge'; (2) Mr Rendel Harris' *Popular account of the Newly-recovered Gospel of St Peter;* (3) Prof. Harnack's text and notes (Texte und Untersuchungen ix. 2); (4) Lod's text and notes (Paris, 1892); (5) Dr Swete's text mentioned above, and my notes of two lectures which Dr Swete delivered on the Fragment in the February of this year—lectures which will, I trust, be soon given to the world in the form of an edition of the Fragment.

The LXX. has οὐκ ἐπιδύσεται ὁ ἥλιος ἐπ' αὐτῷ. The Syriac has of course a simple verb (ܣܝܪ ܕܝ ܪ̈ܠܐ), and Peter has an uncompounded verb μὴ δῦναι: (ii) xxi. 1 'If any one be found *slain* in the land.' The LXX. renders הָלָל by τραυματίας, the Syriac by ܪ̈ܠܝܠܐ (= πεφονευμένος, comp. e.g. Matt. v. 21, Jas. v. 6).

P. 3, l. 17 ff. καὶ ἔλεγον Σύρωμεν τὸν υἱὸν τοῦ θεοῦ...καὶ ἐκάθισαν αὐτὸν ἐπὶ καθέδραν κρίσεως, λέγοντες Δικαίως κρῖνε, βασιλεῦ τοῦ Ἰσραήλ.

Professor Robinson (p. 18) gives the obvious reference to Justin, *Apol.* i. 35 καὶ γάρ, ὡς εἶπεν ὁ προφήτης, διασύροντες αὐτὸν ἐκάθισαν ἐπὶ βήματος καὶ εἶπον Κρῖνον ἡμῖν. As to this passage I remark (1) that Justin seems to have in his mind some passage of the Prophets which has not yet been identified; (2) that Justin, like Peter, has the plural (ἐκάθισαν). It seems probable that in some harmonised account of the Passion the supposed action of Pilate (John xix. 15) was transferred to some part of the history where the people are the actors. But I think there is a further reference to Prov. xx. 8 'A *king* that *sitteth* on the *throne of judgment*'. The LXX. has simply ἐπὶ θρόνου. The Syriac however has ܪ̈ܠܝܢ ܟܘܪܣܝܐ ܕ (comp. Ps. cxxi. 5 'thrones for-judgment'). The Syriac ܟܘܪܣܝܐ literally translates the Hebrew כסא, but it also represents καθέδρα in the three places where the latter occurs in the N.T. (Matt. xxi. 12, xxiii. 2, Mark xi. 15). For the phrase 'to-cause-to-sit on the-throne of' comp. 2 Chron. xxiii. 20. It may be added that the Syriac versions transliterate βῆμα (ܒܝܡ) in the Gospels[1].

P. 4, l. 16 ἦν δὲ μεσημβρία καὶ σκότος κατέσχε πᾶσαν τὴν Ἰουδαίαν.

Dr Swete compares Amos viii. 9 'And it shall come to pass in that day, saith the Lord God, that I will cause the sun to go down at noon, and I will darken the earth in the clear day.' The Syriac follows the Hebrew closely; the LXX. diverges in the latter clause. Dr Swete also compares the Diatessaron (Ciasca, p. 92) 'Tenebrae *occupauerunt uniuersam* terram'. Should we not also compare Is. lx. 2 'darkness shall cover the earth (land)'? Comp. Is. ix. 19, Ezek. xxxii. 8.

[1] It should be noted that 'the-seat of-judgment' would be a very natural Syriac equivalent of βῆμα, for, besides the compound phrase ܒܥܠ ܕܝܢܐ (= his adversary, Acts xxv. 16, Matt. v. 25, Lc. xviii. 3), we have ܪ̈ܠܝܢ ܕܝܢܐ (= judgment-hall, Acts xxv. 23, Jas. ii. 6, 1 Tim. v. 24).

DATE. BIRTHPLACE. AFFINITIES. 119

P. 4, l. 21 f. *καὶ ἐπλήρωσαν πάντα, καὶ ἐτελείωσαν κατὰ τῆς κεφαλῆς αὐτῶν τὰ ἁμαρτήματα.*

We have here, I believe, two Pauline phrases: (i) Acts xiii. 29 *ὡς δὲ ἐτέλεσαν πάντα.* Syriac ܟܕ ܓܡܪܘ ܟܠܗܝܢ. The verb ܓܡܪ represents *πληροῦν*, e.g. Acts xiii. 27, xiv. 26; comp. Jn. xviii. 32, xix. 24. Note also the Greek and Syriac of Jn. xix. 28, 30. The Syriac brings all these passages into line. Dr Swete compares the words of our Lord on the cross in the Diatessaron—'consummata sunt omnia' (Ciasca, p. 92). (ii) 1 Thess. ii. 16 *εἰς τὸ ἀναπληρῶσαι αὐτῶν τὰς ἁμαρτίας* (Syriac, ܠܡܫܡܠܝܘ ܚܛܗܝܗܘܢ). The phrase *κατὰ τῆς κεφ. αὐτῶν* is an O.T. phrase; compare Ezek. ix. 10, xi. 21, xxii. 31, Joel iii. 4, 7.

P. 4, l. 29 *καὶ ἡ γῆ πᾶσα ἐσείσθη.*

Dr Swete compares Jer. viii. 16, where the LXX. has these words, though in a different order.

P. 6, l. 2 *ἐπέχρισαν ἑπτὰ σφραγῖδας.*

Compare Apoc. v. 1, 5.

P. 6, l. 4 f. *ἦλθεν ὄχλος ἀπὸ Ἱερουσαλὴμ καὶ τῆς περιχώρου ἵνα ἴδωσι κ.τ.λ.*

Compare John xii. 9 f., Acts v. 16.

P. 6, l. 8 ff. *μεγάλη φωνὴ ἐγένετο ἐν τῷ οὐρανῷ καὶ εἶδον ἀνοιχθέντας τοὺς οὐρανοὺς καὶ δύο ἄνδρας κατελθόντας ἐκεῖθεν, πολὺ φέγγος ἔχοντας.*

Compare (1) Apoc. xi. 12, 15 *καὶ ἐγένοντο φωναὶ μεγάλαι ἐν τῷ οὐρανῷ*: (2) Apoc. xxi. 10 f., *τὴν πόλιν...καταβαίνουσαν ἐκ τοῦ οὐρανοῦ ἀπὸ τοῦ θεοῦ, ἔχουσαν τὴν δόξαν τοῦ θεοῦ· ὁ φωστὴρ αὐτῆς κ.τ.λ.* It may be added that the Syriac translates the last words thus: 'while there-was to-her (*i.e.* having) the-glory of-God *like a-bright light*'.

P. 6, l. 22 ff. *καὶ φωνῆς ἤκουον ἐκ τῶν οὐρανῶν λεγούσης Ἐκήρυξας τοῖς κοιμωμένοις· καὶ ὑπακοὴ ἠκούετο ἀπὸ τοῦ σταυροῦ τὸ Ναί.*

Compare Apoc. xiv. 13 *καὶ ἤκουσα φωνῆς ἐκ τοῦ οὐρανοῦ λεγούσης Γράψον Μακάριοι οἱ νεκροί...ναί, λέγει τὸ πνεῦμα.* Comp. xi. 12.

P. 7, l. 8 ff. *συμφέρει γάρ, φασίν, ἡμῖν ὀφλῆσαι μεγίστην*

120   THE BEZAN TEXT OF THE ACTS.

ἁμαρτίαν ἔμπροσθεν τοῦ θεοῦ, καὶ μὴ ἐμπεσεῖν εἰς χεῖρας τοῦ λαοῦ τῶν Ἰουδαίων καὶ λιθασθῆναι.

Peter puts into the mouth of the Jews a blasphemous parody of David's words. Compare 2 Sam. xii. 13 ἡμάρτηκα τῷ κυρίῳ (the Syriac has 'before the-Lord'); 1 Chron. xxi. 8, 13 ἡμάρτηκα σφόδρα...ἐμπεσοῦμαι δὴ εἰς χεῖρας κυρίου...καὶ εἰς χεῖρας ἀνθρώπων οὐ μὴ ἐμπέσω. With λιθασθῆναι compare Lc. xx. 6, Acts v. 26.

P. 8, l. 12 f. καὶ ἕκαστος...ἀπηλλάγη εἰς τὸν οἶκον αὐτοῦ.

Compare [John] vii. 53. Note the singular, and compare the note on Acts v. 18.

Thus in this short fragment of the Petrine Gospel we have, it would appear, instances of assimilation to passages in Deuteronomy, the historical Books of the O.T., the Prophets, the Acts, a Pauline epistle, the Apocalypse, a non-canonical fragment. We see the same tendency at work which we have so often noticed in Codex Bezae, the tendency to incorporate in a Scriptural narrative phrases and ideas derived from other parts of Scripture. Such a tendency would be the outcome of a peculiar habit of teaching and thought prevailing in a particular church at a particular time[1]. If that church were a bilingual church, such a tendency would be active among both classes of its members. And in a work like the Petrine Gospel, which probably, through the influence of oral teaching, grew up gradually in the church, these accretions from external sources would be added at different stages of its growth, and would therefore bear the stamp now of this class, now of that class, in the Christian community. The facts seem to be in harmony with this view as to the probabilities of the case. These embedded passages from parts of Scripture other than the Gospels appear sometimes to supply evidence of the use of a Syriac authority, some-

[1] In this connexion a special interest attaches to Ignatius' language in regard to the old Prophets: see Magn. IX., Philad. v. (τοὺς προφήτας δὲ ἀγαπῶμεν, διὰ τὸ καὶ αὐτοὺς εἰς τὸ εὐαγγέλιον κατηγγελκέναι...ὄντες ἀξιαγάπητοι καὶ ἀξιοθαύμαστοι ἅγιοι), viii., IX. (οἱ γὰρ ἀγαπητοὶ προφῆται κατήγγειλαν εἰς αὐτόν), Smyrn. v. These expressions of affection towards the Prophets are very remarkable.

DATE. BIRTHPLACE. AFFINITIES. 121

times to point to the Greek, whether of the LXX. or of the New Testament, as their source. The point however which I am anxious to emphasise is this. The presence of this characteristic, i.e. assimilation to other parts of Scripture, in a marked degree both in Codex Bezae and in the Petrine Gospel, and the fact that the latter certainly arose at Antioch or in its immediate neighbourhood about the time when the Bezan text was formed, confirm the *prima facie* probability that Antioch was the birthplace of the Bezan text.

(ii) In the second place I shall collect and discuss the indications, which the text of the Petrine fragment affords, that behind parts of it there lie portions of an Old Syriac text of the Gospels.

Previous workers in the field have noted points of affinity between our fragment and Syriac authorities, especially the Diatessaron. They have, as I understand, argued from this evidence that the fragment depends on some kind of Gospel-harmony, and that between the Syriac authorities and our fragment there exists some textual kinship. I hope to be able to add to the number of these coincidences, and to make it probable that, at least as far as the Scriptural phrases are concerned, through the Greek soil which our fragment presents to our view there protrudes in many places a Syriac stratum.

P. 3, l. 11 f. εἰ καὶ μή τις αὐτὸν ᾐτήκει, ἡμεῖς αὐτὸν ἐθάπτομεν, ἐπεὶ καὶ σάββατον ἐπιφώσκει.

Dr Swete points out that a reference at this point of the history to the approaching Sabbath is found in the Diatessaron (Ciasca, p. 93) : 'Iudaei autem, quia Parasceue erat, dixerunt : Non remaneant corpora haec super lignum, *quia aurora sabbati est.*' This reference to the Sabbath, which survives in the Syriac Vulgate of Jn. xix. 31, is doubtless due to assimilation to Lc. xxiii. 54.

P. 3, l. 16 οἱ δὲ λαβόντες τὸν κύριον.

On λαβόντες see the note on Acts ii. 23.

122   THE BEZAN TEXT OF THE ACTS.

P. 3, l. 20 ff. καί τις αὐτῶν ἐνεγκὼν στέφανον ἀκάνθινον ἔθηκεν...καὶ ἕτεροι ἑστῶτες ἐνέπτυον αὐτοῦ ταῖς ὄψεσι, καὶ ἄλλοι τὰς σιαγόνας αὐτοῦ ἐράπισαν· ἕτεροι καλάμῳ ἔνυσσον αὐτόν.

I will take the several points in order. (1) The contrast between the action of 'one of them' and that of 'the others' takes us back to Matt. xxvii. 48 καὶ εὐθέως δραμὼν εἷς ἐξ αὐτῶν καὶ λαβὼν...καὶ περιθεὶς καλάμῳ...οἱ δὲ λοιποὶ εἶπαν. But I believe that the difference in phraseology points to the supposition that the passage has passed through the medium of a Syriac version. The Syriac Vulgate has : 'There-ran one from-them and-took (ܢܣܒ)...and-put-it (ܣܡܘ)....... The-rest (ܪܫܐ) saying were...'. (2) ταῖς ὄψεσιν. I believe that this reading is due to assimilation to Mc. viii. 23 καὶ πτύσας εἰς τὰ ὄμματα αὐτοῦ (ܘܪܩ ܒܥܝܢܘܗܝ, and-He-spat in-his-eyes); comp. Jn. ix. 6. The Lord's work of mercy is parodied and paid back to Him in the mockery of the Jews. The variation of the word (ταῖς ὄψεσιν, εἰς τὰ ὄμματα) points again to a Syriac medium. (3) τὰς σιαγόνας. This detail (probably due to O.T. associations—Micah v. 1: 'They shall smite the judge of Israel with a rod upon the cheek,' Lam. iii. 30, Job xvi. 10, 1 Kings xxii. 24, Isa. l. 6) has a place in the Diatessaron (Ciasca, p. 88) 'Conspuerunt in faciem eius, et percusserunt illum, et illudebant ei. Milites autem, *percutientes genas eius*, dicebant'. It survives in the Syriac Vulgate of Jn. xix. 3 'And-saying were-they, Peace to-thee, King of-the-Jews, and-smiting were-they Him *on His-cheeks*'. (4) καλάμῳ ἔνυσσον αὐτόν. The word used in this connexion in Matt. xxvii. 30, Mc. xv. 19 is ἔτυπτον, which the Syriac Vulgate renders by ܡܚܐ ܗܘܐ. But this Syriac expression would be very naturally rendered by ἔνυσσον αὐτόν, for in Jn. xix. 34 the same Syriac verb with the suffix added (ܡܚܝܗܝ, 'he-struck-Him') is used to render ἔνυξεν. Compare the note on Acts xii. 10 (p. 88).

P. 4, l. 5 καὶ ἤνεγκον δύο κακούργους.

Compare the word used by St Mark (xv. 22) of the *leading* to the Cross—καὶ φέρουσιν αὐτόν. The Syriac Vulgate has the perfect— ܘܐܝܬܝܘܗܝ.

P. 4, l. 6 f. αὐτὸς δὲ ἐσιώπα, ὡς μηδὲν πόνον ἔχων.

There is a remarkable parallel to this gloss in a gloss inserted in the Old Syriac (Curetonian) Version of Lc. xxiii. 9 'And he [Herod] was

DATE. BIRTHPLACE. AFFINITIES. 123

asking Him with cunning words; but Jesus returned him not any answer, *as though He had not been there*'. The strangeness of the phrase μηδὲν πόνον ἔχων has caused difficulty. Prof. Robinson prints μηδένα, Lods μηδέν[α]; Harnack in his critical notes gives Hartel's conjectures 'μηδένα? μηδέ?'. Dr Swete suggests μηδ᾽ ἔυπονον. But may we not follow out the hint given by the fact that we have a parallel in an Old Syriac gloss? May not the phrase under consideration be a somewhat literal translation of the following Syriac words[1]?

ܠܗ ܗܘܐ ܠܝܬ ܕܟܐܒ ܡܕܡ ܐܝܟ
to-him was-not of-pain any-thing as if

A further point of great interest may be noticed in connexion with these words. Prof. Robinson (p. 19) writes: 'Observe that, to make room for this [sentence], the words "Father, forgive them: for they know not what they do" must be omitted.' If however Peter is following, as I believe, the Diatessaron, there is no question about his *omitting* at this point the Lord's prayer for His enemies; for in the Diatessaron it is placed at the very close of the history of the Passion, just before the Lord's final prayer of commendation. I am not aware that attention has been called to this misplacement of the prayer 'Father, forgive them: for they know not what they do' in the Diatessaron. The matter requires full and anxious investigation. But this I may be allowed to say. In proportion as my theory as to the Syriac element in Codex D finds favour—Codex D is one of the authorities which omits the prayer in Lc. xxiii. 34—and in proportion as further examination shews that the influence of the Syriacised text spread widely, so far it will be admitted that a *prima facie* case is made out for the suggestion that the omission of the prayer in Lc. xxiii. 34 by some authorities is to be traced to its displacement in the Diatessaron. Compare Eus. *H. E.* ii. 23. 16.

P. 4, l. 7 f. καὶ ὅτε ἐώρθωσαν τὸν σταυρόν, ἐπέγραψαν ὅτι Οὗτός ἐστιν ὁ βασιλεὺς τοῦ Ἰσραήλ.

Two points require notice. (1) The phrase ὁ βασιλεὺς τοῦ Ἰσραήλ is due to assimilation to Matt. xxvii. 42, Mc. xv. 32 (comp. Jn. xii. 13). Note too the earlier taunt in Peter (p. 3, l. 19 f.) δικαίως κρῖνε, βασιλεῦ τοῦ Ἰσραήλ, with which the phrase quoted above from Mic. v. 1 should be specially compared. (2) The writing of the title, with its mocking assertion of the Lord's royalty, is assigned here to the soldiers. With this compare the remarkable gloss in the Old Syriac (Curetonian) Version of Lc. xxiii. 36 ff. 'And also the soldiers were coming near to Him, and

[1] The original phrase, it thus appears, was free from Docetism. The Greek rendering however suggests, though it does not require, a Docetic interpretation.

saying, Peace to Thee : if Thou be the king of the Jews, save Thyself. *And they had set on His head a crown of thorns*, and also was written a title and placed over Him, This is the King of the Jews.' This gloss appears also in Codex Bezae, and in (the Old Latin) Codex Colbertinus (see Bp. J. Wordsworth's note *in loco*); compare *Gesta Pilati* x. (Rendel Harris, *Codex Bezae*, p. 271 f.).

P. 4, l. 10 ff. εἷς δέ τις τῶν κακούργων ἐκείνων ὠνείδισεν αὐτοὺς λέγων Ἡμεῖς διὰ τὰ κακὰ ἃ ἐποιήσαμεν οὕτω πεπόνθαμεν· οὗτος δὲ σωτὴρ γενόμενος τῶν ἀνθρώπων τί ἠδίκησεν ὑμᾶς;

Again there are several points to be noticed. (1) The phrase τῶν κακ. ἐκείνων is simply a literal translation of the idiomatic Syriac phrase. In Lc. xxiii. 33, 39 the Old (Curetonian) and the Vulgate Syriac Versions have '*those* (ܗܢܘܢ) doers-of evil-things'. The word *those* expresses the definite article (see note on Acts vi. 5). Compare the Old Syriac of Lc. xxiii. 40 'his companion *that* other', xxiv. 9 'and told those words to the eleven, and to the rest of *those* disciples'. Compare below (p. 6, l. 15) οἱ στρατιῶται ἐκεῖνοι, with which compare the Syriac Vulgate of Matt. xxviii. 11 'There came some of *those* (ܗܢܘܢ) guards into the city' (=τινες τῆς κουστωδίας); and perhaps p. 8, l. 4 τὸν σταυρωθέντα ἐκεῖνον (cf. Matt. xxviii. 5). (2) The paraphrase 'because of the evil things which we did' would be a very natural one in Syriac, for the equivalent of κακοῦργοι is ܥܒܕܝ ܒܝܫܬܐ (doers-of evil-things)[1]. On the frequent juxtaposition of these two words in Syriac compare the note on Acts iii. 17, and note the phrases below (p. 5, l. 8, l. 25) γνόντες οἷον κακὸν ἑαυτοῖς ἐποίησαν...ποιήσωσιν ἡμῖν κακά. (3) σωτὴρ γεν. τῶν ἀνθρ. Compare the form of the Scribes' taunt in the Diatessaron (Ciasca, p. 92): '*Aliorum saluator* non potest seipsum saluom facere'. Compare too *the Doctrine of Addai*, p. 18 'He gave Himself and was crucified for all men', p. 20 'God was crucified for all men'.

P. 4, l. 24 ff. καὶ ὁ κύριος ἀνεβόησε λέγων Ἡ δύναμίς μου, ἡ δύναμις κατέλειψάς με· καὶ εἰπὼν ἀνελήφθη.

Two points claim attention. (1) Two arguments lead us, I believe, to conclude that this version of our Lord's cry on the Cross comes immediately from a Syriac version of it. (*a*) The supposition that it is a direct representation in Greek of the current Syriac version of the words is to my mind far easier than the alternative hypothesis that it is

---

[1] With the phrase οὕτω πεπόνθαμεν compare the reading of (the Old Latin) Codex Veronensis 'et nos quidem iuste haec patimur'.

DATE. BIRTHPLACE. AFFINITIES.

the translation of 'Ηλί 'Ηλί, a translation due solely to the influence of the learned (comp. Justin Martyr, *Tryph.*, 125). It will be remembered that in the Syriac versions no interpretation of the Aramaic words was needful, such as was unavoidable in the Greek Gospels (see the Syriac Vulgate of Matt. xxvii. 46, Mc. xv. 34)[1]. (*b*) Mr Rendel Harris (p. 82) notices that 'the second possessive pronoun is wanting,' and 'that Tatian's text had a similar peculiarity, for Ephrem gives it as "God, my God", and the Arabic Harmony has *Yaiil, Yaiili*, where the added suffix belongs to the possessive pronoun'. It should be added that the Syriac Vulgate both in Matt. *l. c.* and Mc. *l. c.* has ܐܠܗܝ ܐܠܗܝ (God, God)[2]. (2) καὶ εἰπὼν ἀνελήφθη. Compare Lc. xxiii. 46 τοῦτο δὲ εἰπὼν ἐξέπνευσε. The words had no place, it would appear, in the Diatessaron. If Peter omits 'this', the Old Syriac (Curetonian) has nothing to answer to τοῦτο δὲ εἰπών. But what of the strange reading ἀνελήφθη? The Syriac equivalent of this word is ܐܣܬܠܩ (Mc. xvi. 19) or ܐܬܬܣܩ (Acts i. 2, 1 Tim. iii. 16). The Syriac equivalent of ἐξέπνευσε is ܫܠܡ (Vulg.), or ܫܠܡܐ (Curetonian). The ease with which ܐܣܬܠܩ (=ἀνελήφθη) might be substituted for ܫܠܡ (=ἐξέπνευσε), would at least facilitate, though we may hesitate to say that it would originate, a change which in the light of Lc. ix. 51 (comp. Jn. iii. 14, viii. 28, xii. 32 f.) may have seemed an innocent and even a devout emendation[3].

P. 4, l. 26 f. καὶ αὐτῆς τῆς ὥρας διεράγη τὸ καταπέτασμα.

Here note two points. (1) The Diatessaron (Ciasca, p. 92) has a note of time at this point: 'Et *statim* facies ianuae templi scissa est in duas partes'. This *immediately* survives in the Syriac Vulgate of Matt. xxvii. 51. But it should be noted that the same note of time which the Petrine Gospel inserts here is elsewhere inserted in the Diatessaron (Ciasca, p. 87): 'Et continuo adhuc illo loquente, bis cantauit gallus. Et *illa hora* conuersus est Iesus, qui foris erat'. In Lc. xxii. 60 παραχρῆμα

---

[1] In Mark indeed an interpretation is added, introduced by the word 'which-is'. But this interpretation differs from the clause interpreted only in its use of ܐܠܗܝ (my-God) and not ܐܠܗܐ.

[2] It is possible that there may be some connection between this interpretation of our Lord's words and the tenets of the book bearing the name Elchasai (חֵיל כְּסַי, hidden power).

[3] Compare *Doctrine of Addai*, p. 7 (Syriac, p. ܐ) 'And when He had completed the will of Him that begat Him, He was taken up (ܐܬܬܪܝܡ) to His Father and sat with Him in glory'.

becomes in the Old Syriac 'at the same hour (ܒܗ̇ ܫܥܬܐ)'. (2) ἐσχίσθη (Matt. xxvii. 51 || Mc., Lc.)= ܐܨܛܪܝ (Old (Lc.) and Vulg. Syr.) =διεράγη (Peter). This Syriac verb is the equivalent of διαρήσσειν in Matt. xxvi. 65, Mc. xiv. 63, Lc. v. 6 ; of ῥήσσειν in Matt. ix. 17, Mc. ii. 22.

P. 5, l. 1 f. τότε ἥλιος ἔλαμψε καὶ εὑρέθη ὥρα ἐνάτη. Mr Rendel Harris (p. 81) compares the words of Ephrem's commentary (ed. Moesinger, p. 257): 'Tres horas sol obtenebratus est, et pǫstea denuo luxit'.

P. 5, l. 4 f. λαβὼν δὲ τὸν κύριον ἔλουσε καὶ εἴλησε σινδόνι καὶ εἰσήγαγεν εἰς ἴδιον τάφον καλούμενον Κῆπον Ἰωσήφ.

Three points here are worthy of notice. (1) Peter has the simple verb εἴλησε. Matt. xxvii. 59, Lc. xxiii. 53 have ἐνετύλιξεν, Mc. xv. 46 ἐνείλησεν. I have collected in the note below[1] a series of passages where Peter has an uncompounded, one or more of our Gospels a compound, verb. This is quite natural if Peter is giving a retranslation from the Syriac, where compound verbs are unknown. Such a phenomenon we have several times noticed in the Bezan text. (2) With εἰσήγαγεν compare the Diatessaron (Ciasca, p. 93): 'Sederunt contra monumentum, uidentes quomodo *introduxerint* et posuerint ibi corpus'. (3) For ἐν τῷ καινῷ αὐτοῦ μνημείῳ (Matt. xxvii. 60) the Syriac Vulgate has : 'in-the-house-of a-new sepulchre which-was-his (ܕܝܠܗ)'. Now this last word of the Syriac is frequently used as the nearest representation in Syriac of ἴδιος (see e.g. Jn. i. 11). Here it seems that Peter uses ἴδιος as its equivalent.

P. 5, l. 8 ff. ἤρξαντο κόπτεσθαι καὶ λέγειν Οὐαὶ ταῖς ἁμαρτίαις ἡμῶν· ἤγγισεν ἡ κρίσις καὶ τὸ τέλος Ἱερουσαλήμ.

(1) Prof. Robinson (p. 23) compares (a) Ephrem (ed. Moesinger, p. 245 f.) Vae fuit, uae fuit nobis, Filius Dei erat hic...Venerunt, ait, iudicia dirutionis Ierosolymorum. (b) The Old Syriac (Curetonian) Version of Lc. xxiii. 48 'Saying, Woe to us, What is this ? Woe to us from our sins'. (c) The Latin Codex S. Germanensis (g₁) Vae nobis,

---

[1] Peter, p. 3, l. 1 ἐνίψατο | Matt. ἀπενίψατο.   p. 3, l. 8, 10 ᾔτησεν | Matt. Mc. Lc. ᾐτήσατο.   p. 3, l. 16 λαβόντες | Jn. παρέλαβον.   p. 3, l. 21 ἔθηκεν | Matt. Jn. ἐπέθηκαν, Mc. περιτιθέασιν.   p. 5, l. 2 δεδώκασι | Matt. ἀποδοθῆναι, Mc. ἐδωρήσατο.   p. 5, l. 5 εἴλησε | Matt. Lc. ἐνετύλιξεν, Mc. ἐνείλησεν. p. 5, l. 29 κυλίσαντες | Matt. προσκυλίσας, Mc. προσεκύλισεν.   p. 6, l. 13 κυλισθείς | Matt. ἀπεκύλισε, Mc. ἀνακεκύλισται.

DATE. BIRTHPLACE. AFFINITIES. 127

quae facta sunt hodie propter peccata nostra : appropinquauit enim desolatio Hierusalem. Mr Rendel Harris (p. 77 f.) also compares the *Doctrine of Addai* (ed. Phillips, p. 27) 'For, behold, except they who crucified Him knew that He was the Son of God, they would not have proclaimed *the desolation* of their city, also they would not have brought down *woes* upon themselves'. (2) When we examine the words of Ephrem as given in Moesinger's translation of the Armenian—iudicia dirutionis— we see that this reading must have arisen (i) from the vocalization of ܪܠܢ as plural (see e.g. Mc. xiii. 9); (ii) from the confusion of ܘ (and) and ܕ (of); compare note on Acts xix. 29. By this double confusion 'the judgment *and* the desolation' has become transformed into 'the judgment*s of* the desolation'. (3) As Ephrem, Addai, and Cod. g_1 all attest the reading 'the *desolation* of Jerusalem', it must be regarded as the original reading. How then can we account for the Petrine phrase τὸ τέλος Ἱερουσ.? A reference to the Syriac suggests the answer to this question. The Syriac word meaning *desolation* is ܚܘܪܒܐ (Lc. xxi. 20); that meaning *end* is ܫܘܠܡܐ (Lc. xxi. 9). In the Syriac original which lies behind the quasi-Scriptural phrase of Peter, the latter word has been substituted for the former. (4) The cry of the Jews in the Diatessaron is in part founded on our Lord's words recorded in Lc. xxi. 20.

P. 5, l. 10 ἐγὼ δὲ μετὰ τῶν ἑταίρων μου ἐλυπούμην, καὶ τετρωμένοι κατὰ διάνοιαν ἐκρυβόμεθα· ἐζητούμεθα γὰρ ὑπ' αὐτῶν ὡς κακοῦργοι.

Here two points call for remark. (1) With μετὰ τῶν ἑταίρων compare 'The Apostles my companions', 'His disciples, my companions....I was chosen, with my companions' (*Doctrine of Addai*, pp. 27, 39, 21). (2) I venture to suggest that this description of the Apostles hiding themselves has been evolved from a phrase of a passage in the Diatessaron (Ciasca, p. 93):—'Venit uir nomine Ioseph, diues et decurio, ab Arimathaea ciuitate Iudaeae, qui erat uir bonus et rectus, ac discipulus Iesu ; *qui occultabat se, timens a Iudaeis*' (Jn. xix. 38)[1]. This reference to 'the fear of the Jews' would connect the phrase with Jn. xx. 19, and would suggest that Joseph hid himself *after the Passion*. The mention of Joseph's *bold* entrance into Pilate's presence, it may be added, has no place in the Diatessaron—'Accedens ergo iste introiuit ad Pilatum'. That this interpretation of the phrase in the Diatessaron was the current

---

[1] The Syriac Vulgate has: 'Because a-disciple was-he of-Jesus *and-hiding was-he* (ܗܘܐ ܘܡܛܫܐ) *from fear of-the Jews*'.

one seems clear from a later passage in the fragment where Mary Magdalene is described in language borrowed from St John's description of Joseph (p. 7, l. 14) μαθήτρια τοῦ κυρίου φοβουμένη διὰ τοὺς Ἰουδαίους ἐπειδὴ ἐφλέγοντο ὑπὸ τῆς ὀργῆς οὐκ ἐποίησεν κ.τ.λ.

P. 5, l. 18 εἰ τῷ θανάτῳ αὐτοῦ ταῦτα τὰ μέγιστα σημεῖα γέγονεν, ἴδετε ὅτι πόσον δίκαιός ἐστιν.

The significance of the signs which were connected with our Lord's death is emphasised at considerable length in the *Doctrine of Addai*, p. 27. The phrase ὅτι πόσον has caused difficulty. Dr Swete banishes πόσον to the foot of the page. Harnack gives the emendation ὁπόσον in his text. Is not the strange ὅτι πόσον of the MS. a literal representation of the Syriac ܐܝܟ ܡܐ (Duval, p. 298, Nöldeke, p. 254)?

P. 5, l. 22 ἵνα φυλάξωμεν τὸ μνῆμα αὐτοῦ.

The verb φυλάσσειν is used in the same connexion again in l. 27; p. 6, l. 3, l. 7. In Matt. xxvii. 64, 65, 66 the verb ἀσφαλίζεσθαι is no less consistently employed. The Syriac equivalent of ἀσφαλίζεσθαι is the Ethpeel of ܙܗܝ. But this Syriac verb is also the equivalent of φυλάσσειν in Lc. xii. 15, 2 Tim. iv. 15. In such a context as that in Peter, φυλάσσειν would be the most natural translation of the Syriac verb. The difference then between the word of Matt. and the word of Peter is probably due to the medium of the Syriac.

P. 5, l. 25 ἐκ νεκρῶν ἀνέστη.

The corresponding words in Matt. (xxvii. 64) are ἠγέρθη ἀπὸ τῶν νεκρῶν. The difference of order and of wording is explained if we regard Peter's phrase as derived from Matt. through the medium of a Syriac translation. The Syriac Vulgate of Matt. *l. c.* is ܩܡ ܡܢ ܒܝܬ ܡܝܬܐ (from among the-dead He-rose).

P. 5, l. 29 ff. καὶ κυλίσαντες λίθον μέγαν κατὰ τοῦ κεντυρίωνος καὶ τῶν στρατιωτῶν ὁμοῖ [*lege* ὁμοῦ] πάντες οἱ ὄντες ἐκεῖ ἔθηκαν ἐπὶ τῇ θύρᾳ τοῦ μνήματος.

What of the strange phrase κατὰ τοῦ κεντυρίωνος? Robinson, Harnack, and Lods have admitted into their text the emendation μετὰ τοῦ κ., an emendation which appears to me unfortunate just in proportion as it seems at first sight natural and necessary. The κατά of the MS. is, I believe, a most valuable indication of the faithfulness of the transcription and an evidence of Syriac influence. Our passage is the result of the conflation of two passages in St Matthew, both of which have a place in the Diatessaron. These are (i) Matt. xxvii. 60 προσκυλίσας λίθον μέγαν τῆ θύρᾳ τοῦ μνημείου. The Syriac is: 'And-*they-rolled a-great stone* they-placed (it) *at* (lit. *upon*, ܠܥܠ) the-door of the sepulchre'.[1] (ii) Matt. xxvii. 66 σφραγίσαντες τὸν λίθον μετὰ τῆς κουστωδίας. The Syriac is: 'And-they-sealed that stone *with* (ܥܡ) the-guards'. I think that it can admit of little doubt that the κατά is a literal translation of ܠܥܠ (upon), which clung to the words 'they rolled a great stone', and kept its place in its new context, before the words 'the centurion and the soldiers', partly because it resembled ܥܡ (with), which should have been substituted for it.

This link with the Syriac is specially valuable, because it seems to shew that the true view as to the origin of the Petrine Gospel is, not that the work was the patching together of Greek renderings of Syriac phrases, but rather that a conglomerate narrative, consisting largely of words from the Evangelists, existed in Syriac, and that on this narrative was based the Greek Peter, though without further investigation it is not possible to reach definite conclusions as to the amount of editing and of adding which accompanied the work of translation.

P. 6, l. 7 τῇ δὲ νυκτὶ ᾖ ἐπέφωσκεν ἡ κυριακή.

Compare p. 7, l. 13 ὄρθρου δὲ τῆς κυριακῆς. Dr Swete compares the Diatessaron (Ciasca, p. 97) 'Et post dies octo, in *dominica* altera'.

P. 6, l. 10 f. δύο ἄνδρας κατελθόντας ἐκεῖθεν...καὶ ἐπιστάντας τῷ τάφῳ.

The germ of the fuller account of the descent from heaven of the two angels may perhaps be found in the Syriac (Old and Vulgate) of Lc. xxiv. 4: 'they saw two men which(-are)-standing *above them* (ܠܥܠ ܡܢܗܘܢ)'.

P. 6, l. 18 f. τρεῖς ἄνδρας, καὶ τοὺς δύο τὸν ἕνα ὑπορθοῦντας, καὶ σταυρὸν ἀκολουθοῦντα αὐτοῖς.

This triumphal procession after the Resurrection seems designed to recall the procession to Calvary as described in the Diatessaron (Ciasca, p. 91): 'Et suscipientes crucem, imposuerunt ei, ut portaret illam, et *ueniret* post Iesum. Iesus enim praecedebat, et crux eius erat post illum[2]'.

[1] In Mc. xv. 46 the word 'and-put-it' has not been inserted—'And-he-rolled a-stone upon the-door of-the-sepulchre'.

[2] There is a passage in the *Doctrine of Addai* (p. 18 f.) which seems to shew knowledge of, but to reject, the statement of our Fragment that the soldiers saw the actual Resurrection. It runs thus: 'He arose and went forth with many. And those who guarded the grave saw not how He went forth from the grave; but the angels of heaven were the preachers and publishers of His resurrection.'

C. C. B. 9

It is perhaps worth while to compare the description of the two Angels and of Him Who was led by them with the description of the two 'Angels' —the one the Son of God, the other the Holy Spirit—in the myth of the Syrian Elchasaites (Hippol., *Omnium Haer. Refut.*, ix. 13).

P. 7, l. 6 f. ἐδέοντο αὐτοῦ καὶ παρεκάλουν.

The phrase occurs in the Old Syriac (Curetonian) Version of Matt. viii. 5, a verse which has a place in the Diatessaron (Ciasca, p. 19, where however the phrase has been assimilated to the text of the Syriac Vulgate). See the note on Acts viii. 19, and compare above (p. 5, l. 21 f.) δεόμενοι αὐτοῦ καὶ λέγοντες.

P. 7, ll. 7, 11 κελεῦσαι τῷ κεντυρίωνι,...ἐκέλευσεν οὖν ὁ Π. τῷ κεντυρίωνι.

Dr Swete gives the text thus. But the MS. reads τω κεντυριων...των κεντυριων. The form κεντυριων in an oblique case is not here a mere blunder of transcription; this seems clear because the form occurs twice, and because there is in the second clause the *itacism* των, the form of the article being assimilated to that of the noun which follows. I would suggest that, as the word is to some extent of the nature of a proper name, the Greek represents the unchangeable Syriac ܩܢܛܪܘܢܐ; compare the note on Acts iii. 4.

P. 7, l. 19 ὅπου ἦν τεθείς.

The phrase comes from the Syriac of Matt. xxviii. 6 'Come, see the-place in which our-Lord *was placed* (ܐܬܪ ܕܣܝܡ ܗܘܐ).' The Greek is ὅπου ἔκειτο. The phrase has a place in the Diatessaron (Ciasca, p. 94). In Jn. xx. 12 (Ciasca, p. 95) the verb in the Greek and in the Syriac is the same as in Matt. *l. c.*

P. 7, l. 22 ff. τίς δὲ ἀποκυλίσει ἡμῖν καὶ τὸν λίθον τὸν τεθέντα ἐπὶ τῆς θύρας τοῦ μνημείου;

For τὸν τεθέντα compare the Syriac of Matt. xxvii. 60 'And-they-rolled a-great stone *they-placed* (ܣܡܘ, iniecerunt) (it) *at* (lit. *upon*) the-door of the sepulchre.' The verse has a place in the Diatessaron (Ciasca, p. 93). The word interpolated in Matt. *l. c.* probably suggested the phrase just below (l. 27) κἂν ἐπὶ τῆς θύρας βάλωμεν ἃ φέρομεν.

P. 8, l. 6 f. ἀνέστη γὰρ καὶ ἀπῆλθεν ἐκεῖ ὅθεν ἀπεστάλη.

Prof. Robinson (p. 29, n. 1) writes thus "With this we must compare the 20th Homily of Aphrahat (ed. Wright, p. 385), 'And the Angel said

DATE. BIRTHPLACE. AFFINITIES. 131

unto Mary, He is risen and gone away to Him that sent Him' (cf. Jn. xvi. 5)." The following passages from the *Doctrine of Addai* should also be compared: 'But as to that which thou hast written to me...I am going up to my Father, who sent me' (p. 4 f.). 'He...descended by Himself, and ascended with many to His glorious Father' (p. 9).

P. 8, l. 11 ἡμεῖς δὲ οἱ δώδεκα μαθηταί.

Compare the *Doctrine of Addai* (p. 44), 'the Acts of the Twelve Apostles', and Cod. D (Acts i. 26) καὶ cΥΨΗΦΙϹΘΗ ΜΕΤΑ ΤΩΝ ΙΒ̄ ΑΠΟϹΤΟ-ΛΩΝ. In the N.T. itself note 1 Cor. xv. 5.

The examination of the fragment of the Petrine Gospel has thus led to quite definite results. In the *first* place, we have seen that it contains several remarkable instances of the incorporation in the narrative of phrases which occur in different parts of Scripture. In the *second* place, it appears that immediately behind those parts of the fragment which are based on the Canonical Gospels there lie the corresponding sentences of the *Syriac* Diatessaron. Thus *mutatis mutandis* the fragment reveals the same phenomena which we have already noticed in the Bezan text of the Acts.

The fact that the Petrine Gospel is closely connected with Antioch confirms the hypothesis, which had a strong antecedent probability, viz. that Antioch was the birthplace of the Bezan text of the Acts.

(3) Affinities of the Bezan text of the Acts.

Any one who has thought out a theory, which he believes to be established by the evidence collected and considered, and to the importance of which, if true, he is fully alive, cannot but ask himself what light his conclusions throw on wider questions. He will however be wise if he checks the impulse to deal with the ultimate issues of his work, and submits his conclusions and his interpretation of the evidence, on which those conclusions are based, to the judgment of his fellow workers.

It is not therefore my intention to enter upon a full discussion of the many and intricate subjects which are embraced by the title *Affinities of the Bezan text of the Acts*. It must suffice to notice briefly these affinities, so far as they throw some light on (1) the genesis of the Bezan text; (2) the origin of the 'Western' text of the New Testament.

(1) The genesis of the Bezan text of the Acts.

(*a*) The Old Syriac text of the Acts.

'Of the Old Syriac Acts and Epistles nothing as yet is known'—so wrote Dr Hort in 1881 (*Introduction*, p. 85). I am not aware that the twelve years which have elapsed since these words were written have witnessed any discovery of an Old Syriac version of these portions of the N.T. Our investigation however into the Bezan text of the Acts has brought to light a large number of Old Syriac readings in this Book, and has enabled us to see that a system of harmonizing and glossing, which is possibly in part due to the influence of the Diatessaron, moulded to no inconsiderable extent the Old Syriac text of the Acts. But further, these Old Syriac readings in the Acts supply clear indications of the existence of an Old Syriac version (*a*) of the Prophets (see on Acts v. 38, vii. 43, xii. 10, xix. 29, and comp. pp. 117 f.), probably of the Psalms (see on iv. 24), and the Pentateuch[1] (see on vii. 24, and comp. p. 117); (*b*) the Pauline Epistles (see on Acts vi. 10, xi. 2, xiii. 15, xv. 29,

---

[1] In *c.* vii. there are several cases of assimilation to passages of the Pentateuch. (*a*) *v.* 18 ΟC ΟΥΚ ΕΜΝΗCΘΗ ΤΟΥ ΙωCΗΦ (so Cod. E) from Gen. xl. 23. (*b*) *v.* 21 ΠΑΡΑ (Cod. E ΕΙC) ΤΟΝ ΠΟΤΑΜΟΝ from Ex. ii. 3, 5 (*bis*). (*c*) *v.* 24 ΚΑΙ ΕΚΡΥΨΕΝ ΑΥΤΟΝ ΕΝ ΤΗ ΑΜΜω from Ex. ii. 12. (*d*) *v.* 35 ΕΦ ΗΜω̄ (Cod. E ΕΦ ΗΜΑC) from Ex. ii. 14. In these passages the Bezan phrases coincide with those of the LXX. As the Bezan scribe was well acquainted with the LXX. (see on iii. 1, v. 39), it may be plausibly suggested that he here used LXX. phrases in rendering Syriac glosses derived from a familiar passage of O.T. history. This suggestion tallies with (1) the general phenomena of the Bezan text; (2) the gloss ἐκ τοῦ γένους (note on vii. 24); (3) the fact that Cod. E varies from Cod. D in *vv.* 18, 35. Still, if we consider these glosses by themselves, the existence of a Syriac medium in their case cannot be considered as proved.

and comp. p. 119); (c) probably also of some work (perhaps the *Exposition* of Papias) containing extra-Canonical narratives which at a later time attached themselves to St John's Gospel (see on v. 15, 18, and comp. p. 120).

A comparison of the Bezan text with that of Codex E (see on v. 39, vi. 10), and with that supplied by the quotations of Tertullian (see pp. 103 ff.) and of Irenaeus (see pp. 105 ff.), shews that variations of reading existed in the Old Syriac text of the Acts at that period of its history with which we are dealing. In one passage (v. 39) Codex E seems to represent an earlier form of the Old Syriac text than that implied in Codex D. This impression is confirmed when we compare the texts represented by the two MSS. generally. The growth of harmonistic glosses would doubtless be progressive. Though we have no right to assume that Codex D and Codex E reproduce all the characteristic readings of the Old Syriac texts on which they are respectively based, yet these glosses are so conspicuously more frequent in Codex D than in Codex E, that we may safely conclude that the Old Syriac text implied by the former is a later text than that implied by the latter. Further, such corruptions as we have noticed in ii. 17 ($αὐτῶν$), ii. 47, iii. 14, iv. 1, 6, 24, v. 29, vi. 1, vii. 4, 16, xiii. 1 (p. 74 f.), 8 (p. 43), xix. 29 prove that, before it reached the form in which it was used by the Bezan scribe, the Old Syriac Version of the Acts had had a long textual history. It is impossible at this point not to ask ourselves two questions of paramount importance. How far back does the necessity of allowing time for these stages of textual development oblige us to place the date of the primitive (unglossed) *Syriac* text of the Acts? And again, how far back are we thus constrained to push the date of the primitive *Greek* text of the Acts?

With these conclusions as to the character of the Old Syriac text of the Acts it is very instructive to compare Dr Hort's words (*Introduction*, p. 84) as to the 'imperfect Old Syriac copy of the Gospels' discovered by Cureton. 'The character of the fundamental text confirms the great antiquity of the version in its original form; while many readings suggest that, like the Latin Version, it degenerated by transcription and perhaps also by irregular revision. The rapid variation which we know the Greek and Latin texts to have undergone in the earlier centuries could hardly be absent in Syria; so that a single MS. cannot be expected to tell us more of the Old Syriac generally than we could learn from any one average Old Latin MS. respecting Old Latin texts generally.'

(*b*) The Greek text of Codex D and of Codex E.

A comparison of Codex D with Codex E reveals several points of importance.

We have discussed many passages[1] in which these two MSS. incorporate the same Old Syriac gloss, but give different Greek renderings of it (see e.g. notes on ii. 14, iii. 8, iv. 32, v. 12, 15, 38 f.). It is clear therefore that we have in these two MSS. two independent attempts to assimilate the Greek text of the Acts to an Old Syriac text.

It is clear further that these two attempts to assimilate a Greek to a Syriac text widely differ. The Old Syriac element in Codex E chiefly appears in the glosses which are adopted into the text. The Greek text in this MS. runs smoothly and is not defaced by solecisms. The case of Codex D is wholly diverse. The disease of Syriacising, which in a mild form has attacked Codex E, has assailed Codex D with peculiar malignity. So violent are the paroxysms that at times the language of the Codex ceases to be coherent. Passage after passage becomes a chaos. These wild utterances indeed are invaluable when they are used as a guide to a right diagnosis of the disease. They shew unmistakeably in what company the Codex has been, and from what country the disease has come. But they are also a measure of its extreme severity.

To drop the language of metaphor, we have in these two

---

[1] Other instances will be found in xiii. 43, xiv. 2, 7, 19.

DATE. BIRTHPLACE. AFFINITIES. 135

codices two Greek texts, each of which is the outcome of a process of assimilation to an Old Syriac text. But this process has been carried out in the one case on principles quite different from those on which it has been carried out in the other. Notwithstanding however this striking difference, there is a considerable number of readings supported by Codd. D E comparatively or absolutely alone. The following is a collection of such readings in Acts i—xii., a collection however which does not aim at being exhaustive. The 'true text' is given within square brackets.

ii. 17 λέγει κύριος [λ. ὁ θεός].
ii. 32 after τοῦτον add οὖν.
ii. 37 after ἀδελφοί add ὑποδείξατε ἡμῖν.
iv. 1 after λαόν D has τὰ ῥήματα ταῦτα. E ταῦτα τὰ ῥ.
iv. 9 after ἀνακρινόμεθα add ἀφ' ὑμῶν.
v. 32 τὸ πνεῦμα...ὃν [ὃ] ἔδωκεν.
v. 34 ἐκ τοῦ συνεδρίου (E αὐτῶν) [ἐν τῷ συνεδρίῳ].
vi. 10 after σοφίᾳ add τῇ οὔσῃ ἐν αὐτῷ.
vii. 17 ἧς ἐπηγγείλατο [ὡμολόγησεν].
vii. 18 οὐκ ἐμνήσθη τοῦ [οὐκ ᾔδει τὸν] Ἰωσήφ.
vii. 24 after ἀδικούμενον add ἐκ τοῦ γένους (E αὐτοῦ).
vii. 29 ἐφυγάδευσεν [ἔφυγεν].
vii. 39 ταῖς καρδίαις (om. ἐν).
viii. 23 θεωρῶ [ὁρῶ].
x. 21 τότε καταβάς [καταβὰς δέ].
x. 26 after εἰμί add ὡς καὶ σύ.
x. 29 after μεταπεμφθείς add ὑφ' ὑμῶν.
xii. 11 ὅτι ἀληθῶς [ἀλ. ὅτι].

These coincidences of reading suggest, though perhaps they do not prove, that in Codex D and in Codex E alike we have two strata of Syriacisation; that, while the upper and more recent stratum in Codex D differs widely from the corresponding stratum in Codex E, there is a lower and earlier Syriacised stratum common to the two texts. In other words, the phenomena seem to point to the following as the history of the two texts. (1) There was first the common basis of the 'true (Greek) text.' (2) This text was in a few unimportant points assimilated to an Old Syriac text. (3) This text, thus slightly Syriacised, was subjected to two further processes of Syriacisation, the one resulting in the text of Codex E, the other, more thorough and more reckless, resulting in the text of Codex D. The problem of the relation of the two Codices requires, and will amply repay, more careful examination. The theory given above, I believe, fits the facts.

Besides the well known Graeco-Latin bilingual MSS. of the Gospels, the Acts, and the Pauline Epistles, we possess fragments of two Graeco-Thebaic bilingual MSS. of the Gospels (see Scrivener, *Introduction*, pp. 142, 395). The supposition then that there were current among the Christians at Antioch, where both Greek and Syriac were spoken (see above, p. 116), Graeco-Syriac bilingual MSS. of different parts of the N.T. is a hypothesis not only natural in itself, but also in strict analogy with known facts about other Churches. I venture then to offer the conjecture, as one which will explain the facts, that in the Greek texts of Codex D and Codex E we have the Greek texts of two such Graeco-Syriac bilingual MSS.; and that, just as the Latin texts which have been placed side by side with these Greek texts, were conformed to them (see especially Scrivener, *Bezae Codex*, ch. iii.), so, in the earlier stage of their history, these Greek texts were themselves conformed respectively to their companion Syriac texts.

One more point I must emphasise. Physical science has taught us that the changes in the earth's surface, which the philosophers of former and less instructed days traced to sudden upheavals and violent catastrophes, are due to age-long processes of development. The science of criticism, I believe, enforces in its own province an analogous lesson. It tells us that the great changes in the early texts of the N.T. are the result not of the cataclysm of a single bilingual, whether Graeco-Syriac or Graeco-Latin, but of the continuous

DATE. BIRTHPLACE. AFFINITIES. 137

work of schools of scribes at the great centres of Christian life. To pass from the general to the particular, the consideration of the evidence presented to us in Codex D, Codex E, the quotations from the Acts in Tertullian and Irenaeus, points to the conclusion that the Greek text of Codex Bezae in the Acts must not be regarded as originally an isolated phenomenon, but rather as one of the surviving representatives of a large family of similar documents.

(2) The origin of the 'Western' text of the New Testament.

The wide influence of that class of codices to which Codex Bezae belongs is beyond dispute. In the days when the 'Western' text was in process of growth, no attempt was made to isolate or to disinfect a Greek codex attacked by the foreign disease of Syriacisation. Indeed it is more than likely that the strange excrescences, which were conspicuous symptoms of the malady, gave the codex additional value in the eyes of pious men[1]. One notable instance of the way in which this disease was propagated has a special interest for Englishmen. At the beginning of the eighth century there was a severe outbreak of the Syrian epidemic in the Northumbrian monastery of Jarrow. Bede's *Expositio Retractata* of the Acts embodies a text whose characteristic readings are due to the influence of the Old Syriac. There appears to be little doubt as to the medium of infection. Theodore of Tarsus, when he came to England as Archbishop of Canterbury, brought with him many Greek MSS. Among these it

[1] It is impossible to wonder at the charm which such a text as that of Codex D had for Christians of the second century, when we observe that the harmonistic glosses of this MS. have deceived so scientific an investigator as Professor Ramsay; see *The Church in the Roman Empire*, e.g. pp. 151, 153. The partiality of Prof. Ramsay's treatment of the readings of Codex D is exemplified in his discussion of xix. 28. He lays stress (i) on the anarthrous Ἄρτεμις (p. 140), (ii) on the gloss 'and ran into the street' (p. 153). But he is content to leave the Greek words (which he quotes)—καὶ συνεχύθη ὅλη ἡ πόλις αἰσχύνης—unnoticed, except that he translates them 'And the whole city was thrown into confusion.'

is highly probable that Codex E had a place (Scrivener, *Introduction*, p. 160; Dr Hort, *Introduction*, p. 153).

To describe the widespread influence of Codex Bezae and kindred texts I will use other than my own words. For this purpose I quote a passage from a remarkable review of Mr Rendel Harris' *Study of Codex Bezae* which appeared in the *Guardian* of May 18 and May 25, 1892. The review is evidently the work of one of the little group of Oxford scholars who have made the Latin text of the N.T. a special study. Though I do not think that it is hard to identify the writer, I shall content myself with referring to him in the following pages as the 'Reviewer'[1]. 'It is a well-known saying of Dr Scrivener's,' he writes, 'that the "worst corruptions to which the New Testament has ever been subjected originated within a hundred years after it was composed." A brief study of the *apparatus criticus* at the foot of Tischendorf's, or Tregelles's, or Alford's Greek Testament will soon serve to verify this. It will show that there is a certain large group of authorities which repeatedly diverges in a more or less erratic manner from the rest. At its head stands a solitary Greek MS., Codex Bezae (D), but this frequently carries in its train the whole regiment of Latin MSS., of which as many as twelve or fourteen are extant in some parts of the Gospels; these are also often joined by one or more of the Syriac versions; and the line will extend so far as to include even the version of Upper Egypt and the Æthiopic. The proof that these eccentric readings are of early date is supplied by the Fathers. Many of them are found in Justin Martyr; further traces appear in Tatian; they abound both in the Greek and the Latin of Irenaeus, and are very conspicuous in Tertullian. But in greater or less proportions they extend as far as the versions which present the same readings, from extreme West to extreme

---

[1] I notice that Professor Armitage Robinson (*Expositor* for January 1893, p. 67) quotes a passage from this review as 'the words of another of the ablest of living critics of the N.T. Text.'

East, from Hilary of Poitiers to Aphraates on the banks of the Tigris.'

This widely spreading textual affinity cannot be accounted for by the influence of casual errant codices such as we have seen that Codex E was—an exile in the cell of an Anglo-Saxon monk. The influence of the Syriacised type of text is far too early and far too deeply seated in the 'Western' text to admit of this explanation. We must rather enquire to what conclusion the evidence points as to the district in which the 'Western' text took its rise. I need make no apology for quoting at length the 'Reviewer's' treatment of this question.

'What,' he asks, 'is the origin of the Western text? We may say, broadly speaking, that three answers to this question are possible—(1) That it originated in the West—Professor Harris gives us the choice of Rome, Lyons, or Carthage; (2) that it originated in Asia Minor; or (3) in Syria, which might perhaps be narrowed down to Antioch.'

(1) The first of these answers the 'Reviewer' rejects. After criticising at some length the arguments which Mr Rendel Harris urges in its favour, he gives his verdict in these words: 'The fundamental error, as we cannot but think it, in Professor Harris's theory appears to be (1) that he has formed an exaggerated idea of the amount of Latinising in Codex Bezae generally; (2) that he refers too much of this Latinising to the parent MS. of the group, the "primitive bilingual." On the face of it Mr Harris's contention that readings found in Upper Egypt originated in the West, though possible (for Rome was a centre from which any part of the empire might be reached), is not probable; and when the necessary deductions are made it does not seem to us that the arguments for it are very strong.'

At this point I shall quote the 'Reviewer's' words *in extenso*, adding from time to time footnotes of my own.

'(2) But if the so-called Western readings did not arise in the West, where did they arise? The first alternative which we have to consider is the view which Mr Harris attributes to Dr Hort, that they "had their origin in Asia Minor[1]." Any opinion of Dr Hort's deserves the greatest attention. We suspect that it will have been the experience of many others besides ourselves that, although they may begin by differing from that eminent scholar, they often end by agreeing with him, the reason being that his published opinions frequently rest upon facts and arguments which are not fully stated, but which the inquirer discovers for himself painfully by degrees.

'For Asia Minor, as the birthplace of the Western text, there is, on the face of it, much to be said. For the century 70—170 A.D. the most active centre of Christianity was the Roman province of Asia. At the beginning of the period falls the organising work of St John, of which the results are seen in the flourishing communities revealed to us by the Ignatian Letters. Then comes the ministry of Polycarp, with the circle of "Elders" round him, the school from which issued Irenaeus, the nursing-ground for the Gallic Churches. To Asia practically belongs Justin Martyr, whose text has the Western character clearly stamped upon it. Not far away from Pontus came Marcion, whose text is also conspicuously Western. Towards the end of the period we have a number of names, among the most prominent of their time —Claudius Apollinaris, Melito, Sagaris, Polycrates. The Paschal controversy was not a missionary movement; but Montanism, on the other hand, was a movement which soon began to assume the aggressive, and might easily (as Mr Harris argues that it did) diffuse a particular type of text. The Monarchians, again, made their first settlement at Thyatira with Theodotus of Byzantium. From the same region

---

[1] Mr Rendel Harris (p. 181) writes 'They [Western readings] are supposed by Dr Hort to have had their origin in Asia Minor.' It should be observed that Dr Hort (*Introduction*, p. 108) quite distinctly gives the second place in the order of probability to Asia Minor. 'On the whole,' he says, 'we are disposed to suspect that the "Western" text took its rise in *North-western Syria or* Asia Minor ...*From North-western Syria* it would easily pass through Palestine and Egypt to Ethiopia.' In the last sentence, it will be noticed, Dr Hort leaves out of account the alternative suggestion of an Asiatic origin of the 'Western' text.

came Praxeas and Noetus; and there was clearly a constant stream of intercourse between Asia Minor and Rome, the effects of which extended as far as Carthage. If we assume that the Western text originated in the province of Asia, it would be easy to understand the course of its diffusion—Westwards to Rome and the Latin-speaking Churches, Eastwards through the Cilician Gates into Syria. It would also be specially easy to account for the traces (if they exist) of Marcionitism and Montanism.

'The main difficulty would be to account for all the phenomena of the Latin Version. Mr Harris thinks that these are sufficiently met by his hypothesis of the "primitive bilingual." And there would, it is true, be no difficulty in explaining these, if all the forms assumed by the version could be really traced up to a single MS. We do not contest the view that there is but one fundamental version; and this would naturally represent a single Greek text, which, it might be urged, could be carried to Rome or Carthage or Lyons, and there be translated. But the relations of the Latin MSS. among themselves, and yet more to the Syriac versions, do not seem to us to be satisfied by a hypothesis quite so simple. It seems to us that the starting-point must have been not a single MS., bilingual or otherwise, but a *work-shop of MSS.* —that at the very threshold of the Latin Version there must have been several MSS., copied in near proximity to each other, and affected by allied, but yet different, Greek texts. How else are we to account, for instance, for the considerable amount of divergence in the Greek which underlies *d* and *k*? Both are primitive; both, we may believe (though this is not obvious), go back to the same fundamental Latin; both also have a number of common readings in the Greek; but both also have a number of Greek readings in which they are divided, and in which *k*, as a rule, goes with the purer Greek MSS., *d* with the more corrupt (see the instances collected in Old Latin "Biblical Texts," Part II., p. 97 ff.). The same thing would appear, though not quite so marked, if another MS. were taken, such as *b*, which has not a few individualities of the earliest type in its underlying Greek text. And a like phenomenon may be observed, though again with somewhat shifting relations of agreement and difference, in the oldest form of the Syriac Version.

'This last point is the one to which we should be inclined to attach the most importance. It seems to us that the Syriac Version took its rise in the very midst of the development of the Latin Version. A single Graeco-Latin MS. carried to the East and used in the construction of the Syriac Version will not, we think, satisfy the facts. The problem is no doubt highly complex, and needs clear-sighted workers. We only state what seems to us probable, and leave it to the judgment of others.

'(3) We are brought then to the third hypothesis, that the Western text originated at such a centre as Antioch. And we observe at the outset that this is given as an alternative by Dr Hort:—

"On the whole," he says, "we are disposed to suspect that the Western text took its rise in North-Western Syria or Asia Minor, and that it was soon carried to Rome, and thence spread in different directions to North Africa and most of the countries of Europe. From North-Western Syria it would easily pass through Palestine and Egypt to Ethiopia."

'For "North-Western Syria" we would venture to substitute "Antioch," because what we want is, in the strict sense, a "centre," a manufactory where a succession of MSS. might be produced in near juxtaposition to each other. Antioch satisfies this condition better than any other Church; and it is all in its favour that it was the oldest established Church of first-rate importance outside Palestine. The Antioch we mean is the Antioch almost, we are tempted to think, of Ignatius himself.

'To make this theory complete it needs an assumption which will seem quite as paradoxical as that of Mr Harris's, which seeks for the origin of readings circulating at Antioch or Edessa in regions so far to the west as Italy or Africa.

Our assumption is just the opposite of this—that the Latin Version itself may have been made in Syria, and we will say boldly at Antioch. This is, of course, an addition to the view just quoted from Dr Hort, for which he must not be held in any way responsible. He apparently contemplated what is, no doubt, at first the more probable view, that the Western character was imprinted on Greek MSS. in Syria; that these Greek MSS. travelled to Rome or North Africa and there were used in the making of the Latin Version. But the paradoxical character of our assumption will, we cannot but think, be greatly diminished on examination, while there are positive arguments of weight to be urged for it. In what class was the version most likely to arise? Was it not in the class of the *notarii*, public writers and copyists— and especially in that branch of the *notarii* which had to do not only with copying, but with translating? And where would this class of copyists congregate most thickly but in the suite of the Governor of one of the most important provinces? The administration of a province like Syria must have involved a large amount of office work. This would be in the hands of slaves, who would be employed to translate official documents into the language of the ruling nation. All kinds of notices in "Aramaic, Greek, and Latin," like the inscription upon the Cross, would be of common occurrence; and the writers of them would be at the same time more or less skilled penmen. Was it not in just such a circle that the idea of copying out bilingual MSS. was most likely to arise?

'But when once we begin to entertain this hypothesis, positive arguments are not wanting for it.

'(1) There are traces that the Western text, and with it the Old Latin Version, was the work of some one who possessed a special acquaintance with the administrative arrangements of Palestine. In Luke iii. 1 the common and undoubtedly the right reading is ἡγεμονεύοντος Ποντίου Πειλάτου τῆς Ἰουδαίας. Here for the vague and general ἡγεμονεύοντος D with Eusebius, the Old Latin, and the Vulgate has substituted ἐπιτροπεύοντος *procurante*, from which we may infer that the author of the reading knew that the proper title of the Governor of Palestine was "procurator." The distribution of the reading is interesting; the presence of Eusebius showing that the reading is more likely to have been introduced in the East than in the West. A similar and striking case occurs in Mark xii. 14, where for κῆνσον (ἔξεστιν κῆνσον Καίσαρι δοῦναι ἢ οὔ;) D has ἐπικεφάλαιον, *k capitularium*[1]. We look up *capitularium* and we find that it is a poll-tax levied specially upon the Jews (*capitularium Iudaeorum*, Orell., Inscr. 3345). D is above suspicion of Latinising here, because the Latin column has the ordinary rendering *tributum*: for what is probably the true text we have to combine the Greek of D with the Latin of another MS. which preserves very ancient readings, Codex Bobbiensis (*k*). The common rendering of ἡγεμών in the Gospels is *praeses*, which is quite correct; but in one place, Luke xx. 20, Codex Palatinus (*e*), a MS. allied to *k*, has *legato*. And it is noticeable that this rendering occurs frequently in the Würzburg palimpsest of the Old Testament—*e.g.*, throughout the chapter Gen. xxxvi. 15 ff. (A.V. and R.V. "dukes"). The veteran editor, Ernst Ranke,

[1] The supposition that Codex Bezae has a Greek text assimilated to a Syriac text throws fresh light on the genesis of these readings. (i) In Lc. iii. 1 the Syriac Vulgate and the Old (Curetonian) Syriac alike, transliterating the Greek ἡγεμονία, read 'in-the-government of-Pontius Pilatus.' The Bezan scribe retranslating this Syriac phrase into Greek, and avoiding, as he so often does (see e.g. on Acts iii. 1, vi. 10), the most obvious word, not unnaturally selects the word which was technically correct. (ii) The Bezan reading in Mc. xii. 14 is still more instructive. The word κῆνσος occurs in the N.T. only in Matt. xvii. 25, xxii. 17, 19, Mc. xii. 14. In the passages of Matt. the Syriac Vulgate and the Old (Curetonian) Syriac translate κῆνσος by the Syriac words (ܟܣܦ) ܟܣܦ ܪܫܐ (money-of the-head). In Mc. *l.c.* (where the Curetonian fragments fail us) the Syriac Vulgate has the same phrase. The word φόρος (φόροι) is so translated by both Syriac Versions in Lc. xx. 22, xxiii. 2; by the Syriac Vulgate in Rom. xiii. 6 f. In Acts v. 37 the words ἐν ταῖς ἡμέραις τῆς ἀπογραφῆς are rendered in the Syriac Vulgate by the paraphrase 'in-the-days (in)-which-written were the-men in-the-money-of the-head.' In Mc. xii. 14 then Codex Bezae gives a somewhat literal translation (ἐπικεφάλαιον) of this common Syriac phrase.

DATE. BIRTHPLACE. AFFINITIES. 145

remarked on this that it looked as if the version was made in an imperial province governed by a *legatus*, and not in a senatorial province governed by a *proconsul*. This would agree well with Syria, but not with Africa, or we may add with Italy or Asia Minor. (See also Rönsch, *Semas. Beit.*, p. 40.)

'(2) Another point which comes out about the author or authors of the Western text is that he or they possessed a knowledge of Hebrew and Aramaic. The details of this evidence must be left to the Hebraists; but it is, we believe, quite clear from the variants in Matt. xxvii. 46, Mark xv. 34, Mark v. 41. On the alternatives in the first passage, Ἐλωί ἐλωί λεμὰ σαβαχθανεί and Ἠλεί ἠλεί λαμὰ ζαφθανεί, Dr Hort observes that the latter is "probably an attempt to reproduce the Hebrew as distinguished from the Aramaic forms, ζαφθανεί standing roughly for *azavthani*." In Mark xv. 34 ἠλεί and ζαφθανεί are again set down as Western readings. In Mark v. 41 κούμ and κούμι represent respectively the fuller written and the shortened form as pronounced in the current Aramaic. Then, again, Eleazar is, of course, Hebrew for Lazarus. Mr Harris notes the form *Lazar* in *a d* of John xi. 14. Here *e* has *Lazarus*, but in Luke xvi. 20 ff. the regular form is *Eleazarus*, and even in Prudentius we find *Eleazar* (Trench, *Sacr. Lat. Poetry*, p. 289).

'Professor Harris propounds to himself the question, "Does the Codex Bezae Syriacise?" And he answers it in the affirmative[1]. The examples which he gives are very interesting, notably his explanation of the curious reading Σαμφουρείμ interpolated in St John xi. 54[2]. This he takes to be "a cor-

---

[1] I would add that Mr Rendel Harris defines his own position thus (p. 188); 'We cannot then say that they [Michaelis and Harvey] or we have brought forward any clear evidence of wide-spreading Syriacizing in the Codex Bezae. Sporadic traces there may be, and perhaps a few Tatianisms; but not much beside.'

[2] *A Study of Codex Bezae*, p. 184. It seems probable that in some Old Syriac copy one line ended with the word ܪܝܚܪܐ (= εἰς τὴν χώραν), and that at the end of the next line there were crowded the words ܢܣܝܒܪ ܡܫܡܠ܂ (whose-name

C. C. B. 10

ruption from the Syriac words answering to 'Whose name is Ephraim,'" and he compares it with a passage in Ephrem's *Commentary on the Diatessaron* :—"Patres nostri in hoc monte adoraverunt. Haec de Iacob et filiis eius dixit, quia in Monte Sichem aut in Bethel aut in Monte *Samgriazim* adorarunt." It is certainly both neat and simple to take this strange compound as standing for the Syriac, "whose name is Gerizim." It does not, however, appear to us that the account which is given of these Syriasms is so satisfactory. Assuming that the Western text was formed in the West, Professor Harris naturally looks for Syrians in the West, and to a certain extent, no doubt, he finds them. We know that in Juvenal's time the Syrian Orontes flowed into the Tiber, and even in Gaul there is evidence to show that Syrian traders were more numerous than we might have expected. (Harris, p. 178; comp. also Hauck, *Kirchengesch. Deutschlands*, pp. 8, 67.) Some influence from these sources we might be justified

(was) Ephraim); that these words in a corrupt form slipped up into the line just above and so took their place after the word ܐܪܥܐ. Cod. D has cαμφογρειν (= ܣܦܘܪܝܢ); for the Syriac plural form see note on Acts vii. 16. The Bezan Latin has Sapfurim.

On p. 178 Mr Rendel Harris calls attention to the Bezan reading in Mc. viii. 10, εις τα ορια Μελεγαδα. He suggests that the common reading Δαλμανουθά arose from the word ܡܢܬܐ ($= \epsilon$ἰς τὰ μέρη) being dittographed, and adds that 'if this explanation be the right one, we have lighted upon a case in which all Greek MSS. except D have a Syriac error!' Here I venture to remark (1) that there is no evidence, so far as I know, that the Syriac word 'parts' was used in a *local* sense like the Greek τὰ μέρη. In point of fact this Greek phrase is translated in the Vulgate and Old (Curetonian) Versions by the words 'the-place', 'the-places' (see note on Acts vii. 43), the only exception, I believe, being Matt. xv. 21, where both the Syriac Versions have 'boundary', a reading due to assimilation (Matt. xv. 39): (2) that the Bezan reading in Mc. *l. c.* is clearly a corruption of the reading in the Diatessaron, where Mc. *l.c.* has no place. See Ciasca, p. 41, Et uenit *in fines Magheda* (Matt. xv. 39). It would seem that the right-hand stroke of the ܠ in ܡܢܬܐ was carried up somewhat high and so generated a ܕ; hence the Bezan Μελεγαδα. This suggestion, it will be noted, is strongly confirmed (i) by the Bezan εἰς τὰ ὅρια, (ii) by the fact that several MSS. have the Tatianic reading in an uncorrupted form—'28 2^{pc} μαγεδα, d *magidan*, a ff^2 *magedan*, b i *magedam*, c *mageda*' (Tischendorf *in loco*).

in assuming; still it may be questioned whether the facts can be adequately accounted for in this way. The Aramaising element seems to be too deeply seated in the heart of the Western text. It is not merely a casual contact at this point or at that, but the very authors of the text seem to have possessed a first-hand knowledge both of Aramaic and of Hebrew.

'We may note, too, by the way, that their knowledge is not only linguistic but extends to the topography of Jerusalem itself. It is, perhaps, probable that $B\eta\theta\zeta a\theta \acute{a}$, or $B\eta\zeta a\theta \acute{a}$, is the right reading in St John v. 2. This is the only name which would have distinct verification from without, as Josephus gives to the quarter of the city where the pool with its five porches seems to have been situated the name "Bezetha." The authorities for this reading are ℵ, L, 33, Eus., and with slight variations the group D, *a, b, e, l*, Vulg. *codd*. If the reading is right the author (or authors) of the Western text knew enough of Jerusalem to retain it; if it is wrong they must have known still more to invent it.

'(3) Yet another important consideration appears to tell in favour of the Antiochene origin of this very primitive form of text. It is, as it is well known, distinguished by its interpolations. But those interpolations are remarkable for the fact that many of them at least are not merely such as would arise from reflection upon the context in which they occur, but they seem to point to some external source. What this source is must for the present be regarded as an open question: whether it is a still living, oral tradition, like that preferred by Papias, or whether it is extra-canonical writings like the Gospel according to the Hebrews, or whether it is, as Dr Resch maintains, some older pre-canonical form (such as the original "Logia") of our present Gospels. But whichever of these possibilities we adopt, in any case it seems far more probable that the interpolations were made in the East than in the West, and we may say most probable that they were made within the bounds of the province of Syria. If they were brought in from oral tradition where else would that tradition circulate in such strength and volume? If from apocryphal Gospels what other region was so prolific in those Gospels? If from pre-canonical texts those texts can hardly have travelled outside the district in which they arose.'

So far the 'Reviewer.' To these three arguments[1] for an Antiochene origin of the 'Western' text I venture to add two further arguments.

(i) If we are led to adopt this hypothesis, we have an explanation of a phenomenon which demands more careful investigation than has as yet been accorded to it, viz. the survival of rare 'Western' readings in the works of Chrysostom. They lingered in Antioch, the place of their birth. Some of these I have collected in a little work on Chrysostom published a few years ago (p. 87 f.)[2].

(ii) The hypothesis of an Antiochene origin of the Western text of the N.T. is supported by the *geographical* argument. The Orontes, on which Antioch stood, flowed

---

[1] In view of the conclusions of the first chapter of this essay as to interpolations in the Bezan text of the Acts, the last argument of the 'Reviewer' must be to some extent, I venture to think, restated. The interpolations are a road which leads to Antioch, but it is a more direct road than the 'Reviewer' thought.

[2] One of these readings I may be allowed briefly to discuss. In x. 153 E (see Field's note *in loco*) Chrysostom commenting on 1 Cor. vi. 20 quotes the text thus—δοξάσατε δή, ἄρατε τὸν θεὸν ἐν τῷ σώματι ὑμῶν καὶ ἐν τῷ πνεύματι. The reading is found in Tert., *de Resurr.*, c. 16, glorificate et *tollite* Deum in corpore uestro (comp. *c.* 10, *tollere* et magnificare Deum in corpore nostro): *adv. Marc.* v. 7, honorabimus...*tollemus* Deum in corpore: in Cyprian, *de Hab. Virg.* 2, *de Orat. Dom.* 11, clarificate et *portate* Deum in corpore uestro: in the Latin Vulgate, glorificate et *portate* Deum. I would suggest the following explanation of the gloss ἄρατε (tollite, portate) as in complete analogy with what has been seen to be the true solution of many similar problems in Cod. D. I believe that the gloss ἄρατε is due to assimilation to (i) Gal. vi. 17 τὰ στίγματα τοῦ Ἰησοῦ ἐν τῷ σώματί μου βαστάζω. (ii) 2 Cor. iv. 10 τὴν νέκρωσιν τοῦ Ἰησοῦ ἐν τῷ σώματι περιφέροντες. But it comes through the medium of a Syriac version. In Gal. *l. c.* βαστάζω=ܫܩܠ ܐܢܐ. In 2 Cor. *l. c.* περιφέροντες=ܛܥܝܢܝܢܢ. But ܫܩܘܠܘ (bear-ye) would be naturally translated by ἄρατε, see e.g. Mc. iv. 15, vi. 29, Jn. i. 29, xx. 2, 13, Acts xxvii. 17, 1 Cor. v. 2.

into the sea some 16 miles westward of the Syrian capital at the port Seleucia. Hence Antioch must have been in direct commercial communication with all the great trading centres of the Roman world. Vessels must have been constantly sailing for, and arriving from, Ostia, South Gaul, Alexandria and Carthage[1]. Christianity and the Christian Scriptures followed in the wake of trade. Hence we can easily understand how an Antiochene text of the N.T. was in the hand of Irenaeus at Lyons and of Tertullian at Carthage; how it passed to Alexandria, and from Alexandria to the native Egyptian Churches.

Thus the 'Reviewer' finds in Antioch the birthplace of the 'Western' text. In Antioch I found (see above, pp. 115 ff.) the birthplace of Codex Bezae and of similar Syriacised texts. Our lines of argument are wholly independent. Our conclusions converge. The theory of the 'Reviewer' as to the origin of the 'Western' text and my theory as to the origin of Codex Bezae interpret and confirm each other.

Thus I bring to a close a long and intricate discussion of the character of the Bezan text, its date, its birthplace, its affinities. I would fain find an indication that my work may prove a starting point for further investigation of the early history of the text of the New Testament in the fact that in its final stage it is merged in the well considered conclusions of one who speaks with authority, conclusions which are the restatement in a more definite form of an opinion expressed by Dr Hort.

[1] Comp. Acts xi. 20 ἦσαν δέ τινες ἐξ αὐτῶν ἄνδρες Κύπριοι καὶ Κυρηναῖοι, οἵτινες ἐλθόντες εἰς Ἀντιόχειαν κ.τ.λ. xiii. 1 ἦσαν δὲ ἐν Ἀντιοχείᾳ...Λούκιος ὁ Κυρηναῖος.

APPENDIX.

NOTE ON [MARK] XVI. 9—20.

THE object of the following note is to review certain arguments, closely connected with the subject of the Bezan text, which appear to establish the *antiquity* of this section.

In the note on Acts i. 2 I gave some reasons for the belief that the gloss καὶ ἐκέλευσε κηρύσσειν τὸ εὐαγγέλιον is derived from an Old Syriac version of [Mark] xvi. 15, 19, identical, as far as *v.* 19 is concerned, with the Curetonian fragment, a fragment which unfortunately only extends from *v.* 17 to *v.* 20. This suggestion as to the source of the Bezan gloss in Acts i. 2 has been confirmed by the subsequent discussion of other glosses in the Bezan text of the Acts.

We now are in a position to reap the advantage of having reached what I believe to be certain conclusions as to the date of the Bezan (Greek) text, and of the implied Old Syriac text, of the Acts. The former must have 'existed at least as early as 180 A.D.'; the latter 'shortly after, and perhaps even some time before, the middle of the second century' (see above, p. 115).

These general conclusions we are able to apply to the particular passage under consideration. If this Old Syriac text of the Acts contains a gloss derived from an Old Syriac text of the Gospels, the latter text must have been already in existence when the former took the shape which is implied in the Bezan text. But the Old Syriac text of the Gospels implied in the Bezan gloss is, as we have seen, identical, as far as the reading in *v.* 19 is concerned, with the Curetonian text. We conclude therefore that an Old Syriac text of [Mark] xvi. 9—20, identical with, or closely allied to, that from

NOTE ON [MARK] xvi. 9—20.

which the Curetonian fragment was taken, must have been in existence very shortly after the middle of the second century.

But we may go a step further. I pointed out (p. 4 *n.*) that the Curetonian reading 'after that He had *commanded* His disciples' ([Mc.] xvi. 19) is probably due to assimilation to Matt. xxviii. 20 (see the Syriac). But a glossed text implies an earlier unglossed text. The primitive Syriac text therefore of [Mark] xvi. 9—20 must have been in existence in the earlier half of the second century. Further, before this primitive Syriac version of the *pericope* was made, the Greek text must have been already in existence, and must have had some kind of evangelical authority attaching to it.

These conclusions are confirmed by the consideration of four other pieces of evidence.

(i) Of the twelve disputed verses we have seven in the text of St Mark's Gospel given in Codex Bezae. The MS. breaks off towards the end of *v.* 15 with the words τὸ εὐαγγέλιον. An investigation into the Bezan text of [Mark] xvi. 9—15 will elicit evidence, unless I am mistaken, which will prove the peculiarities of that text to be due to assimilation to a Syriac text.

Before starting on this enquiry one preliminary statement must be made. It is most unfortunate that, while the Bezan text extends only from *v.* 9 to *v.* 15, the Curetonian fragment commences with the closing words of *v.* 16 'that believe in me'. Thus the Greek fragment and the fragment of the Old Syriac (Curetonian) text do not overlap.

I will take the divergencies from 'the true text' in order.

v. 9. ΕΦΑΝΕΡѠϹΕΝ ΠΡѠΤΟΙϹ ΜΑΡΙΑ ΜΑΓΔΑΛΗΝΗΝ.

The true text has ἐφάνη πρῶτον Μαρίᾳ τῇ Μαγδαληνῇ.

(1) What of the strange ἐφανέρωσεν? The Syriac Vulgate has 'He-was-manifested', the same word as in *vv.* 12, 14. Did an Old Syriac text assimilate its rendering of the word ἐφάνη—unique in the N.T. as applied to a 'manifestation' of the Risen Lord—to the phrase used in Jn. xxi. 1 ܚܘܝ ܬܘܒ ܢܦܫܗ (He-manifested again Himself (lit. His-soul)), and Acts i. 3 ܚܘܝ ܠܗܘܢ ܢܦܫܗ (He-manifested to-them Himself (lit. His soul))? The phrase would then run ܚܘܝ ܠܘܩܕܡ ܢܦܫܗ (He-manifested first Himself (lit. His-soul)). In that case the word 'His-soul', separated from the

verb by the word 'first', might *either* fall out in a carelessly written Syriac MS. (comp. Jn. xxi. 1 *b*) *or* be overlooked by the Bezan scribe. Whether this be the true explanation or not, the Bezan ἐφανέρωσεν gives the impression of being a careless retranslation from a version. (2) πρώτοις seems to be a retranslation of the Syriac ܩܕܡܐܝܬ, the common translation of πρῶτον; it is also the rendering of ἐν πρώτοις in 1 Cor. xv. 3. (3) For the omission of the article before Μαγδαληνῇ see the note on Acts vi. 1; compare p. 101 *n.* 1.

v. 10. ΑΠΗΓΓΕΙΛΕΝ ΑΥΤΟΙΣ
ΤΟΙΣ ΜΕΤ ΑΥΤΟΥ ΓΕΝΟΜΕΝΟΙΣ.

The true text has ἀπήγγ. τοῖς μετ' αὐτοῦ γενομένοις.

The Syriac Vulgate naturally renders the true Greek text by the words ܗܘܘ ܥܡܗ.ܕ ܠܐܝܠܝܢ (to-them who-with-Him were). The Bezan phrase is a close translation of the Syriac phrase. Compare the notes on Acts ii. 1, iii. 2.

v. 11. ΚΑΙ ΟΥΚ ΕΠΙΣΤΕΥΣΑΝ ΑΥΤΩ.

The true text has ἠπίστησαν.

(1) What of the καί? The Syriac Vulgate has 'And-they when they-heard...did-not believe them.' It may be conjectured that the Old Syriac Version read 'And-they heard ..*and*-did-not believe her.' See below on *v.* 15 and the notes on Acts vii. 4, viii. 1, xiii. 27; see also the Bezan reading in Acts iii. 4, xiii. 29, as compared with the Syriac. (2) οὐκ ἐπίστευσαν. The Syriac, having no compound verbs, is obliged to render ἀπιστεῖν by prefixing the negative to the verb 'to-believe'. This is the Syriac rendering here and in *v.* 16, Lc. xxiv. 11, 41, Rom. iii. 3, 2 Tim. ii. 13; in Acts xxviii. 24 a different verb (they-did-not assent) is used. The Bezan phrase here is thus an exact translation of the phrase necessarily used in the Syriac. (3) The αὐτῷ is discussed in the note on Acts viii. 27. Conversely the Jerusalem Syriac in *v.* 10 takes ܥܡܗ (see above) as feminine, and reads 'who-were mourning and-weeping *with-her*'.

v. 12. ΚΑΙ ΜΕΤΑ ΔΕ ΤΑΥΤΑ.

The true text has μετὰ δὲ ταῦτα.

The Syriac Vulgate has 'After these-things'. The Old Syriac doubtless had a literal rendering of the true Greek text—ܒܬܪ ܗܠܝܢ ܕܝܢ

NOTE ON [MARK] xvi. 9—20. 153

(and-after these-things). This 'and', being the first word in the sentence, is retranslated by the Bezan καί, but the δέ retains its place in the sentence (comp. Acts ii. 14 τότε σταθείς δέ). For somewhat similar cases of double renderings see the notes on Acts i. 5, iii. 2.

v. 15. ΚΑΙ ΕΙΠΕΝ ΠΡΟC ΑΥΤΟΥC
ΠΟΡΕΥΘΕΝΤΕC ΕΙC ΤΟΝ ΚΟCΜΟΝ
ΚΑΙ ΚΗΡΥΖΑΤΕ ΤΟ ΕΥΑΓΓΕΛΙΟΝ.

The true text has καὶ εἶπεν αὐτοῖς Πορευθέντες εἰς τὸν κόσμον ἅπαντα κηρύξατε τὸ εὐαγγέλιον.
(1) πρὸς αὐτούς. The true text αὐτοῖς = ܠܗܘܢ (comp. e.g. Mc. xiv. 27, 48) = πρὸς αὐτούς (comp. e.g. Lc. ii. 49, iii. 13). (2) As to the omission of ἅπαντα, it may be said (though it is of course a matter of impression) that the Syriac ܥܠܡܐ would not be unlikely to fall out after ܠܥܠܡܐ (into-the-world). At least it would be more likely to fall out than ἅπαντα in the Greek. (3) καὶ κηρύξατε. The intruded καί is explained by the Syriac. The Syriac Vulgate, unable to translate the participle πορευθέντες except by an imperative, is obliged to render the true text thus : ' Go-ye...and-preach.'

Thus an examination of the Bezan text of [Mark] xvi. 9—15 leads to a clear and important result. The Bezan text of this section implies an Old Syriac text.

It is antecedentally probable that the Bezan text and the implied Syriac text of the Gospels are as old as, probably older than, the Bezan text and the implied Syriac text of the Acts, the dates of which we have been able approximately to fix (see above, p. 115). This is confirmed by the fact that Bezan readings in the Gospels are found in Justin (see Bp Westcott, *Canon*, p. 149; Dr Sanday, *Gospels in the Second Century*, p. 133 f.). The conclusions then to which we are brought are these: (1) That about 150 A.D. a Greek text of [Mark] xvi. 9 ff. was assimilated to a Syriac text; (2) That before this time there existed a Syriac text of this section : by combining this result with that reached in the note on Acts i. 2 we are able to assign an approximate date to the Curetonian version of this section; (3) That before this date there existed, ready for the process of assimilation to a Syriac text, a Greek text of this section.

(ii) It is clear from Ciasca's Arabic Tatian (p. 95—p. 99) that the section [Mark] xvi. 9—20 had a place in the Diatessaron. It must be especially noted that phrases and sentences from this section are woven by Tatian into the text of the Harmony throughout the area of history covered by the section. This fact is a clear proof that Tatian found this section already attached to the Gospel. Had he received it as a narrative external to the Gospels and himself been the first to attach it to the Gospels, we should not have expected that he would have used it in precisely the same way as any undoubted section of the Gospels, interweaving into the text of the Harmony one verse of the section here, another verse there: in that case we may conjecture either that it would have been inserted in a mass or that it would merely have supplied one or two glosses.

(iii) There is some early evidence in the Apologists which has hardly been rated at its full value. The most important passage is in Justin, *Apol.* i. 45. After quoting Ps. cx. 1—3 he adds τὸ οὖν εἰρημένον 'Ράβδον δυνάμεως ἐξαποστελεῖ σοι ἐξ Ἱερουσαλὴμ προαγγελτικὸν τοῦ λόγου τοῦ ἰσχυροῦ, ὃν ἀπὸ Ἱερουσαλὴμ οἱ ἀπόστολοι αὐτοῦ ἐξελθόντες πανταχοῦ ἐκήρυξαν. Compare [Mark] xvi. 20 ἐκεῖνοι δὲ ἐξελθόντες ἐκήρυξαν πανταχοῦ. Dr Hort (*Introduction*, pp. 28, 39) did not consider the reference as certain. The combined force however of the following four arguments will seem to many to dissipate the doubt. (*a*) The impression that Justin is here *more suo* weaving a quotation into his own words is confirmed by the fact that two lines further on he repeats the word πανταχοῦ—ἡμεῖς πανταχοῦ καὶ ἀσπαζόμεθα καὶ διδάσκομεν—as if it were a word occurring in an authority quoted by him. (*b*) The language of Justin elsewhere should be noticed. In *c.* 39 Justin writes: ἀπὸ γὰρ Ἱερουσαλὴμ ἄνδρες δεκαδύο τὸν ἀριθμὸν ἐξῆλθον εἰς τὸν κόσμον...ἐμήνυσαν παντὶ γένει ἀνθρώπων ὡς ἀπεστάλησαν ὑπὸ τοῦ Χριστοῦ διδάξαι πάντας τὸν τοῦ θεοῦ λόγον. The impression produced on my mind is that Justin is characteristically weaving together words and ideas derived from [Mc.] xvi. 15 (πορευθέντες εἰς τὸν κόσμον ἅπαντα κηρύξατε τὸ εὐαγγέλιον πάσῃ τῇ κτίσει) and words and ideas derived from *v.* 20 (see above). We should also compare *c.* 42 ὁ καθ᾽ ἡμᾶς δὲ Ἰησοῦς Χριστός...ἀνέστη καὶ ἐβασίλευσεν ἀνελθὼν εἰς οὐρανόν, καὶ ἐπὶ τοῖς παρ᾽ αὐτοῦ διὰ τῶν ἀποστόλων ἐν τοῖς πᾶσιν ἔθνεσι κηρυχθεῖσιν εὐφροσύνη ἐστί (cf. [Mc.] xvi. 15, 19); *c.* 49 οἱ ἀπὸ Ἱερουσαλὴμ ἐξελθόντες ἀπόστολοι αὐτοῦ ἐμήνυσαν τὰ περὶ αὐτοῦ. (*c*) Dr Hort considered the reference to [Mark] xvi.

doubtful, partly because '*v*. 20 does not contain the point specially urged by Justin, ἀπὸ Ἰερουσαλήμ...ἐξελθόντες (cf. *Ap.* i. 39, 49), which is furnished by Lc. xxiv. 47 ff.; Acts i. 4, 8' (*Introduction*, p. 39). Since his note was written the Arabic Tatian has been brought to light. From this it appears that in the Diatessaron [Mark] xvi. 20 stood immediately after Lc. xxiv. 52 f., so that the whole passage runs thus (Ciasca, p. 98 f.): 'Et ipsi, adorantes eum, regressi sunt *in Ierusalem* cum gaudio magno; et omni tempore erant in templo laudantes et benedicentes Deum. Amen. Et, *inde* egressi, praedicauerunt ubique.' It will be, I think, generally admitted that the probability is that there is some kind of connexion, more or less immediate, between Tatian's Diatessaron and Justin's N.T. quotations. I have pointed out (p. 112 *n*.) that there is some reason for thinking that Justin used a Syriacised text. It is not then too much to say that in the light of the evidence of the Diatessaron the connexion of the words ἀπὸ Ἰερουσ....ἐξελθόντες in Justin rather favours the belief that he had [Mark] xvi. 20 in his mind[1]. (*d*) In regard to the text of the N.T. Irenaeus is an authority akin to Justin; both, as I believe, used texts more or less Syriacised. Irenaeus (iii. xi. 6) refers to [Mc.] xvi. 19 as a passage from St Mark (*in fine autem evangelii ait Marcus*).

I do not know that attention has been called in this connexion to a passage in Aristides' *Apology* xv. 'And after three days He revived and went up into Heaven (εἰς οὐρανοὺς ἀνῆλθεν). The glory of His coming, thou, O king, mayest know from what is called among them [the Christians] the evangelical holy Scripture, if thou readest it. He had twelve disciples, who after His ascent into Heaven (τὴν ἐν οὐρανοῖς ἄνοδον αὐτοῦ) went out (ἐξῆλθον) into the provinces of the world (τῆς οἰκουμένης), and taught (ἐδίδαξαν) His majesty; even as one of them visited our districts, preaching the doctrine of the truth.'

I own that I cannot resist the impression, an impression which is strengthened by the fact that in the immediately preceding context he has referred the Emperor to evangelical writings, that in the closing sentence of this extract Aristides is translating into a rhetorical form his remembrance of [Mark] xvi. 15, 19, 20.

---

[1] Since writing the above I have noticed that Mr Rendel Harris (*The Diatessaron of Tatian*, p. 57 f.) has called attention to this point.

(iv) Lastly we turn to the newly discovered fragment of the 'Gospel according to Peter.' Here when we read (p. 5, l. 14 f.) ἐκαθεζόμεθα πενθοῦντες καὶ κλαίοντες νυκτὸς καὶ ἡμέρας ἕως τοῦ σαββάτου, it is well nigh impossible to doubt that the writer has in mind [Mark] xvi. 10 τοῖς μετ' αὐτοῦ γενομένοις πενθοῦσι καὶ κλαίουσιν. In connexion with this passage another (p. 8, l. 11 f.) must be noticed—ἡμεῖς δὲ οἱ δώδεκα μαθηταὶ τοῦ κυρίου ἐκλαίομεν καὶ ἐλυπούμεθα. Have we here the same phrase, the order of the words being reversed, retranslated from the Syriac? The Vulgate Syriac in v. 10 has ܡܫܬܐ ܗܘܘ ܡܠܝܐ܂ (who-mourning were and-weeping). Here it will be noted that (1) the imperfects ἐκλαίομεν καὶ ἐλυπούμεθα are a very natural rendering of the Syriac 'mourning were and-weeping'—a phrase which (with the prefixed relative) is the natural Syriac equivalent of the simple participles of the true Greek text; (2) the Syriac ܗܘܘ ܡܠܝܐ would naturally suggest the Greek ἐλυπούμεθα; for this Syriac verb, though commonly the equivalent of πενθεῖν, is used to translate ποιεῖν κοπετόν in Acts viii. 2; in 2 Sam. iii. 33 it answers to the LXX. θρηνεῖν, in Esth. vi. 12 to the LXX. λυπεῖσθαι; the derived noun is used to translate ὀδυρμός in 2 Cor. vii. 7. If this account of this phrase in Peter is correct, we have another proof of the existence about the middle of the century of an Old Syriac version of the disputed section[1].

The results of the preceding investigation are as follows: (1) The section [Mark] xvi. 9—20 was used in the same way as any undisputed section of the Gospels by Tatian in the Diatessaron. (2) The evidence of Codex Bezae (Acts i. 2, [Mark] xvi. 9—15), reinforced by that of the fragment of the Gospel according to Peter, shews that at Antioch (see above, pp. 115 ff.), at least as early as the middle of the second century, this section in an Old Syriac version and in a Greek text assimilated to that version, was current and was regarded as part of St Mark's Gospel; that consequently the primitive Greek text must have existed before this Old Syriac version was made, at least some years before the middle of the century. (3) The section was known to, and was used by, Justin before the middle of the century. Probably still earlier it is alluded to by Aristides.

[1] It will be noticed that (i) Peter used the Diatessaron (see above, pp. 121 ff., 154); (ii) Mark xvi. 8 (see Ciasca, p. 94) is referred to in Peter (p. 8, l. 7 f.) τότε αἱ γυναῖκες φοβηθεῖσαι ἔφυγον.

NOTE ON [MARK] xvi. 9—20.   157

Thus the evidence guides us backwards if not into, at least to the confines of, the first quarter of the second century.

If however we are tempted boldly to set aside later evidence and, relying on the very early evidence which we have collected and reviewed, to take the decisive step and assert the *genuineness* of the section, we are checked by two considerations. (1) The section, it appears, has no place in the Old Syriac text of the Gospels recently found by Mrs Lewis at Mount Sinai. Before however we can estimate the exact significance of this omission, it is necessary that we should know many facts about the MS. and, if possible, have before us photographs of the MS. (2) The Old Syriac (Curetonian) text and the Bezan text present some remarkable interpolations— interpolations some at least of which may be derived from reliable sources (see above, pp. 52 ff., comp. p. 120). The section in question may be one of these interpolations.

In bringing this investigation to a close I may be allowed to point out two coincidences between this section and passages in the Apostolic epistles, coincidences which appear to confirm the verdict of this section's antiquity. They are these :

Col. i. 23.
τοῦ εὐαγγελίου...τοῦ κηρυχθέντος ἐν πάσῃ κτίσει τῇ ὑπὸ τὸν οὐρανόν.

[Mark] xvi. 15.
κηρύξατε τὸ εὐαγγέλιον πάσῃ τῇ κτίσει.

Hebr. ii. 3 f.
ἥτις (σωτηρία), ἀρχὴν λαβοῦσα λαλεῖσθαι διὰ τοῦ κυρίου, ὑπὸ τῶν ἀκουσάντων εἰς ἡμᾶς ἐβεβαιώθη, συνεπιμαρτυροῦντος τοῦ θεοῦ σημείοις τε καὶ τέρασιν καὶ ποικίλαις δυνάμεσιν.

[Mark] xvi. 19 f.
ὁ μὲν οὖν κύριος ['Ιησοῦς] μετὰ τὸ λαλῆσαι αὐτοῖς ἀνελήμφθη...ἐκεῖνοι δὲ ἐξελθόντες ἐκήρυξαν πανταχοῦ, τοῦ κυρίου συνεργοῦντος καὶ τὸν λόγον βεβαιοῦντος διὰ τῶν ἐπακολουθούντων σημείων.

These coincidences must not be considered apart from the general subject of coincidences between the Epistles and the Gospels (see *The Lord's Prayer in the Early Church*, pp. 19 ff.). They shew *either* that the section is founded on language current at a very early period, *or* that the section itself, at least substantially, was known in the Apostolic age.

INDEX.

Acts of the Apostles, passages incidentally referred to, ii. 3, 31; ii. 17, 104; ii. 33, 105; iv. 4, 31; iv. 8, 106; v. 31, 106; v. 42, 107; vii. 18—35, 132 n.; ix. 20, 108 f.; x. 16, 6; x. 25, 34 f.; x. 41, 5, 86; xi. 3, 6; xiii. 1, 75; xiii. 6, 71; xiii. 7, 64; xiii. 8, 43; xiii. 10, 3 n.; xiii. 44, 83; xiii. 45, 64, 77; xiii. 46, 57 n.; xiv. 2, 69; xiv. 27, 59; xv. 8, 62 n.; xv. 11, 107; xv. 15, 8; xv. 18, 107; xv. 20, (29), 114; xv. 27, 107 f.; xv. 28, 104, 114; xvi. 4, 95 n.; xvi. 10, 99; xvi. 40, 59 n., 83; xvii. 13, 79; xvii. 15, 99; xviii. 2, 33; xviii. 28, 67; xix. 26, 16 n.; xix. 28, 137 n.; xx. 3 f., 98.

Acts of the Apostles, assimilation to passages of, 25, 28, 34, 36, 43, 51, 59, 61, 67, 69, 77, 83, 84, 85, 86, 95 n., 96, 97, 98, 99, 101; comp. 119.

Addai, the Doctrine of, 60 n., 124, 125, 127, 128, 129 n., 131.

Alternative glosses, insertion of, 68, 91.

Antioch, birthplace of Bezan text, 115—131; birthplace of 'Western' text, 142—149.

Aphrahat, Homilies of, 80, 86, 130.

Apocalypse, glosses from (in Gospel of Peter), 119; ii. 20, 36.

Aristides, Apology of, 114, 155.

Article (Greek), Syriac equivalent of, 64 f., 124; in Bezan text, omitted, 62, 101 n., 152; added, 10, 11, 62.

Bede, text of the Acts in, 61, 137.

'Behold', the Syriac word interpolated, 13 and n.

Bilingual MSS., 136, 143.

Chrysostom, 'Western' readings in, 148 and n.

Colossians, Epistle to the, i. 13, 157; i. 17, 113.

Compound (Greek) words, Syriac representation of, 6, 20, 32, 78, 90, 118, 126 n., 152; comp. 40, 42.

Context-glosses, 22, 30, 44, 61, 101, 109.

Corinthians, First Epistle to the, vi. 20, 148.

Cyprian, text of N.T. in, 11, 148 n.

Deuteronomy, xxi. 1, 22 and xxiv. 15, 117 f.

Diatessaron, the, 5, 8 and n., 20, 23, 24, 34, 38, 46, 48, 55, 61, 91, 94, 121—131 *passim*, 132, 146 n., 153 f., 155.

Didaché, 114.

Docetism, 123 n.

Double renderings, in Syriac and 'Western' texts, 78 f.; comp. 130.

Duplicate renderings of Old Syriac in Bezan text, 7, 16 and n., 31, 37, 59, 91, 153; comp. 62, 75.

ܠ, 39, 41, 44, 73, 91, 92, 112; confusion with ܩ, 7, 15, 92, 101, 127. Comp. 12, 31, 36, 65.

INDEX. 159

E, Codex (Laudianus), 11, 19, 24, 32, 33, 34, 37, 38, 40, 42, 43, 44, 45 n., 47, 48, 50 and n., 51, 58, 60, 65, 67, 71, 72, 79 n., 94, 97, 100 n., 132—138; witnesses to a different Old Syriac reading from Cod. D, 41, 60, 61, 69, 133; comp. 95, 104, 105, 106, 107.
Elchasai, the Book, 125 n., 130.
Ephrem, 112, 126, 127.
Epistles (Pauline), assimilation to passages of, 7, 68, 83, 89, 95, 106, 132; 119 (Gospel of Peter).
Extra-Canonical narrative, assimilation to, 52, 53, 133; 120 (Gospel of Peter).
Ezekiel, xl. 6, 86 f.

Feminine plural in Syriac, equivalent of Greek neuter plural, 5.

Gospels, assimilation to passages of, 4, 5, 7, 9, 19, 23, 24, 33 f., 34 n., 36, 37, 38, 46, 48, 54, 55 n., 61, 65 f., 68, 71, 74, 80, 86 n., 90, 91, 94, 95 n., 97, 100 and n.; 122 (Gospel of Peter).

Harnack, Prof., 117—131 *passim*.
Harris, Mr Rendel, 78, 117 n., 124, 125, 126, 127, 139, 140 n., 141, 142, 145 n., 146 n., 155 n.
Harvey, Editor of Irenaeus, 10, 38 n., 110.
Hebrews, Epistle to the, ii. 3 f., 157; iv. 4, 92.
Hort, Dr, 132, 133, 138, 140 n., 142, 145, 149, 154 f.

Jerome, 9.
Jerusalem Syriac, 152.
Ignatius, 82, 115, 120 n.
Impersonal use of 3rd person fem. sing. of Syriac verb, 50.
'Indeterminate third person' (Syriac idiom), 45, 91.
St John, Gospel according to, i. 13, 10; xi. 54, 145 and n.; xix. 38, 127; xxi. 21, 8.
Irenaeus, 10, 95, 105—113, 155.
Justin Martyr, 112 n., 118, 153 f.
ἴδιος, 14 and n., 126.

Latin Text of Codex Bezae, 2, 3, 4 f., 5, 7, 10, 12, 14, 15, 19, 39, 45, 49, 50, 56, 57, 64, 73, 88 n., 95 n., 99, 109 n.
Lewis, Mrs, Old Syriac Gospels discovered by, 157.
Lightfoot, Bp, 82 n., 85 n., 113.
Lines, confusion of, in Old Syriac, 22, 63, 77, 107, 111 n., 145 n.; comp. 41.
Lods, M., 117—131 *passim*.
Lord's Prayer in the Early Church, 62, 157.
St Luke, Gospel according to, i. 21, 36; i. 70, 41; iii. 1, 143, 144 n.; viii. 8, 79; x. 21 f., 110 f.; xi. 2, 62; xix. 42, 6; xxii. 52, 42 n.; xxiii. 34, 123; xxiii. 41, 40; xxiv. 42 ff., 86 n.; xxiv. 49, 7, 74.

St Mark, Gospel according to, viii. 10, 146 n.; ix. 15, 38; ix. 27, 34; xii. 14, 144 n.; xiv. 64, 90; xiv. 72, 80, 81 n.; xvi. 11, 81; xvi. 19, 4 n.; xvi. 9—20, 150—157.
St Matthew, Gospel according to, viii. 5, 78; xi. 25 f., 110 f.; xxvii. 41, 16.

Names, proper, in Bezan text of Acts, 32 f., 71; comp. 130.
νύσσειν, 88 and n., 122.

Old Latin MSS., 124 and n., 126, 141.
Old Syriac text, Gospels (Curetonian), 4, 13 n., 14 n., 46, 111, 122, 123, 124, 126, 130, 133, 146 n., 150 f., 157; corruptions in Gospels, 8, 38 f., 91, 111, 112, 151, 152, 153; corruptions in Acts, 7, 9, 15, 16 n., 17, 18, 19, 22, 24, 26, 28, 38, 42, 46, 53, 56, 57 n., 58, 63, 70, 75 and n., 85, 90, 92, 94, 97, 101, 107, 133; comp. 85 n., 125, 127, 129.

Old Testament, assimilation to passages of, 21, 32, 60, 73, 86 f., 101, 117, 118, 120, 122, 132 and n.; comp. 46.
Origen, 49 n.

Papias, 54; comp. 52, 120, 157.
St Paul and St Peter, glosses assimilating histories of, 25, 28, 43, 47, 52, 83, 84; comp. 67.
St Perpetua, Passion of, 104.
St Peter, Fragment of Gospel according to, 116—131, 156; Preaching of, 47.
Philoxenian Version, 6, 50, 67, 69.

Ramsay, Prof., 137 n.
Rénan, description of Antioch, 116.
Reviewer in *Guardian*, 138—149 *passim*.
Robinson, Prof., 104, 117--131 *passim*, 138 n.
Rönsch, 103.

Sanday, Dr, 153.
Scrivener, Dr, 3 and n., 90, 136, 138.
Septuagint, Bezan scribe's knowledge of, 30, 60 n., 61, 80; use of in Gospel of Peter 117—121.
Serapion of Antioch, 116.
'Son of', expressed in Syriac, 10.
Swete, Dr, 117—131 *passim*.

Tatian, Encratite views of, 8; see *Diatessaron*.
Tertullian, 95 n., 103—105, 112 n., 148.
Theophilus of Antioch, 114, 116 n.
Third person plur. of Syriac verbs, 10, 41.
Timothy, First Epistle to, i. 4, 113.
τότε, 16, 23, 53, 100; comp. 72, 125.

Verb-constructions, Bezan rendering of Syriac, 3, 4, 16, 27, 33, 37, 39, 49, 55, 56, 62, 64, 72, 74, 75, 84, 90, 92, 93, 94, 96, 98, 152, 153; comp. 82, 111.
Vocalization of Syriac words, 18, 55, 58, 64, 81, 94 n., 111, 127, 152.
Vulgarism in Old Syriac text, 71, 146 n.
Vulgate, Syriac, especially 13 and n., 21, 22, 29 f., 42, 76 f., 81 n., 88, 92, 96, 121, 122, 125, 127 n., 130.

Westcott, Bp, 48, 112 n., 153.
Wordsworth, Bp, J., 124.

www.ingramcontent.com/pod-product-compliance
Lightning Source LLC
Chambersburg PA
CBHW062002180426
43198CB00036B/2139